URSULA

A voyage of love and drama

EILEEN NASEBY

PIER 9

Dedication

For Ursula and Nigel who gave me much more than I ever realised
And for David who holds my hand every day

Contents

Ursula, 1941

for Ursula

I STILL THINK of you every day although you've been gone now for more than twelve years. Today, as I was ironing a shirt, I spread the sleeve flat to avoid making a crease. I always think of you as I do this, no matter how many shirts I iron in my life. You taught me this ironing trick more than fifty years ago. I smile when I think of such pedantry in the midst of the household chaos you created. For a long time it didn't make me smile, but now I have come to a different stage in my life, and part of my amusement relates to the fact I am continuing to obey your rules.

Who taught you to iron so carefully anyway? Was it Mama, my grandmother? I'm sure it was. She was the fastidious one, in her tailored suits and handmade shoes which lasted for decades. Mama was the one who wore stockings to do her housework. You, on the other hand, rarely did housework. You were always too ill from a variety of ailments, the most debilitating of which was melancholy. You delegated the chores to your succession of children, some of whom showed more diligence than others in their attempts to please you.

And how you could sew. When did you learn to do that? Was it before or after you escaped from Nazi Germany, or in Palestine? You made the curtains for every one of our houses. Do you remember the red and grey ones in the house in Nambour? You loved bright colours—you wore blues and greens and above all red. Mama never wore bright colours. A generation later I have reverted to the autumn colours of my grandmother. You made most of your own clothes despite all that trouble with your hip, all that pain you were in.

I should have been impressed because, even though I took a sewing course when I was first married, I still can't sew a straight line. Once when I was thirteen you made me a beautiful lemony summer dress. It was called an H-line and it swung from my hips as I walked. I don't think I ever told you how much I loved that dress. You taught me to knit the German way, the fast way, the needle curling into the wool instead of the wool being wrapped over the needle. I still have the jumper you made me when I was forty-five. Its heavy cable is too hot for this climate. Even when I thought I hated you, I couldn't throw it away.

You didn't actually teach me how to read. Reading came along with everything else in our household: table manners, compassion for those less fortunate and breathing. By the time I was six I was as addicted to books as you were. Remember how you said I wasn't allowed to read For Whom the Bell Tolls until I was fifteen. I must confess now to stealing it off the bookshelf long before that birthday arrived. You were probably right. I think I missed most of what was important while I was scanning the book for the illicit parts you were trying to keep away from me.

You always limped, even before the hip replacement. Sometimes the kids next door would imitate you behind your back. I couldn't work out who was to blame for my humiliation, you or them. Something happens when you move countries. In England I already knew our differences set us apart from our neighbours, and no matter how hard I tried I was only ever half-English, and you were something else even more foreign—exotic, but threatening at the same time. There used to be a Jewish café called Scheherazade in

Melbourne. I went there occasionally when I was in town. It was in a street they call 'Cake Street'. When I was there I would shut my eyes and listen to the old people arguing. Then I would be back with you and Mama in the kitchen in the little housing commission house in Brisbane, listening as the two of you throw your love and your anger back and forth across the table.

How did you and Nigel find love in the midst of all that wartime chaos? How did it become so strong it withstood the life that lay ahead—the poverty, the disappointments, the arguments? You began your life studying ballet. By the time you finished school you could speak five languages, and you could write and paint. Then he took you to live on cow farms, first in England and then Australia. Every time he had to move on you became something else for him. You nurtured his belief in these dreams and everybody knew you loved him just as much when the dreams were gone. You were the strong one and I never really understood.

You were lost to me for such a long time.

Eileen Naseby

Ursula and Cila, Frankfurt, 1928

Chapter One

A PERFECT
ANGEL

Life is God's novel.
Let him write it.

—Isaac Bashevis Singer, *Love and Exile*

Frankfurt, 1933

MY GRANDMOTHER IS picking her way along the wide footpath between the tall buildings in the city centre. An icy March wind carrying a dark bank of clouds is spiking in from the north. She wishes she hadn't decided to wear the good shoes with the high heels because her knees are wobbling so much she has difficulty walking fast. She had intended to wear her best coat with the fox fur collar because she has always understood the importance of being well dressed for an interview. Now she is glad she changed her mind. The old brown one is neat enough and far less likely to draw attention as she makes her way through this unfamiliar part of Frankfurt. My grandmother's head is bent slightly into the wind, and this gives her an excuse to avoid eye contact with other pedestrians. She believes some Germans have an instinct that helps them to single out a Jew in a crowd. It has happened to her several times. Her palms are sweating inside her gloves. Every so often, as the pressure builds up under her ribs, she is forced to take in a deep gulp of air so she can get enough oxygen to keep walking. It has been a long time since she has been inside a synagogue, but under her breath she is praying.

'Please don't let anything happen to me now.'

My grandmother Cila Singer is praying not for her own safety but for that of her daughter. She prays she will be able to do her business and get home to Ursula without running into any brown-shirted thugs. She prays the British Consulate will give her the visas she wants. She prays she will have good news to tell her daughter. Her heart beats a little faster when she thinks of Ursula, not because of the particular situation she finds herself in now, but because whenever they are apart and she thinks about her child her heart flutters. Even when she collects Ursula on her way home from work, she has to stop herself from running down the street and rushing up the neighbour's steps. She stops herself only because Ursula gets ashamed if her mother is breathing too heavily when the neighbour opens the door. Cila finds it hard to keep pace with Ursula's reactions to her love. She knows her daughter finds her displays of affection embarrassing. Lately she has begun to ration herself, pulling back, so her feelings are less obvious. The child knows this too, and uses her mother's tentativeness as a weapon.

'Mama, don't you want to kiss me?' she wheedles, and when Cila leans across Ursula snatches her face away. 'No, you're too late now.'

How beautiful and clever her daughter is. Ursula is only eight years old, but already she has attracted the wonder of all those who meet her. Cila is simply in awe of this miracle she has somehow created. She gives no credit to Solomon, the child's father, whom she left before Ursula was born. Instead she is overwhelmed by the weight of the responsibility involved in caring for such a perfect angel. When her daughter is difficult, when she screams or broods, Cila is terrified she has failed as a mother, but whenever Ursula demonstrates some little form of affection, sometimes teasing, sometimes touching, she is filled with pride for both of them.

She remembers last night, and she smiles. It was such a wonderful evening, she even managed to forget the peril they were facing. They had gone through one of their very special rituals. Ursula had to finish her French homework first. Then Cila made her read out loud everything she had written. At the end Ursula read a special little rhyme she had memorised, and she enunciated so crisply, so precisely, as real French people would say it, Cila's eyes filled with tears at the cleverness of her child. '*Un boeuf, der Ox. Une vache, die Kuh / Fermez la porte, die Tür mach zu.*'

Afterwards Ursula put her books away, tidily of course because, although Cila is excessively indulgent, she can't deal with any disorder and is a tyrant when it comes to neatness and cleanliness. Cila had patted a spot on the sofa, and after Ursula sat down Cila knelt to undo her daughter's laces. She slipped off the shoes and socks and began to massage the little girl's feet. Ursula sank deep into the comfort of the soft cushions. The scent of Cila's home-made face cream filled the air. Ursula's feet are long and slender—ballerina's feet, Cila tells everyone. They must be looked after. Thank G-d she does not have to pay for the ballet lessons. Her daughter's talent has taken care of that expense. When Ursula was quite small, Cila's sister Tamara had introduced them to a famous ballet master. Tamara was on the way to becoming a leading ballerina. Of course the two ballet experts had recognised Ursula's potential at once.

'Such grace, such beauty,' the great man had said. 'It would be my privilege to teach her.'

Ursula wriggles about on the sofa and whimpers. 'My hip hurts.'

'I know, my darling. Soon it will be better and you will be able to go back to your lessons.'

In a moment of excessive enthusiasm at ballet practice, Ursula had misjudged the edge of the tiny stage and fallen heavily enough on her left side to dislocate her hip. The orthopaedic surgeon Cila consulted had ordered six months' rest from all strenuous physical activity, especially ballet.

When Cila finished massaging Ursula's feet, she stood up, and picked up a soft scarf that was hanging over the arm of the chair. She went behind the sofa and placed the scarf around Ursula's head. She tied it so her daughter was blindfolded.

'Are you sure you cannot see?' Cila asked.

'I can't see anything.'

'Don't peek.'

'I won't.'

Cila crossed the room and took the dust cover off the shiny gramophone machine in the corner. She picked out a record from a pile, placed it on the turntable. Slowly at first she wound the handle and then gently brought the needle down on the black disc. Music filled the room.

'Mozart!' Ursula said excitedly. 'I knew it straight away, it's ...'

'No, not yet. Wait until it is finished.'

There was only one dim bulb to light the room, so they sat in near darkness, the child slumped back, twitching with impatience, Cila sitting upright, head tilted back, eyes closed in reverie.

When the music was finished Cila picked up the gramophone arm and placed it back in its rest. She held the record up to the light bulb, turning it over and over to check for dust or scratches before putting it back in its cover. Only then did she take the blindfold from her daughter's face.

'Well, now you must tell me everything you know about this piece of music.'

'It is Mozart.' Now she was allowed to speak, Ursula waved her legs up and down in excitement.

Cila nodded.

'It's from an opera ... It's from *The Marriage of Figaro*.'

'Very good, but what part of the opera?'

'It's the bit at the beginning. I know. It's the overture.'

'My clever darling. So what do you remember about how Mozart wrote this piece?'

'That's easy. He was very late—they were going to perform the opera in the concert hall the next day and he hadn't even started to write this part. So he had to work all night. He told his wife not to let him go to sleep, but when he fell asleep she felt sorry for him and decided not to wake him. When he woke up he was very angry with her because now he had to work even faster to get the music written on time. He gave it to the orchestra just after he'd finished it.'

Cila clapped. She was almost dizzy with pride.

'Perfect, perfect. What a memory. Now you shall eat.'

She took a white napkin and placed it across her daughter's lap. 'I have something special. Some chicken. I won't tell you how much it cost.'

She went to the kitchen and came back with a tray. She put the tray on her daughter's lap, and then sat back while Ursula picked at her food. Cila loved these times. She thought of them as their talking times, only she did nearly all the talking. Often she heard herself speaking too quickly, as if she needed to speed up in case Ursula was becoming bored, but the need to hurry often spoilt the telling of the story. Sometimes she felt her voice trailing away just as she had reached the important part and she sensed that her audience was lost to her, maybe forever.

'One day I shall take you to Vienna. Before you were born I saw *Figaro* at the Wiener Staatsoper. Come, you're not eating. No, Ula, don't pull such a face. How many children in Germany are eating chicken tonight? Maybe only you.'

They had ruined Ursula's appetite in the orphanage. Cila's chest tightened when she thought of how she had to leave her daughter in that place, and the terrible things that happened there. It was only supposed to be for a few weeks, but it had ended up being months.

After the stock market crash the restaurant Cila worked for had been forced to close its doors. Without a proper income she had not been able to pay for someone to look after Ursula while she searched for work. Cila had no choice but to put her daughter into temporary care in an orphanage. No one had expected the financial collapse would be so deep and the economic recovery so long. The leader of the National Socialists, Adolf Hitler, started to blame Jewish greed and financial power for the crash. And the German public, beaten down by unemployment and poverty, began to listen. A rank smell of anti-Semitic suspicion seemed to hang in the air. Almost imperceptibly, doors began closing. For months Cila had to support herself with bits and pieces of domestic work until finally she found another restaurant job and was able to bring Ursula home.

But by then the damage had been done. The misery of their separation had opened up a wound that would never heal, and Cila's attempts to make up for the suffering she thought she had caused only compounded her guilt and handed the power in their relationship to her daughter.

It is beginning to rain. Icy spits strike her cheeks and forehead. Even so, she thinks, not even a howling snowstorm would turn her back now. Most of her friends and family who know of her plan to leave Germany have expressed concern about it. They think that in her usual way she is being overdramatic. This change in government doesn't have to spell disaster for the Jews, they say. They believe it inconceivable that Germany will descend into the pogroms of the past. There are too many influential and sophisticated gentiles, many of whom could be counted as friends—they would never allow this to happen. Why, the mayor of Frankfurt is a Jew, elected by the majority of its citizens. Isn't this proof that, despite the rhetoric of National Socialism, the views of its more extreme adherents would never become public policy? Not here, not now, not in the twentieth century, they say.

What was it Axel Furhmann from the butcher's shop had said before the election: 'So what if he comes to power? It won't last more than a few months. People like him don't stay in power for long.'

Cila knows differently. For months Hitler has been roaring from the radio and from the newspaper headlines. He screams about the evils of Jewish capitalism and rages at the Jews as if they are a disease that will eventually infect the whole German nation. Germany could only become healthy when the Jewish spirit has been eradicated, he rants. Why aren't her people listening to what he is saying? The liberal Jews talk in sorrow about insults. The Zionists insist that German Jews must struggle for a new emancipation—as if they have the power to make this a possibility. The orthodoxy speak about trusting our Father in Heaven: 'Be faithful to G-d, because he and his deliverances will not fail,' they preach. The Union of Jewish Veterans write to Hitler on behalf of the ninety-six thousand Jews who participated in the First World War, twelve thousand of them killed. 'Because of our sacrifice of blood and our service for the fatherland, we believe that German Jews have the right to full civil equality in Germany,' they advise the new chancellor and demand he

Aunt Tamara

Ursula's father Solomon

Solomon and friend

Aunt Miriam

Ursula

must recognise their loyalty as German citizens. Only last month one of the Jewish newspapers, under the heading 'Getting Down to Serious Business', had called for a public debate on a comprehensive plan for the future of German Jewry.

Talk. Talk. Talk. Cila cannot believe the naivety of even the most intelligent Jewish leaders. Such optimism, such trust in human nature—as if you could influence a man like Hitler. The man is too crazy to be reasoned with. It should be obvious to everyone. Even as a young man he had said that if ever he got political power, the destruction of the Jews would be his first and most important job. He had railed he 'would have gallows after gallows erected, for example, in Munich on the Marienplatz—as many of them as traffic allows. Then the Jews will be hanged one after another, and they will stay hanging until they stink.'

Cila has never forgotten what she had heard, yet these Jewish leaders believe all they have to do to change the mind of such a man is to have a debate and write him a letter. Is she the only Jew in Germany who has any intelligence?

So she has decided to take her child and leave. Thirty years on when we, her grandchildren, would ask her how on earth she knew when others didn't, she would shrug her shoulders and say, 'I felt it in my bones, but it was not evidence enough for others, and I could not make them change their minds.'

Despite her entreaties to her sisters, aunts, cousins, friends, no one would come with her, and most would not survive the war. She would blame herself forever because she had failed to convince them to leave. And she would never let Ursula forget either, as long as she lived.

The pavement has become foreign territory, peopled by anti-Semitic stalkers who spring from the cracks and the gutters. Occasionally strangers glance at her and then shift their eyes sharply, others ostentatiously walk around her, still others move towards her with such swift ferocity she is forced to sidetrack or be mowed down. She is thankful that most just ignore her.

***

FIFTEEN YEARS BEFORE Hitler came to power, Cila's family had fled a series of anti-Jewish pogroms that followed the collapse of the Austro-Hungarian Empire at the end of the First World War. She had been born in her mother's ancestral home town, Dynów, a little shtetl in Galicia, which was part of Austria before the war. Cila claimed her 'Austrian' heritage proudly and declared there were no better composers than Austrian composers.

In 1999 I went to Dynów, now in Poland. Zdzisław Les, the bookseller from

Kazimierz, the Jewish quarter in Cracow, drove me the two hundred kilometres to Dynów. He was an erudite man, an intellectual who had been employed by the former communist regime as a sort of cultural counsellor at one of Poland's biggest steel factories on the outskirts of Cracow. More than ten thousand people were employed in the factory and it was his job to organise state-sanctioned cultural activities. Les, as he suggested I call him, spoke and read seven languages. After he asked to read a piece I had written about my family's history in Poland, he came straight to the point: 'So many words. Well, I can see you are no Hemingway.'

We were driving west to Dynów. The previous day we had travelled east to Auschwitz. I hadn't wanted to go to the concentration camp but Les talked me into it. I thought I knew enough without having to see it. My mother used to become hysterical at the sight of concentration camp footage on television. My grandmother's most precious possession was an awful book containing a photographic record of Nazi atrocities, which she acquired after I left home. One day I caught Cila showing the book to Naomi and Michael, my youngest sister and brother. They were seven and five years old at the time. It was if she were determined to cast the same shadow across their lives as she had across my mother's. We had a major argument. She accused me of not caring, of not knowing anything about how she and her family had suffered. She was probably right. As a child I had developed a resistance to the emotional outpourings of my mother and grandmother. At its best, my reaction was indifference if not outright intolerance.

'Thank G-d you will never have such terrible trouble in your life,' my grandmother would quiver at me.

It always came back to this, with Cila and Ursula, to the terrible troubles of the war. These troubles were an excuse for everything, for telling too much about some things and not enough about others. They were the reasons they were allowed to scream or weep as the mood took them, while we children had to be constrained and considerate in respect for their suffering. I was still quite young when I realised how much I resented the memories of a family virtually eradicated in the Nazi gas chambers. How could I ever be able to match this?

When I was a child and we were living in Cypress Street at Inala, I would look out the living-room window and imagine Nazi Brownshirts crunching down the streets. They would come tramping along Mrs Foster's neat path with the marigold and violet borders and ring her 'Greensleeves' chimes.

'Any dirty Jews in here?' they would demand, and Mrs Foster would shake her head emphatically. They would stare at her and remind her, 'The penalty for harbouring a Jew is death. You must not help them in any way. Not even a drink of water must be given.'

They would march next door to the Castellis, with the seven children, two derelict cars in the deep grass of the front yard and the constant wafts of garlic floating from the kitchen, up the hall and out into the street. They would look hard at the Castelli family because they were foreigners, dark-skinned, and black of eye and hair. But Mr Castelli would produce his passport and the soldiers would begin to laugh and joke with him because the Germans were good friends with the Italians during the war. Mrs Castelli would bring out some Italian wine she had saved for a special occasion and they would stand around drinking a toast to fascism.

The German commander would whisper into Mr Castelli's ear and they would both turn to look in the direction of our house. Then the Germans would re-form into a column and come crunching towards our house like a giant black centipede, marching across the road, across the footpath, marching up to the front door.

There were so many ways for me to save my family, so many brave heroic acts to perform, but I knew I would never feel the real fear—the violence would never really touch me. The storm troopers were not going to come marching up Cypress Street, something I almost came to regret.

Fifty-four years after its liberation, Auschwitz looked more like an old-fashioned school than a death camp. The buildings had been made into a museum, full of lists of the dead and hills of ephemera. Behind floor-to-ceiling windows there were artfully structured piles of suitcases, spectacles and clothes, which had been stripped from the new inmates as they arrived. The suitcases still had the labels naming the owners and their travel destinations. But none of the labels bore the name of this final destination. In a small room in the museum was a display of baby clothes, little crocheted matinée jackets and bootees. I thought of my own children and lasted only a couple of minutes in that room.

The corridors were lined with photographs of camp inmates—photographs that had been gathered as a memorial to those who died. Underneath each photograph was a typed card giving the biographical details of the individual, the date they arrived and the date they were killed. I found myself scanning the corridors looking for evidence of my grandmother's family. It was a ridiculous exercise since more than a million people had perished in the Auschwitz complex. I came across a photograph of a young woman who looked a bit like a younger version of my grandmother. She was well-dressed and attractive, with bright eyes and clear skin.

I had to read the date of her death several times before I could accept she had died just three weeks after she arrived. I felt dizzy from trying not to cry. How dare I cry over a stranger when I had never cried for those sisters, the aunts, who were permanently lost to my grandmother and mother?

In the pretty little village of Dynów, Les and I explored the streets where my grandmother grew up. The spaces where Cila's people once walked, the benches on which they sat, the rooms where they slept, the songs they sang, had been taken over by another people. I thought the very air her family and friends had breathed had been stolen by those who would later scurry along the narrow passageways between the buildings. These usurpers must have taken a long time to learn how to occupy this quarter before they could straighten up their shoulders. The Jews may have been sucked into a void but their memory would permeate this place for generations to come. Wouldn't it?

We drove out of the village and down past the railway station. A bank of rain was coming in over the hills. During its retreat from the Russians, the German army had blown up the bridge across the river. We drove over its replacement, now more than half a century old. We followed a rough track up the hill to the Jewish cemetery set on a steep slope overlooking the river. The cemetery gate had been pulled off its hinges and lay in deep grass beneath a crumbling stone wall. Covered in brambles, the centrepiece Star of David insignia was almost unrecognisable. I imagined that one of my grandmother's relatives had made this gate. He would have been so proud of it. 'Take me through my gate' might have been the last words he had breathed.

I pushed my way up through the undergrowth, looking for headstones. I blinked, trying to focus. It was late afternoon and a stand of tall oaks cast deep shadows down the cemetery slope. Maybe it was a trick of the light, but no matter how hard I looked I couldn't see a single headstone. My heart began to beat faster. My grandmother's ancestors had been buried here for four centuries and now I could barely make out a single resting place. There are only two left, Les was saying. The Germans took the stones to make roads. It was something they did to demoralise the Jews. Only they didn't re-lay the stones with their inscriptions facing up as in the film *Schindler's List*. They laid them face down to obliterate the names of the dead. Even the paths that had once separated the rows of graves seemed to have disappeared.

I began to scramble up the steep slope, slipping and sliding as I tried to gain a foothold. It had started to rain and my jeans and boots were soon covered in mud. When I reached the top and looked back down the hill I realised Les was right. There was nothing but trees and undergrowth. All that remained were the shattered remnants of one grave and another recently restored by descendants who live in the United States.

Out of the gloom a Polish farmer appeared. He owned the farm next door, Les translated. It was a terrible thing, the farmer said, to take away even the headstones. He was a Christian but had been happy to share his village with his Jewish neighbours. He said we should know about something worse. I didn't think I wanted to hear but he took no notice. It was something he had been telling people all his life. Not long after the Germans came they had gathered all the Jewish people from the village, taken them into the forest and shot them. Later the Germans brought the bodies back here in trucks. The farmer was a boy of eight when this happened, but he and his father and other local men and boys had been forced to dig a deep pit. They were ordered to throw the bodies into the pit. There were more than four hundred people. His family knew most of them, all the old ones, the religious ones, the shopkeepers. There were children as well.

'Would you like me to show you this grave?' he asked, pointing down the slope.

I shook my head, and took off in an unsteady and undignified descent, hoping they weren't watching me and knowing they were. Halfway down my legs slipped from under me and I ended up sprawled on my back. I could feel the mud oozing through the seat of my jeans. I imagined I had fallen on to the mass grave the farmer and his son had dug. I wanted to jump up and run, but instead I could only lever myself up slowly. As I pushed down with my hand I felt something hard and round in the soft slush. My fingers closed around it as I stood up. It was a large acorn fallen from one of dozens of trees that dotted the cemetery. I turned the hard and muddy nut over in my hand and looked up at the shadowy forms of the branches tangled in a dark web against the sky. These oaks had sprung from a soil rich with the remains of my ancestors. One day this patch will be thick woodland and no one will remember that anyone was ever buried here. This graveyard was only ever a temporary shrine to human fragility. I put the acorn in my pocket and plodded slowly back up the slope.

The redrawing of the map of Europe after the First World War and the consequent rebirth of Poland brought havoc to the Jewish communities in the east of the country. Many fled abroad. When a gang from the Polish-American legion attacked a group of his relatives travelling on the train to a family wedding in Dynów, my great-grandfather decided to move his family to the comparative safety of the capital. Hirsch Raff was an *uhrmacher*, a watchmaker, like his father before him. He opened up a new watchmaking business in Warsaw. Cila, his eldest child, took on the role of caring for her brothers and sisters after their mother Ethel died. When her father remarried, Cila became his apprentice. She spent her working days sitting in the shop window trying to master her trade under the watchful eyes of the passers-by. After her father died she left Warsaw for Berlin, where she quickly found work at Meobis, a large watchmaking firm, but her employment was short-lived: she had had limited training and lacked the necessary skills. She worked as a waitress for a few months before being employed by the well-known rabbi Doctor Munk in his famous kosher restaurant Nebenzahl on Strasse 52. She worked at Nebenzahl from 1918 until 1923, rising to the position of manager, which meant she supervised the ritual preparation of the food. At the end of 1923 she married Solomon Singer, who was a salesman at Baecker's, a wool shop, and they moved to Frankfurt. Solomon was a simple man without Cila's intelligence, and she soon became impatient with his lack of ambition and dull conversation. By the time Ursula was born in November 1924, Cila and her husband had separated.

Cila had been able to relax in the wide-open opportunities of German society, away from the comparative anti-Semitism of Poland. In 1918 she had been young and full of hope for her future. Now, fifteen years later, the past had come back to revisit her. She was struggling to raise Ursula on her own and give her child the very best education, which was almost beyond her means. Now the spectre of Nazism had risen up to threaten even this simple existence.

She would tell us how some of her neighbours had begun to spit on the ground as she and Ursula walked past. One day a spit globule landed on my mother's face. She was only eight years old. She was hysterical and it took over half an hour to calm her down. Every time I heard the story as a child, I imagined the stranger's putrid foam landing wet and clinging on my own smooth skin. I remember wanting to throw up. Jewish students were still allowed to attend German public schools, but Ursula started coming home with stories of friends being humiliated by teachers and non-Jewish students. Because of this, and the spitting incident, Cila had withdrawn my mother from the general public school and enrolled her in a Jewish school. Ursula hated it. The classrooms were overcrowded, and there were so few blackboards teachers were forced to paint the walls black. None of Ursula's extra-curricular activities was available at the school. Now more than ever it was time to leave.

***

MARTIN KUPFERBERG IS walking towards Cila. He is the son of her aunt Nechuma, her mother's sister. When she first came to Frankfurt, Cila stayed with the

Kupferbergs. In those days Martin had been a short, skinny adolescent with a dry wit and a serious commitment to family. Now Martin too is worried. They are surprised to see each other. He is on his way to the American Consulate to apply for a visa. He is concerned to find Cila so far from home, and even more concerned that she is planning to go to Palestine of all places.

'It's all right for the young Zionists. They want to work the farms, till the soil, turn the desert into a garden of Eden. But a divorced woman with a child in this primitive place? Forgive me, I have never heard of such a thing.'

'I have no choice,' she tells him. 'Soon I will have no job. Not only are they targeting the department stores but last week two Nazis came and stood outside the restaurant where I work. There were several non-Jews having meals. Some of the regular customers stayed. One even told the owner not to worry about such thugs. But once they finished eating no one else came in, not while the Nazis stood there. I kept saying, don't close it. Don't let them win. It was terrible and my boss became very upset. He was sweating. He was pale as a sheet. I thought any minute he would fall over. I don't know if he has the courage to stay in business much longer.'

'I know, it is terrible. But why Palestine? Why not Australia or America where your brothers are already living? You could go back to Poland even.'

'Poland, what's Poland? We Galicians are Austrians, you know.'

Martin smiles and shrugs his shoulders. 'New York, that's where I'm going. I want to establish myself so I can bring my parents and my brother and sisters to America. You should come with me,' he says.

'You remember my father, Hirsch Raff?'

'How could I forget? He was a good man.'

'Every spring during the Passover Seder he would vow, "Next year in Jerusalem." This memory is like a message from my father.'

He looks at her and shrugs his shoulders in resignation. 'How are we supposed to know what is right or wrong any more?' he says. 'May you go with G-d, you and your child.'

A studio portrait of Ursula

Aunt Tamara

Gila's brother David

Gila, David, Ursula and Tamara

A studio portrait

Chapter Two

THE TRAIN LEAVES AT MIDNIGHT

The aims of LIFE are the best defence against DEATH.

—Primo Levi, *The Drowned and the Saved*

Frankfurt, 1933

URSULA IS WOKEN in the middle of the night by the sounds of voices and doors opening and closing in the room next door. She calls out to her mother, and her heart begins to beat fast when she gets no answer. On the other side of the wall she can hear a man's voice and then her mother's. Their tones are low and urgent, and she can't quite make out what they are saying. What is a man doing in Frau Schweda's apartment in the middle of the night talking to Mama? She thinks it might be her father. It's months since she has seen him—on her eighth birthday. But why would he come to visit at such a late hour? She listens again. The man is talking too quickly to be her father.

The room where Ursula and her mother live is in the attic apartment of a large old house. Frau Schweda, who leases the apartment and sublets the room to Cila, has an eighteen-year-old son, and sometimes the two women joke about Max and Ursula getting married when Ursula grows up. Ursula doesn't like Max. He is often mean to her when the women are out of earshot. He pretends to spit on her schoolbooks and once he hid her best doll Liselotte in the coal box, something he never admitted to. A year from now Frau Schweda will write to Cila enclosing a snapshot of Max wearing the uniform of the Hitler Youth.

Ursula gets out of bed to listen more closely. She peers through the keyhole. She can't see the face of the man Mama is talking to, but she recognises his leather coat.

The local police inspector has one the same colour. He is Mama's friend. Mama is saying, 'Yes, I understand.' Then, 'Yes, I know we have to be careful.' And then, 'She is a good girl, she will do what she is told.'

When the man finally leaves Ursula hurries back to bed. The house is now silent except for some noise her mother makes when she comes back into the room and begins opening and shutting drawers and cupboards.

'Mama,' she calls, 'I want you.'

Her mother comes over to the bed. 'Go to sleep, Ula. There is nothing to worry about.'

Ursula turns over and shuts her eyes. From a long way off she hears the faint sounds of sirens. There are sirens every night now. Mama says it is nearly always about the Brownshirts causing trouble. Once when they saw one of these strangely dressed men on a tram, Mama told her to always keep away from such people because they are very evil. Ursula wonders where the Brownshirts appeared from all of a sudden and why they are so evil. The man on the tram didn't look evil at all. She thought he looked very ordinary, nice even, a bit like the man who comes to do the gardening. She was going to smile at him to see if he would smile back but Mama chastised her for staring and she had to look out of the window instead. What sort of trouble do these men cause to set off sirens in the streets of Frankfurt? Perhaps the police will arrest them and they will all disappear. She is glad no Brownshirts live in her street.

She wishes it had been her father who had come to visit. Mama doesn't like him very much. She says it was the silliest thing she ever did to marry him, except if she hadn't married him she wouldn't have had Ursula. At least that's something she can thank him for. Mama says Ursula's father is not a bad man, just a stupid one. Ursula thinks maybe her father could be bad as well as stupid because once he told her a big lie. Mama says it's wrong to tell lies.

***

PAPA HAD COME to visit her once when she was in the orphanage. He came just after she and the other children had finished lunch in the dining room. The nuns came and took her to the visitors' room. He was sitting in one of the armchairs, perched on the edge as if he were afraid he might do it some damage. She was disappointed it wasn't Mama but she smiled at him anyway. He smiled back and raised his eyebrows.

'So?' he said. He never knew how to talk to her. Mama once told her that her father wasn't used to talking to little girls. Ursula went and sat on the chair beside her father. She rubbed her hand on the rough cloth of his coat sleeve. He moved her hand from his sleeve and pointed to the chair opposite.

'Why don't you sit there where I can look at you? We can talk to each other better that way.'

He spoke to her in the same way shopkeepers do—as if he were a stranger.

'You have grown,' he said. 'How old are you now?'

'Four. Soon I'll be five.'

'Do you like it here?'

She shook her head.

'No? It looks all right to me.' He swivelled his head, peering into all corners of the room. 'It looks very clean. Your mother said it was a very clean place. Do you like the food?'

She shook her head again and pulled a face.

'You should eat what you are given. People only want what's best for you. Your mother sent you here because it is a good place. She could have sent you somewhere cheaper. Here you get much better care, even if they are Catholics.'

When he talked about her mother Ursula wanted to cry. She asked him if he knew when Mama would come. He didn't know.

'Are you being a good girl?'

She didn't answer.

'You need to be a good girl. It will make your mother so happy.'

'I wet the bed,' she said softly without looking at him.

They were silent for a while. He pulled a cigarette out of a pack and lit it. She didn't tell him he wasn't supposed to smoke inside the building. Mama always went outside to smoke when she came to visit. Ursula watched the blue smoke curling through the weak sunrays and up into the ceiling. The aroma reminded her of Mama and home. She hung her head down so he wouldn't see her tears.

'Your mother works hard. She will come soon,' he said at last.

She wanted to tell him about the punishment, but she didn't know how to start. He finished his cigarette and stubbed it out under his heel. It made an ashy mess on the gleaming polished boards.

'What games do you like to play?'

'Any sort,' she shrugged.

'What about marbles? Do you like to play marbles?'

She nodded. 'I did at the other school.'

'Show me,' he said. 'Show me how you flick a marble.'

She bent her thumb into the curve of her forefinger and flicked it out.

'Very professional,' he said. 'I was a good marble player too.'

She flicked her thumb again and again. They both laughed.

'I'll tell you what I'll do. I will go and buy you some marbles right this minute. You wait there. I'll be back very soon.'

She watched him go. He looked quickly over his shoulder and gave her a smile as he went through the door. She waved to him.

She would tell him about the punishment when he came back. She had never told Mama because whenever she visited she always talked about how difficult things were—how sad she was to have to leave Ursula in this place, how she wouldn't be able to go to work if Ursula came home and then they would both be thrown out into the street with nowhere to live.

Ursula didn't know how to tell her mother another terrible thing without making her even sadder and more worried.

She trembled whenever she thought about the punishment. In the depths of the orphanage building was a dark cellar. She had seen it many times as the children were marched in a long crocodile up and down the stairs on their way out to the playground and back again. The upright to one of the stairs was missing and whenever she looked down through the gap she could see into a yawning abyss far, far below. Twice a day she had to use those stairs and each time she imagined she was about to be sucked through that gap and plunged down into those black depths.

One night, after the children had been bathed and were supposed to have settled down in the dormitory, someone started a pillow fight, which quickly descended into a free-for-all. There was lots of laughing and squealing, and the neat dormitory was turned upside down in the process. But Ursula took no part in this. Mama had told her the better she behaved the sooner she would be able to come home. So she lay very still in her bed by the door, being particularly good. Somehow it made her feel special to be the only one not taking part in the pandemonium.

Suddenly the door swung open and in walked one of the nuns. She stood there speechless for a moment surveying the wreckage. Silence fell across the dormitory as the children scrambled back into their beds. She glared at each child in turn until her eyes came to rest on Ursula, whose bed was closest to her. Then she leant forward and grabbed Ursula by the arm, almost pulling it out of its socket.

'I'll show you!' she said angrily, as she pulled the child out of bed.

'I didn't do anything!'

'Now you are not just naughty, you are a little liar as well. Do you know what happens to liars?' She was dragging Ursula into the corridor.

'Really, really, I wasn't being naughty.' Ursula was sobbing.

At the end of the corridor was the laundry hatch. The housekeepers would load up the wooden tray with dirty linen and lower it down into the basement. Now the nun slid up the door of the hatch. She picked Ursula up and pushed her into its dark recesses. She slammed down the door. In the dark Ursula lay sobbing. 'Let me out! Let me out!' Then she heard squeaking and grinding, and the tray began to move. The nun was lowering her down into the basement. Down, down, down, into that black cellar which had been part of her nightmares since the day she had arrived. She screamed and screamed to be let out, but inch by inch the ropes were dropping her lower and lower. She drummed her feet on the wooden tray and tried grabbing hold of one of the ropes to pull herself back, but nothing stopped her downward journey. Suddenly there was a tremendous bump and then nothing. She was at the bottom. Now an even worse terror took hold of her. It stiffened her limbs, it dried out her mouth and it banged her heart against her chest. Down here the light was completely gone. She curled her body into a ball. Even though she could see nothing, she had to shut her eyes against the dark forces she knew were coming to claim her. She could feel their presence as they swirled in the air around her. They blew their chilled breath into her ears and whisked their cold hands across her forehead. There were hundreds of them coming for her now. She stopped screaming, she stopped fighting. She lay motionless, waiting to give herself up to them, which is how the nun found her when Ursula finally was hoisted up.

She would tell her father what the nun had done, and then maybe he would take her away from this place and look after her while her mother was at work.

It was dark in the visitors' room when the nuns came for her for the last time. They told her over and over that her father would not be coming back. They even tried being kind to her, but still she kicked and bit them. She knew they would punish her but she didn't care any more. She wanted to be waiting for him when he came back with the marbles. She had something very important to tell him.

***

IN THE MORNING Cila wakes Ursula with some exciting news.

'We are going on a very long holiday. We will be leaving this evening so you need to pack some things.'

'Does this mean I don't have to go to school?'

Frau Schweda, the landlady

Max Schweda

Ursula, centre, in a school play, Frankfurt

Ursula, second from left, at school, Frankfurt

In costume for the school play

On the beach, Palestine

A studio portrait

'Today you can stay home. You should decide what you want to take. There is not much space in your suitcase. You can take your two favourite books and some pencils for the journey.'

'Liselotte, she must come with us on holiday.' Liselotte has a beautiful china face and dark lashes that close over her brown eyes when Ursula lays her down. The doll has long black pigtails that reach down past her waist. The hair is real. Cila had her own hair cut off when she commissioned the doll-maker to create the most beautiful doll in the world for her daughter.

'Liselotte is too big, my darling. She won't fit in the suitcase.'

'Then I'll carry her.'

Later in the afternoon Frau Schweda and Max come to help them take their suitcases down to the street level. Cila takes one last look around the room. She tells Ursula years later that there were so many things she had to leave behind—her precious gramophone records, her books, most of her winter clothes, all her household goods. Because they have only been granted tourist visas to enter Palestine, they have to make it look as if they are coming for a short holiday. Of course Cila has no intention of returning to live under the National Socialist regime, as Frau Schweda realises. Cila knows that as soon as they are gone her landlady will make short work of claiming everything they have left behind. However Frau Schweda never gets her hands on the goose-feather quilt that Cila had brought with her as a young woman from Poland. The quilt is safely tucked into one of the suitcases.

A man arrives at the front door. It is her mother's friend, the policeman. One of their German neighbours appears from her flat and takes Ursula by the hand. Their luggage is placed in the neighbour's living room. Cila looks anxious. She doesn't know these neighbours very well. Nobody else in the house apart from them and the Schwedas knows her plans.

The neighbour reads the concern in Cila's eyes. 'Don't worry. We'll take good care of her.'

'I'll be back very soon,' Cila replies as the policeman steers her out the front door. Ursula rushes to the window to watch them disappear down the street. The neighbour's husband appears.

'Trust the Jews to have the money to travel,' he says, looking at Ursula.

'Shush now!' says his wife. 'It's not the child's fault.'

It is long past Ursula's bedtime when her mother and the policeman finally return and load the luggage into a waiting car.

At Frankfurt am Main station they are swallowed up in a whirlpool of chaos and confusion. The railway station is one of the largest in Europe. It is such an amazing building that Ursula will remember it for the rest of her life. Just looking up to the ceiling makes her feel giddy. Through the smoke from dozens of huge steam engines, she can see great girders soaring into the huge cavern of the building's cathedral-shaped dome. Ursula has never been out of the house so late before. She hugs Liselotte tightly. The station is shrouded in mist lit only by yellow street lamps. Trains are arriving and departing every few minutes. Everybody has to shout to be heard over the high-pitched howls of whistles and the steamy shrieks of engines braking. She is amazed at the number of languages she hears. She recognises French and English from her school lessons, but there are others she can't understand. With the policeman carrying the heavy suitcases, they make their way through the great swells of travellers flowing across the concourse. They are catching the train to Switzerland and the platform is at the far end of the station. She stays close beside her mother, fearing that if they become separated the mist will swallow up Mama and she will disappear forever. Finally they arrive at their platform and out of the gloom a small cluster of people appear, shouting to them.

'Cila, Ula! Over here.'

Waiting for them are four of her mother's close friends, including the sister of Ursula's father and a woman Mama works with. Aunt Tamara is there as well and hugs her very hard.

'My beautiful girl,' she says over and over. 'You must keep up your ballet practice. As soon as your hip is better you must start again. Promise me you won't waste your talent.'

Ursula makes a promise that fate will not let her keep. She looks around. Someone is missing.

'Mama,' she pulls at her mother's sleeve. 'Mama, where is Papa?'

Her mother looks embarrassed.

'You didn't tell him, Mama. How could you?' She is crying.

'But I did,' says Cila's sister-in-law. 'Look, Ula, look over there.'

Ursula looks up and sees her father standing a few metres away, spotlighted by one of the yellow lamps. His shoulders are slumped and he is holding his hat in his hand. He simply stands there, watching.

Ursula calls to him. 'Papa! Papa! Come over here.'

She beckons him again and again, but he doesn't move. He looks like an old statue in his shapeless black coat and his big old shoes.

Everybody has stopped talking now. No one knows what to do. Again Ursula calls out to her father without a response. Finally they all turn away embarrassed, even his sister. Only Ursula keeps looking. Then Cila turns around and pushes Ursula in her father's direction. 'Give me the doll. Go to him,' she says. 'Go and say goodbye.'

Ursula walks ever so slowly towards him. As she gets closer she can see that tears are streaming down his face. She reaches out her hand to him. He swallows it up into the big ball of his fist. He smells of cigarettes and the sweatiness of damp wool. As he looks down at her he tries to smile, but he cannot hold back his tears or stop his shoulders from shaking. She has never felt so close to him before, or ever feared the prospect of losing him so much. The fog wafts about them as they stand in silence holding hands in this noisy fearsome place. There is nothing she can say to him to ease his sadness, because something tells her this is the last time she will ever see him. The vastness of all that is happening terrifies her—the clanging and crashing of shunting carriages, the sound of people laughing and crying at the same time, the journey to a strange place she and her mother are about to take. It all seems too hard to deal with, but what overwhelms her the most is her inability to comfort her weeping father.

Then finally they are aboard the train, in a compartment with a number of gentiles. Three businessmen and a middle-aged German couple sit opposite each other next to the windows. Cila and Ursula are by the inside corridor, so they can't look out and see their friends on the platform. Ursula whimpers that she can't get near enough to the window to wave goodbye. Guards are shouting and blowing whistles as they run up and down the platforms. Brakes hiss and the carriage jerks. The German couple are unmoved by Ursula's tears. It is obvious they are not going to invite her over to their side of the compartment. The train begins to move now. The station is slipping away. Ursula cranes her neck to see, but the train is moving too fast. She stands up suddenly and throws Liselotte to the ground. Then she begins to scream and pushes her way to the window, knocking against the knees of the other passengers and treading on the feet of the German woman.

She is calling, 'Papa, Papa. Tante, Tante.'

Cila is pulling at her but Ursula struggles hard and clings to the window frame. 'I want to get off the train. I don't want to go to Palestine.'

'Shush,' hisses my grandmother as she heaves her daughter away from the window, but she knows the damage has already been done.

The other passengers are looking away as if nothing is happening. Cila doesn't know who these people are and she is very frightened. She tries to push her daughter back into her seat, but by now the girl is so hysterical it is impossible to stop her struggling. Cila is terrified of Ursula's next outburst. Finally, desperately, she slaps her daughter's face hard. The sound echoes like a whip crack around the small compartment. The effect is immediate. Ursula's hand goes up to her cheek, her eyes are wide open with shock. Mama has never hit her before. She stops screaming. There is a long silence broken only by the sound of the deep gulps of air Ursula is sucking into her chest. Mother and daughter stare at each other for a long time, avoiding eye contact with their fellow passengers. They remain suspended like this as the train clatters and sways on its journey to the south. Finally Cila stands up and takes a small blanket out of her suitcase. She wraps this around her daughter. Neither of them speaks. Then Cila takes a chocolate out of her handbag and offers it to Ursula. She takes the chocolate but doesn't undo the wrapping. Instead she holds it in her hand as she leans her head against the back of the seat. She closes her eyes and a few minutes later the chocolate falls to the floor. Cila picks it up and puts it back in her handbag.

When Ursula wakes up they are alone in the compartment. She gets up and goes to the window. The trees whizzing by are so close she can almost touch them. The train enters a tunnel and at the other end they emerge into bright sunlight. Way off in the distance she can see snow-capped mountains. They are in Switzerland, her mother tells her. It is the place where they make the best watches.

Haifa, 1933

MAMA IS MAKING her wear a hat to keep the sun off her face. Ursula doesn't like Palestine. Even though it's only early spring it is already uncomfortably hot. Everyday when she wakes up she wishes she were back in Frankfurt, wishes she had a footpath to walk on instead of uncomfortable sand that gets into her clothes and shoes as soon as she steps outside, wishes she and Mama had a place of their own to sleep in instead of sharing a room with dozens of other people, wishes she didn't have to listen to all that shouting and laughing in so many languages. The other people in the detention camp come from Turkey, Poland, Russia, the Ukraine, as well as from Germany.

Mama told her how, hundreds of years ago, the Arabs had invaded Palestine, the land Moses had promised to the Jews, and forced them to flee for their lives. Ever since then the Jewish people have had to wander from country to country in search of safe havens. Now, Mama says, their time of wandering is over. 'No longer do we have to behave like gypsies. This is our rightful land.' Mama has tears in her eyes when she talks of these things.

This morning they are going into Haifa on the bus. Ursula is happy to get out of the crowded camp. She has a constant headache from all the noise. Her headache is very bad today. The British soldiers are not very strict about letting people come and go. Atlith is a holding place where illegal immigrants can be looked after and fed until they get the right papers. Mama is sure the British will be happy to get rid of all of them. One of the soldiers on the gate speaks sharply to them in English. A man, a Polish refugee, standing beside them translates what the soldier has said.

'He calls us a bloody nuisance.'

'Who wants to live in a place like this?' Mama shouts at the soldier. 'Do you think we came all the way to Palestine to live in a prison?'

The Polish man tells her to be careful or she'll end up in trouble.

'He doesn't understand what I'm saying. Listen!' she turns to the soldier. '*Verstehen Sie mich?*'

The soldier throws his hands up in exasperation and walks off. Mama gives the Polish Jew her see-what-I-mean shrug.

Every week they go into Haifa. There Mama goes to the post office to check for letters from Germany. Sometimes she uses a public telephone to call a friend in Jerusalem. She would like to get a job in Jerusalem. Once she can get some work they will be able to leave the camp and rent a place of their own. She has a list of contacts in a little book, some distant relatives and some business associates of her former employer. It is always the same. They tell her to be patient, tell her they are looking out for possibilities. She doesn't always believe them. She thinks that after they have put the telephone down they probably forget all about her. Mama always takes Ursula down to the docks to watch the ships come in. If a refugee boat has arrived, they will wait by the gangplank and search for familiar faces among the passengers lining the deck rails. Qualifying to be admitted under the tight British immigration regulations is extremely difficult, and arrangements are often made between the refugees and the Jews on the docks to falsely claim they are relatives. Sometimes 'grandmothers' or 'aunts' will be handed children who at least will not end up being stateless even if their parents are shipped on to a detention camp in Cyprus or Mauritius.

Mama goes to a store she has discovered in the back streets. There she hands over some of her precious coins for some little treasures. Her money supply is dwindling. Because of the restrictions on moving currency she has had to leave most of her money in her bank account in Frankfurt. Today she buys a small piece of salami, some pickles and a handful of olives. When they get back to the camp they will find a quiet corner in the grounds. Mama will spread an old blanket on the sand and they will eat their picnic away from the hungry eyes of the poorer refugees.

The bus ride along the coast back to Atlith takes longer than usual because they have to pass through two British checkpoints. The soldiers get on board the bus. They are looking for weapons. A week ago Arab intruders had lobbed a home-made bomb into a house in the Jewish settlement of Nahalal. A man was killed and his son injured. There has been much talk about this event in the camp and the British military are anxious to prevent any tit-for-tat reprisals. The last thing they need is an escalation of the conflict between the Jews and Arabs.

'Why are you searching us?' some of the passengers ask the soldiers. 'Go and find the real culprits, the Arabs.'

They are made to wait under a shadeless sky while the soldiers check every last piece of paperwork and baggage. The temperature inside the bus soars and Ursula's throat is so dry she finds it hard to breathe. Mama gives her some water she has brought in a bottle, but it hurts Ursula to swallow and she coughs violently.

Mama feels her daughter's brow. 'Mein G-d, child, you are burning up!'

The camp at Atlith is divided into two sections. Refugees are housed in army barracks in one section. In the other is the infirmary in a primitive wooden building that is a converted barracks.

The doctor feels his way around Ursula's neck. His touch is painful.

'Her glands are very swollen,' he says to her mother. 'It is not a good sign.'

Cila tries to stay calm.

'I will have to take a swab and send it into Haifa for confirmation, but I have seen three similar cases already this week. I think it's diphtheria.'

'This is very serious, isn't it?' Cila's voice quavers.

'Yes. We will have to put her in isolation and try to control the infection.'

The diphtheria races through Ursula's body, attacking its weakest parts. It is severe and powerful. There are times when all they can do is keep her alive until the next crisis. Then her body begins to spasm, but it isn't the disease which is the cause. By mistake she has been given a double dose of treatment. She is paralysed now. They cannot tell if she will survive, let alone if she will walk again.

There is little that Ursula remembers after it is all over. Occasionally it comes back to her in a dream, first gripping her throat and turning off her breathing, then striking at her limbs until she can feel nothing except its heat and her fear. People come and go in the dark room at the back of the old barracks building. They are faceless shadows that she recognises only by their voices—the head doctor and his young Romanian assistant, the brusque nurse and the kind one.

And through it all she hears Mama's trembling plea: 'Ula, don't die, my darling. Please don't die.'

Each time she wakes she can hear the boom of the waves through the open window of the infirmary. She clings to this sound. Sometimes she imagines pushing a small boat out past the surf and rowing it back across the Mediterranean, back past Greece and on to Naples. From here she will catch the night train to Frankfurt, where the air is crisp and clean and she can walk through the rows of sweet-scented spring flowers in the park.

When she is fit to be moved, the doctor issues Ursula with a medical certificate which allows them to travel to Jerusalem for further treatment. The Austrian specialist Cila takes her daughter to puts Ursula in a plaster cast from her chest to her hips. He says it is to protect her from further damage to her infection-ridden bones. Over several months her body gradually recovers, except for her left hip which leaves her with a permanent limp. The specialist tells them diphtheria always attacks the body at its most vulnerable point. In her case it is her old ballet injury, and he cannot guarantee she will make a full recovery from the damage that has been done to the bone tissue.

In Jerusalem Cila gets a live-in job as a housekeeper for a British family, which means she is able to look after Ursula and work at the same time. Eventually Ursula recovers enough to be able to go school. With the help of her employers Cila enrols her daughter in the British School, where she excels in all subjects. Cila is so proud of Ursula, her happiness more than makes up for the financial burden.

'All I want is to give her a good education,' she tells her employers when they raise concerns about the cost of the school fees. 'I will sacrifice everything to make sure she can do anything in life she chooses. She should never have to want for anything or have to struggle as I have done.'

Nigel Hall, aged sixteen, 1930

Chapter Three

A RANCH IN CHILE

Picnic time, Chisuayante

The days of our future
stand in front of us
like a row of little
lit candles
  golden, warm, and
    lively little candles

—Constantine P. Cavafy, *Candles*

Chisuayante, Chile, 1921

HE STAGGERS UNDER the weight of the saddle. The stable boy would help but the younger boy won't let him. He has strict instructions from his father. Unless he can saddle his own horse, he is not allowed to ride. The stable boy is sixteen, black-haired and olive-skinned like his Araucanian Indian ancestors. The boy trying to lift the saddle is a skinny seven year old. Fair with blue eyes, his name is Nigel Hall, the son of the ranch owners. It takes him three attempts to get the saddle over the back of the creole pony.

'You are too weak,' the peon teases the boy.

'When I grow up, I will be stronger than you,' Nigel answers back and they both laugh.

They speak in Spanish. It has been the language of this country since the arrival of the conquistadors centuries before. The English boy who was born in Chile has grown up with the children of the ranch workers for playmates, and his Spanish is as good as any native Chilean's.

Today his mother Elsie is supervising the ranch's medical clinic and Nigel has a few hours off from his school lessons. He and the stable boy will head along the tree-lined Alameda and out on to the open plains. They will have to turn back before they reach the hills. Nigel will want to go on at this point for it is the most beautiful part of the Chisuayante ranch, but he is only allowed to climb the slopes with his father—an event that happens rarely because his father is always too busy with the business of the ranch.

✳✳✳

EARLY IN SPRING when the hills had been at the height of their spectacular colour, he and his father spent the whole day exploring the ridges and gullies that rose out of the flat coastal land and up into the towering Andes. They were forced to make many detours along paths that criss-crossed the steep slopes. Two rivers fed the melting snows from the great mountain peaks into the irrigation canals. They were fast-flowing and dangerous to cross, except at the shallowest of fords. Each time the boy eased his horse down a steep embankment into the river he expected they would be swept downstream into the icy torrent. But the pony's wild ancestors had spent centuries adapting themselves to the rugged slopes of this great mountain range. The horse had confidence even if the boy didn't. A creole pony has hooves so hard they never need to be shod, and this one could pick its way through the tumbling water and slippery rocks with the sure-footedness of a cat. With each successful crossing the boy's confidence rose, and he urged the pony into a canter, racing ahead of his father, his heart beating and his cheeks flushed with exhilaration. All morning they climbed until they reached their objective, a peak over a thousand metres high which gave them breathtaking views of the ranch below. Here they rested their horses and ate a lunch of bread and sausage. His father lit a pipe and they sat in silence watching a pair of eagles twist and turn in the air above them.

On their return the two riders passed by the dairy yard where cows were queued up for milking. On the other side of the dairy, pigs were squealing for their share of the milk. They rode past the main corral, stopping for a moment to look for action. It was in this corral that Nigel had seen his first wild horse broken.

Although the horse was owned by the ranch it had spent its life far from the reach of men. With their short sturdy bodies and great stamina, the creoles had become the perfect horses for the *huasos*, the cowboys who loved the tough little beasts even more than they loved their wives. If money were short the horses were generally fed before the women and children. Only once before had this pony been touched by a human, when it was brought into the corral to be lassoed, branded and castrated. Afterwards it had been turned loose to run back to the wild herd until it was considered mature enough to be broken.

Nigel stood by his father watching the creature through a gap in the fence. The horse was snorting and prancing to dodge its captors. Even at this age the boy could tell when a creature was angry. There were two men in the corral with the pony. They were the specialists—strong-backed and young, for horse-breaking was not a job for the weak or the slow. In contrast to the English word horsebreaker, or the Argentinean term *domedor*, 'dominator', the Chilean horsebreaker is called *mancador*, or 'gentler'. The *mancadors* talked softly to the horse. They worked in partnership, one on another horse and one on the ground with the wild creole. First the pony was lassoed and blindfolded by the man on the ground, who deftly fastened first the reins and then the saddle to the quivering animal. Then the *mancador* mounted it quickly, removing the blindfold at the same time. The horse was terrified. It broke into a frenzy of bucking, with its head down, crashing in a stiff-legged action as it tried to unseat the rider.

The boy was awed by both the man and horse. He had been told many times that one day he would have to break in a horse. The thought was absolutely terrifying. The battle seemed to last for hours, but it was probably only ten minutes before the animal conceded defeat and came to a standstill sweating and quivering. The spectators, who never tired of this drama, cheered enthusiastically.

This time the main corral is empty as the boys pass by and head off into the open pastures, cantering through fields of alfalfa, skirting the edges of the wheat fields, then off into barer cattle zones. For an hour they put their horses through a series of races as the sun climbs higher in the sky. The peon always wins but Nigel is never far behind. He dreams of being a jockey, of riding in the English Grand National, the greatest race of all. They are about to turn for home when they hear a great rumble coming from beneath the earth. The peon jumps from his horse, his face contorted with terror.

'*Tremblor!*' he screams. 'Get off your horse now!'

Nigel leaps from his horse, and looks to where the stable boy is pointing, still screaming '*Tremblor! Tremblor!*'

A great ripple is tearing through the earth, travelling towards them at enormous speed, like a tsunami racing over the surface of the ocean. Within seconds it has reached them, the ground moving with such force they are tumbled off their feet. Only the horses remain upright, their legs spread wide.

Shaken but unhurt, Nigel and the peon head straight back to the ranch. His sisters Brigid and Joyce rush out to meet them. Everyone has been concerned the boys might have been lying injured out on the pampas. The ranch has survived the earthquake relatively unscathed. Some minor damage to a few buildings will keep the carpenters busy for a few days, but there have been no injuries. The most serious outcome is that Nigel's mother has lost her false teeth. She last saw them on the washstand in the bathroom when she went to clean up after the clinic. Despite hours of searching by the family and servants, they are never seen again. The loss of her teeth means she will have to undertake the arduous journey into Concepcion so the British dentist can make her another pair. It is not long before they are all laughing about it, saying there are not many people who could claim to have lost their false teeth in an earthquake.

***

IN 1906, at the age of eighteen, she had taken herself off on a ship to Uruguay to marry her childhood sweetheart. Elsie is a devout member of the Church of England and has a rare ability to combine virtue with humour and compassion. She is descended from the Schofields of Rochdale, a Protestant family who pledged allegiance to Henry VIII. One of her ancestors, Cuthbert Schofield, lent money to Elizabeth I to finance the defence of England against the Spanish Armada. As a young woman, Elsie had once said something unkind about a family friend. The repercussions were so serious that she had decided never again would she speak ill of anyone and, as a reminder to keep her vow, she determined she would never sit on anything but a straight-backed chair. When she died in her eighties she had broken neither of these promises. Such was the legacy she left to her youngest child and only son, Nigel.

When Stephen Hall goes back to his birthplace in Uruguay to make his fortune, he is following in the footsteps of his father Charles, who had made a profitable income as an *estanciero*, 'farmer', in the country. Charles had been inspired by the adventures of his relation Captain Basil Hall, a navy commander who became famous in the early part of the nineteenth century when he published chronicles of his many voyages. In addition to documenting his explorations, Basil Hall had written the *Abbotsford Journal*, an observation of the life of his good friend Sir Walter Scott, and he interviewed Napoleon Bonaparte on St Helena. Bonaparte asked Basil why he was not yet married and Basil told him he was too poor. The explorer recorded Napoleon's response: ' "Aha!" he cried, "I now see—want of money—no money—yes, yes!" and laughed heartily, in which I joined, of course, though to say the truth, I did not altogether see the humorous point of the joke.'

But it was Basil Hall's *Extracts from a Journal Written on the Coasts of Chili, Peru and Mexico, in the Years 1820,1821 and 1822* that created his reputation as an author and fired Charles's imagination. The book contains fascinating accounts of the people and cultures of South America as well the events of the war of independence between the colonies and Spain. Along with a number of his cousins, Charles Hall set off for Uruguay. Having become quite wealthy, he eventually returned to England where he retired and finished raising his twelve children.

Charles's son Stephen returns to Uruguay in his early twenties and eventually becomes the manager of a large ranch. As soon as he can, he sends for Elsie.

Stephen and Elsie move to Chile and set up home on Chisuayante, a ranch near Concepcion not far from where some other members of the Hall clan have settled. Joyce is born in 1908, Bridget ('Biddy') in 1910 and Nigel in 1914. Stephen is amazed at how quickly and efficiently Elsie takes over the affairs of a household that extends beyond their little family to include the house servants and the gardeners. She sets up the medical clinic, dishing out castor oil, cleaning and bandaging cuts and bruises, and all the time running the gauntlet of the local medicine women. She supervises work in the large garden and orchard, ensuring constant supplies of the fresh produce that are a necessity because of the ranch's isolation. She organises the fruit picking and drying along with the jam-making. Her early attempts to speak Spanish are often met with roars of laughter from the servants, but she soon gains their respect for she is a fast learner with a quick wit as well as a gentle but firm employer.

The peons and their families live on Chisuayante in small, verandahed adobe brick houses on a few hectares with an orchard and enough room for pigs and cows and several horses. The house servants sleep in the main house with the family. Elsie is intrigued by their rituals and superstitions. Descendants of the native Indians mixed with Spanish conquistadors, the workers are deeply religious Catholics. She happily serves food and wine to the local priests whenever they visit to conduct Mass for the workers on the estate. She is always astonished by the weeping and wailing that erupts from the congregation as the priests castigate the worshippers for their sins and warn them of the perils of hell.

The servants are equally perplexed by Elsie's perceived lack of religious faith, although she and Stephen and the children maintain their own Anglican form of worship. They are a devout family. Each of them observes the ritual of kneeling in prayer, hands folded, beside the bed before going to sleep. One day Nigel tells his mother he has seen an angel hovering over the orchard, except he cannot exactly describe its features to her. He continues the bedtime prayer practice for forty years, until he embraces a new form of worship.

The household may be devout but they are not gloomy, mainly because Elsie Hall has an irrepressible sense of humour. One day when the woman who is employed as a nursemaid goes to visit some relatives some distance away, Nigel is left in his mother's care. Elsie decides to play a practical joke on the nursemaid and uses watercolours to paint Nigel's blond hair and eyebrows black. When the nurse returns she is devastated to see a dark-haired baby lying in the cot. Her piteous screams bring the whole household into the nursery.

'What is it?' Elsie asks, pushing her way through the servants crowded around the cot.

'The gypsies have stolen him!' the nurse wails, falling to her knees.

'What do you mean, stolen him?'

'They changed him for one of their own!' She crosses herself several times.

Elsie looks over the railing of the cot. She licks her finger and runs it over one of her baby's eyebrows. She holds up the finger for all to see the black smudge. The nursemaid falls quiet and her eyes grow big with astonishment. Elsie produces a wet flannel from behind her back and wipes both eyebrows clean. Then a look of understanding comes over the nurse's face. She snatches Nigel from the cot and covers his face with kisses. The rest of the servants squeal with laughter. The nurse turns on Elsie and lets out a stream of Spanish invective. All that Elsie understands are the words for wicked woman.

Every year brings its own hardships. Invasions of the terrible weed galega, which seeds three times a year, choke the alfalfa and clover pastures. A rust disease is a constant threat to wheat crops. The worst scourge of all is the dreaded foot and mouth disease, which occurs on an annual basis and is likely to wipe out the complete stock of cattle unless dealt with quickly. At this time cattle are treated, not slaughtered. No one can afford to lose all the infected beasts. So weeks of grinding work have to be undertaken. The terrible ulcers that occur as a result of the disease prevent the animal from eating and if not treated it will starve to death. Each infected animal has to be identified in the early stages, lassoed and brought to the ground to be treated with acid to break the blisters in its mouth. If the disease is caught and treated in time, the animal has a chance of surviving.

The early 1920s bring great financial stress and, with the question of the children's education looming, Stephen and Elsie reluctantly decide to sell up and move back to Europe. They set sail for England early in November 1922. When the ship reaches Rio de Janeiro the steward brings Stephen a wireless cable. Elsie reads the concern in his eyes. Cables are unusual enough and they rarely contain anything but the most serious news. Stephen goes up on deck so he can assess the contents out of sight of the children. When he comes back, his face has a white pinched look of despair. He gives Elsie the cable to read. It is from his cousin in Concepcion. On Armistice Day, 11 November, a powerful earthquake measuring 8.5 on the Richter scale had devastated parts of central Chile near the Argentinean border. The home they have just left has been destroyed, along with most of Chisuayante's buildings. There have been many deaths and injuries. That they themselves have been saved is little comfort when they think of the suffering of those they have left behind. Thus it is with a mixture of sadness and guilt that the family finally disembarks at Southampton.

The wanderlust that struck Stephen Hall as a young man has not been satisfied by his time in Chile, and within a year of arriving in England, he is off again. This time it is to Spain. Elsie and the girls go with him, but Nigel is enrolled in Connaught House, a preparatory boarding school in Weymouth, Dorset. He is nine years old and this is the first time he has ever been separated from his family. He is so broken-hearted he cries every night in bed for weeks, but he muffles his tears so neither the teachers nor his fellow boarders ever discover his sadness. He cries for his mother and he cries for Chile. He cries for the horse he left behind, he cries for his friends. He cries for the sun coming up over the Andes. He even cries for the Spanish language. Spain may be closer than Chile but it is still too far to allow Nigel to make frequent visits home. Most of his school holidays are spent at his grandparents' big house in the beautiful village of Mickleton in the Cotswolds. In that house, with its grand staircase and beautiful gardens, he finds a sanctuary that sometimes softens the pain of his homesickness and the separation from his family, but it never makes up for what he feels he has lost. His grandparents have housemaids, a cook, a gardener and a chauffeur. Every night the family dresses for dinner, and when Nigel goes up to his room the maid always has his clothes laid out for him. Despite their comfortable circumstances, there is a strict household discipline and Nigel's grandmother sets rigid rules that must be adhered to on pain of punishment. At mealtimes she keeps a long wooden spoon beside her on the dining-room table. The spoon is used to crack the elbows of ill-mannered grandchildren who might forget the arms-off-the-table rule.

Twice Nigel finds himself in serious trouble with his grandparents. The first transgression happens not long after his parents move to Spain. For a reason even he will never be able to explain, he takes his grandmother's biggest, sharpest pair of scissors from her sewing room and cuts off all the heavy drapes in the dining room to windowsill level. When a maid discovers the evidence of his wanton destruction lying in little mounds of red velvet up and down the dining room, there is hell to pay.

*Nigel with his father Stephen, mother Elsie and sisters
Biddy and Joyce*

A studio portrait

In Chile

Nigel and Joyce

*Nigel and Biddy on horse,
Joyce in foreground*

His grandparents are shocked that such an apparently well-behaved boy could be so destructive. He is confined to his room for the rest of the holidays. The second incident happens when he is twelve. One day he decides to take his grandfather's car for a drive around the grounds of the house. He doesn't understand how the gears of a car work and ends up crashing into, and destroying, a trellis of his grandmother's prize roses. The gardener rushes out after hearing the crash. He takes off his cap and scratches his head and says, 'Eeh, Master Nigel, thou didn't ought to 'ave done that.'

But his grandparents' initial belief in Nigel's good character is not unfounded, and the rest of his schooldays pass without incident. In 1928, when he is fourteen, he is sent to the prestigious Malvern College in Worcestershire, where he makes a name for himself for academic proficiency and outstanding sporting achievements. He is captain of the school's rugby and cricket teams as well as a sergeant-major in the Officer Training Corps. According to everyone who knows him, the ground has been laid for success in whatever career he might choose. But world economic events intervene to interrupt this smooth trajectory. His father Stephen, who has always had difficulties maintaining the family's lifestyle, becomes one of the millions of casualties of the 1929 economic crash. For four years he struggles to find his son's school fees but in the end it seems Nigel will not be able to complete his final year's schooling. His housemaster Mr Robinson, who has no children of his own, steps in and pays the fees out of his own pocket so his favourite student is able to matriculate. But when he leaves Malvern Nigel is told his parents' financial situation means they will not be able to support him at university. He is going to have to get a job.

He is sanguine enough to realise he doesn't need a university education to do what he really dreams about. All he thinks of are the sounds and smells of the pampas, of horses and cattle, of pastures so broad they disappear into the horizon. He doesn't need, or want, some office job where he has to sit at a desk scratching at paper all day. What he really wants is a place like Chisuayante of his own. A place where he can jump on a horse and ride for hours without interruption, not some little green English farm of patchwork squares with ditches and hedges and little trains puffing across the landscape from village to village. He decides to find a job that will give him some farming experience and allow him to save some money. Then he will jump on a ship bound for South America and see where destiny leads him. But in the middle of the Depression even a poorly paid farm labourer's job is hard to come by, especially for an over-educated nineteen year old with no experience except for an early childhood spent on a ranch in Chile. After a year of unemployment, and having failed the colour-blindness test needed for entry to the navy, he is accepted into the London Metropolitan Police Force.

The Mediterranean, 1939

FOUR YEARS LATER, and six months before the outbreak of the Second World War, Nigel is on a passenger liner heading for the Middle East. As the SS *Comorin* edges its way through the Straits of Gibraltar into the Mediterranean, he is asking himself if he isn't making another mistake. He had left the Metropolitan Police in order to follow a dream. Now here he is again in a brand-new uniform—khaki shirt and bloomers—heading for another commission, this time three years with the British Palestine Police Force in the hope he will be transferred to its mounted division.

He is beginning to recognise a pattern of lost opportunities. He should never have resigned from the London force to take up a position on a ranch in Argentina. His action had been impulsive and driven by the old dream of returning home—if not to the exact place, at least to the continent.

Even after seventeen years he remembers everything about South America. He remembers the soaring mountains with their giant redwoods and the carpets of fuchsias. He remembers the oranges from the Chisuayante cool store, all running with sweet nectar. He remembers going on family picnics with rickety horse-drawn carts loaded with bread, sausage and avocadoes and plump muscat grapes. He remembers one horse in particular, a stock bay, the soft warmth of its breath against the back of his arm, its flesh trembling with impatience. He remembers the feel of the horse as they tear home across the pampas, the wooden stirrups clanking in tune with the sound of its hooves, the snort of the little beast's nostrils as it recognises the first of the ranch outbuildings. He remembers the aromas from the cooking stoves in the peon households. He remembers his mother waiting on the verandah. All through those dark winter evenings patrolling in narrow London lanes smelling of rum and urine, as the sun dropped out of the sky at four o'clock and a damp chill gripped him to the bone, he had warmed himself with these memories.

Elsie understood. It was a melancholy she herself had admitted to once. She had told him how during all the years in Chile she had longed to be back in England. She had found it difficult to adapt to the landscape and the culture. Nigel had been shocked. Everybody had always talked about how marvellous she was and how she had always seemed so happy.

'I was for the most part,' she had told him. 'But every now and again a sight or a smell could set me off, some little blossom in the orchard or just brushing against that old lavender bush. I would feel a tug so hard it was almost unbearable. But I had a job to do. I had made a commitment to your father and I had to make the best of it. I prayed for patience and God helped me to learn to live with it, and you may have to do this as well.'

Stephen was less lyrical: 'I shouldn't waste your time with these ideas of farming, especially in any country in South America. Uruguay, Chile, Argentina—those places can break a man's heart. If you take this job, you'll probably be sorry.'

He should have listened to them because, like many things South American, the Argentinean offer had fallen through the minute he had resigned from the force. Now here he is in another police force, a different one to be sure, but he has joined up for the same reason as before. He is here because he has run out of options, and he has no idea whether he is going to like these duties any more than he did his job as a London bobby. His superiors at the Metropolitan Police were happy enough with him because he was always conscientious and thorough, but he found much of the work tedious and uninspiring. It wasn't so much that he wasn't suited to the job as the work didn't suit him. Maybe it is simply that he dislikes being in a city. So is his only alternative a farming career? He still doesn't know. He feels as if he has let everybody down, especially his housemaster who has been so generous. It seems his whole education has been a waste. What has it actually fitted him out for? The Palestine Police interviewers might have been impressed with his athletic proficiency, first at Malvern and then as a member of various Metropolitan Police teams. Sport is certainly important because it teaches you character and fair play, it gives you some rules about living life. But you can't earn a living from it. What did all that mean, being head prefect and captain of this and that, if at twenty-five he still cannot work out what he wants to do with his life?

They are steaming toward Haifa under a clear blue sky. It has been an exceptionally mild night and Nigel has come up on deck early. He is leaning on the ship rail watching the coastline rising out of the horizon. On one side of a beautiful curved bay he can make out an old fort, its cupolas and minarets shining pink in the sunrise. Towering above the bay is a mountain decorated with white sandstone buildings and green gardens.

'Mount Carmel,' a voice says at his elbow. 'Somewhere up there the prophet Elijah lived in a couple of caves.' His fellow traveller is another Palestine Police recruit, Tony Piercy. They had joined up at the same time and within days were on their way to Jerusalem.

'Really?'

'Yes, really.'

'Are you a student of the Bible?' Nigel asks.

'Not exactly. My mother gave me a travel book as a going-away present and I've been boning up. Place is full of biblical stuff. After all, it is the Holy Land.'

Nigel conjures up pictures from his illustrated children's Bible. 'Of course it is,' he answers. 'Hadn't thought of it like that.' It has not really occurred to him to put his destination into an historical context. Because he is not on his way to a ranch in South America, he hasn't given much thought to the country at the end of his voyage.

'Ever been to the Middle East?' Piercy asks.

'Never, but I think it's going to be an interesting experience.'

'Damned dangerous work, though, for eleven quid a month.'

'Don't forget you get a free rifle and fifty rounds of ammunition.' They laugh.

'Everybody says that this is as tough a situation as anything the French Foreign Legion has to deal with. Those Oozelbarts are an extremely dangerous enemy.'

'Oozelbarts?' Nigel asks.

'It's what the British call them. It's a nickname. The Arab fighters call themselves "Ursabi". Means gang. They've lived on their land for hundreds of years, and they're not going to give it up without a decent fight. It's bloody good luck for us there's a bit of a truce at the moment. Although I must admit I'm up for a bit of action whenever it comes my way.'

'You seem to be well informed.'

'Make it my business,' Tony smiles.

As the ship edges closer to the Palestine coast, a gull lands on the railing next to the two men.

'Cheeky bugger,' laughs Tony and turns to face Nigel. 'You know, I'm glad we met. I think we have a lot in common. We're all going to need friends out here. We are going to be in for a rugged time.'

'Looks like a pretty peaceful sort of a place to me.'

'Aha,' says Tony. 'Looks are deceiving. It's what is bubbling along under the surface that you have to watch out for. That's where the real threat lies.'

The Hall family, Chisuayante

Nigel on a polo horse

Malvern College, Nigel at far left

Gila and Ursula, Jerusalem, 1940

Chapter Four

THE STORY WEAVER

The truth is

that from an early age most people found my looks disturbing and many of them were strongly attracted to me on account of my appearance. This again is one of those things I say without pride or humility, without vanity or self-satisfaction.

—Laurens van der Post, *The Seed and the Sower*

Laurens van der Post

King David Hotel, Jerusalem, 1941

SHE KNOWS WHY he is looking her. It's because she is beautiful. This isn't vanity—everybody is aware of her beauty. All her life she's heard people telling Mama that her daughter is so beautiful and she had better take very good care of her otherwise there is bound to be a lot of trouble ahead.

'Painters and photographers, they all want to make portraits of my Ula,' Cila boasts to her sister Nina when they visit her in Tel Aviv. Nina, who has no children of her own, seems bored with all this talk of beauty.

It is September 1941 and Ursula is sixteen. She sits at a table on the upper terrace of the King David Hotel. It is still very hot and she is wearing a floral dress with a high collar and Mama's little brooch. Her straw hat lies on the chair beside her. Mama is at work somewhere in the heart of the hotel where Ursula is not allowed to go. Elijah is supposed to be keeping an eye on her. He's the lobby manager and has been here since 1936. He allows her access to this part of the hotel only because, he says, she is a good girl with a very strict mother. Still, if she wanted to choose any part of the hotel to sit, it would be out here. Through the french doors she can watch the comings and goings at the reception desk.

Elijah is always saying that everything important that happens in the Middle East happens in the King David. Built from the local pink limestone, the hotel's interior is decorated in the ancient Semitic style, harking back to the court of King David.

It is a beacon of opulence in an impoverished landscape. It is the place where kings and generals come to discuss affairs of state, where political enemies come together to work out compromises in lowered voices, where the rich dine without the restrictions of wartime rationing, where they seclude their lovers. Its polished brass and marbled foyers create an atmosphere of gentility. In all of Ursula's life she has never known a place like this. One day, she dreams, she will be able to come here as a guest.

The south wing of the hotel has been commandeered for the headquarters of the British military. There are many police and military personnel out here enjoying the sunshine on the terrace. Ursula has noticed one officer in particular. He is very handsome. A bit too old, she thinks, but she likes the colour of his eyes and his height. He was here yesterday. Several times she has caught him watching her, and he holds her gaze instead of turning away like some of the other Englishmen.

The handsome British officer is with a group of fellow soldiers. He sits facing her, and each time she looks up he grins. She can't help smiling back in spite of the fact she already has a boyfriend, also an Englishman.

Eventually the officer leaves his friends and comes over to her table.

'Are you waiting for someone?' he asks, and she realises he is not English at all. His accent is South African.

Mama keeps saying she should be careful when talking to strangers. Mama thinks that most men have bad characters. Ursula looks this man up and down. He is neat and polite, he looks trustworthy. She shrugs, and smiles. He sits down beside her and introduces himself. His name is Laurens van der Post. He tells her he is a lieutenant colonel in the British army.

He calls over one of the Sudanese waiters and orders drinks, a whisky for himself and fresh lemonade for her. He asks her again if she is meeting someone, but she doesn't want to tell him her mother works in the hotel and she is waiting so they can go home together. Instead she says she is expecting a family friend. He compliments her on her perfect English. Better than his own, he grins.

'But I can hear just a slight accent. You aren't English, are you?'

'No,' she smiles, arching her eyebrows, inviting him to guess.

'You weren't born in Palestine. Were you?'

She shakes her head again.

'So English isn't your first language. There's just a slight hint of something else. I know what it is. My mother's people were German. So I am guessing you are from Germany. Am I right?'

She holds up her hands to express congratulations, and they clink their glasses to his cleverness.

He asks how long she has lived in Jerusalem. She tells him that she and her mother have fled to Palestine to escape the Nazis. Since the war began they have heard nothing from the family they left behind. Now, she tells him, every day her mother prays that her sisters, Ursula's aunts, are not dead. He finds her story sad and intriguing. He's amazed her mother had the intelligence and bravery to leave when she did.

'It is not an easy thing to decide to leave your homeland and travel into the unknown. I know I did this myself, but I was a young man on my own, not a mother with a child. Is your mother happy, now she's here?'

Ursula shrugs her shoulders. It is a question she can't answer. As long as she can remember Cila has been unhappy. Her life is too hard, there is never enough money, people treat her unfairly and the Germans have driven her out of her home. Ursula has no idea if her mother is any happier in Palestine than she was in Frankfurt. Still, the question makes her feel uncomfortable. This is something she has never thought about until now, and she has a passing feeling of guilt.

Laurens tells her of his own miserable time, when he had first gone to live in England in the late 1920s. For a few months he ran a dairy farm in Gloucestershire while trying to write his first novel. She tells him she would never want to live on a farm, she is terrified of large animals. Yes, he says, it was a hard life, looking after the cows at all hours then working into the night on his book. It was impossible to make money. He was so hungry he stole potatoes from his neighbours.

Despite his poverty his new life did have a bright side. It was during this period, Laurens says, that he had been invited into the exclusive Bloomsbury group and had become friends with many of England's literary elite. In 1931 Virginia and Leonard Woolf had published his first book.

'Virginia killed herself in March,' he says, his eyes misting over. 'She was so horrified by this wretched war, she filled her pockets full of stones and walked into the River Ouse. Of course it's all the fault of that madman Hitler. She was one of my best friends. So we share something, you and I, a tragedy brought upon us by the same awful individual.'

Ursula has heard of Virginia Woolf but confesses to never having read any of her books. Laurens has discovered a bookshop in Ben Yehuda Street which has a big selection of English books. He is sure he can find one of Virginia's novels. Maybe they will even have a copy of the book he wrote, although he doubts it. He tells her

In a Province is a story about the friendship between a white man and a black man. It was well received in literary circles but wasn't a commercial success.

Ursula has never heard of most of the famous friends he talks about such as E.M. Forster, T.S. Eliot and some people he calls the Sitwells.

'I tell you what. I shall be your teacher. From me you will learn about the great books of English literature.' He claps his hands and laughs. She laughs with him.

She wants to know how he came to be in the British army when he is a South African.

He puts his finger up to lips. 'I can't tell you very much, but I have what you would call a special role. You will understand what I mean.'

She nods and her heart flutters a bit, not only because he is so charming but he seems to be hinting he is a spy as well.

He has just come out of Abyssinia, where he tells her he played a major role in restoring the emperor Haile Selassie to his throne. Laurens explains that when Mussolini invaded Abyssinia in 1935, the emperor had fled to England, where he had lived in exile in a place called Bath.

'Bath?' she laughs. 'That's a funny name for a place.'

He has been to Bath, he tells her, and describes the ruins of the ancient Roman bathhouses where hot water bubbles up from a sacred spring. 'Maybe I could take you there one day,' he says.

She tries not to show her excitement at the prospect of him taking her to this far-off romantic place, but she guesses her eyes must be gleaming because he raises his eyebrows and laughs.

'I can tell you something else interesting about the emperor. He stayed in this very hotel.'

'You mean here?'

'Right here, just after he was driven out of his kingdom. By all accounts he would have sat on this very terrace. Looked out at all this.' He stretches out his arm and points to the breathtaking views over the Old City and the Temple Mount, to the Mount of Olives and Mount Scopus. In the distance the Judean hills roll down to the Dead Sea.

'The emperor would have hated being here. It was his darkest time. The Italians had betrayed him. First they had signed a peace agreement with him which they had no intention of keeping. Then the king of Italy put himself on the Abyssinian throne. Nobody would come to his aid, not until Mussolini was everybody's enemy. Only then did the British decide to do something.

'They came up with plan to get the emperor back into his country behind enemy lines. This involved a long trek across deserts and up through mountain passes to ensure the route was safe and then the establishment of a base inside the borders of Abyssinia. They needed someone with experience in this kind of terrain to lead the expedition. General Wavell, who was in charge of the Middle East command, handpicked me because of my African knowledge. Before I knew it I'd been promoted and was sailing up the Nile on a barge to Khartoum.'

Ursula is riveted. She wants him to go on and on, but she is also worried that Mama might come out any minute and discover her talking to another soldier. What if she makes a scene in front of him? All Mama cares about is what her friends say to her. They talk about the British soldiers as if they are all awful people. How could you know what anybody is like if you haven't talked to them first? Her mother and her friends don't understand these men are lonely and far from home. They are brave as well, especially this one, Laurens.

'The only way the expedition could carry the supplies and ammunitions through such terrible terrain was to use camels, fifteen thousand of them,' he tells her. The British command assumed that, because he comes from Africa, Laurens would know how to look after camels. So on top of his other duties he became the camel-keeper. At the end of every day, no matter how exhausted he was, he tended the tired and footsore beasts. He understood how important they were to the success of the mission.

She says she thinks he is very brave to even go near a camel. They are everywhere in Palestine, and they spit and kick and bite. They are also very ugly. She asks herself what sort of a man is this who even cares about ugly creatures? He must be a good man, a man of integrity who can be trusted.

'We had to take supplies from Umm-Idla, which is on the Sudan border. Sleeping sickness was one of the dangers we faced going up to the steep Ethiopian escarpment that leads to Gojjam. Then we transferred the heavy loads from the camels to mules, which were waiting for us there—they are better adapted to the mountainous terrain.' The places trip off his tongue: Abyssinia, Khartoum, Gojjam, Bath. She imagines herself sailing up the Nile on a barge with this handsome prince at her side.

At Shaba where the expedition was assembling, Haile Selassie had arrived to wish the men luck. He was much smaller than any of them expected. 'The men called him Tiger Tim,' Laurens says.

Laurens describes the Abyssinian country to Ursula, how it glares with whiteness, then becomes a blazing yellow. The sky appears black in the heat. His

shirt burnt against the back of his neck and it was hell to handle a machine gun. 'There were all sorts of unexpected hazards. One day the buzzards pinched my bully beef. Have you ever seen a buzzard?'

She shakes her head.

'Buzzards are a kind of hawk. One minute they're high in the sky doing these amazing graceful loops with their wings pinned back. The next they're shooting down on to their prey. I didn't know what hit me when this one dropped on me like a bomb.'

Laurens suggests they go for a walk. He stands up and extends his hand to her. She stalls for a second or two and he takes her hesitation for shyness. He does not know she is trying to stand up without him realising there is something wrong with her hip. Through her will alone she manages a movement that appears so effortless she might have simply floated into the crook of his arm.

They wander into the rambling hotel gardens, where the beds are ablaze with marigolds and petunias and the perfume from hundreds of roses lies heavy on the air. Arab gardeners are busy sweeping and chipping and weeding. The gardeners do not speak to one another. They move noiselessly like a bevy of ghosts inhabiting this garden of Eden. Ursula asks him if he knows anything about the history of the hotel.

'Very little,' he says, 'but you do, don't you?'

She smiles and nods.

'Would you like to tell me?'

They sit down on a bench that has been carved out of the cliff side. She tells him that soon after the First World War ended a consortium of Egyptian Jewish bankers decided to build a luxury hotel in Jerusalem. It took many years for the hotel to be finished and it was not opened until January 1931. 'The Swiss decorator was given special instructions to include the styles of our ancestors, the Phoenicians, the Hittites and the Assyrians.'

He smiles at the way she choreographs her hands to enhance her descriptions and how her eyes flash when she catches him watching her. He can recognise a fellow storyteller anywhere, but rarely is one so beautiful. He is enchanted. When she has exhausted her knowledge of the hotel, he is almost disappointed. But she begs to hear more about how he saved the emperor.

And so the afternoon proceeds. He is at the beginning of his illustrious career as one of the twentieth century's great storytellers. He weaves his magic spell so beautifully that by the end of it she has fallen in love.

When they climb back through the tiered gardens to the terrace Cila is waiting. Even from a distance Ursula can see her mother's body is rigid with anger. She is terrified Cila will embarrass her, but before she has time to say a word Laurens intervenes with a flourish.

'Frau Singer, I bring your beautiful daughter safely back to you. My apologies if I caused you concern. She has been singing your praises. It is my pleasure to meet such a brave woman as you.'

Despite her determination to rebuff him, Cila is won over by Laurens's charm. She agrees to the couple meeting the next day. But when they get home to their little house in the Street of the Prophets she is not so sure. 'I don't know what is going to happen to you. You have already this bad reputation because of the other Englishman, the major, now there is another one.'

'He's not English. He's South African.'

'Neither of them is Jewish.'

'What does it matter if he's Jewish or not? You're just prejudiced. Would it be all right if he were a good Jewish boy wearing a yarmulke?'

'The English protect our enemies. They take the weapons away from the Jewish people but let the Arabs keep theirs.'

'You just don't want me to be happy.'

'What is this obsession with men? You are only sixteen. You have your whole life ahead, Ula. Don't waste it on such things, men and marriage. Remember what happened to me. Look at my life now.'

'Don't get married and weigh yourself down with a child. Is that what you mean? Maybe I should run away and you would be rid of me. Then you can have the life you always wanted without a child.'

Cila turns away to hide the wetness of her eyes. Being a mother is harder than she ever envisaged. Why is love never enough on its own? Too much love makes Ursula angry, and not enough has the same effect. How can it be that a child can dictate where love's balance lies?

Of course Mama lets Laurens take Ursula dancing. Ursula even allows her mother to help her choose what to wear. Laurens takes her to places in the hotel she has never been allowed to enter. They have high tea in the main restaurant of the King David. Waiters, Berbers from Egypt, serve them from trolleys piled so high with cakes that she could easily imagine there is no wartime rationing. Sweetmeats from Syria, soft ripe cheeses from Beirut, thin slivers of chicken and tiny little apricots slide gently on to her plate. It is the best food she has had in her life.

'Wonderful, isn't it?' he says, as the waiter pours her another coffee.

The orchestra plays smoochy Broadway love songs. He asks her to dance. At first she refuses, because of her limp, but he is persuasive, and when he takes her in his arms he is so gentle, so accomplished, she forgets herself, forgets the pain in her hip and forgets the wagging Jewish tongues. She will follow wherever he leads with elegance and grace, even beyond the boundaries of the dance floor. The third time he takes her dancing he asks her to marry him, and she knows her happiness has been cemented forever.

Now Mama will have to accept him completely, she will have to be as enchanted with him as Ursula is. They will travel the world together, this prince of Africa with her the princess by his side. They will go far away from this terrible place with all its fighting between the Arabs and the Jews, from this horrible harsh landscape, from the suffocating tightness of her mother's hold.

Then a month after the Japanese attack on Pearl Harbor, Laurens disappears from Jerusalem. Ursula is devastated. Nobody can tell her what has happened to him. She suspects he has been called away on one of his secret missions. Someone who knows him suggests perhaps he may have been killed. Every day she weeps for her dead prince.

They are perfectly matched. She is beautiful, intelligent, untouched, naive and vulnerable. He is her Errol Flynn. He should have been her future.

Only many years later would Ursula discover that Laurens had been ordered by General Wavell, the commander-in-chief of the Allied forces in South-east Asia, to report to his headquarters at Lembang on the island of Java. Wavell, who had been impressed with Laurens during the Abyssinian expedition and knew he had spent some time in Japan, was charged with stemming the Japanese invasion.

My mother always believed that Laurens would have married her if he had not been sent away with such haste and secrecy. Because she thought he was dead she married another man. She said once she had heard Laurens had come back to look for her after the war was over, but by this time she was long gone from Palestine. What Ursula never found out was that, at the time of his proposal to her, Laurens had a wife and two children in South Africa as well as a lover in London, Ingaret Giffard, whom he later married.

Eileen, Ursula and Tony Piercy, 1943

Chapter Five

A MARRIAGE

PAST and to come seems best; things present WORST.

—William Shakespeare, *Henry IV*

Jerusalem, February 1942

BEFORE SHE CAN begin to love a man, she needs to fall in love with his stories. He has to make his words dance in her head. It is his vision of something much bigger than himself she is hungry for. In her own imagination she has no past she can return to and no future in this country that is moving inexorably towards civil war.

The second storyteller is Tony Piercy, a member of the British Palestine Police Force. He follows swiftly on the heels of the vanished Laurens van der Post. Unlike his predecessor, who was in his thirties, Tony is young, just five years older than Ursula. Despite his youth he already has his own fantasy to tempt her. On a fine day in January 1942, a few days after they meet, he manages to borrow a police staff car and takes her on a picnic into the desert.

She laughs at the idea at first. 'Where can we make a picnic in this country? There's nothing but rocks and sand to sit on. We have to have trees to give us shade and green grass to make us comfortable.'

But he insists they go anyway. She wears her best dress with the puffed sleeves and a narrow leather belt. He is a tall slim redhead and she thinks he looks very smart in his policeman's uniform.

'One day when the war is over I would like to take you on a picnic on my family estate,' he says, as she is climbing into the car.

'Estate? Is this in England?' she asks.

'No, it's on the island of Sardinia, which the Italians call Sardegna. It lies off the west coast of Italy. Everybody falls in love with my beautiful island. You and I will walk along the sands of Alghero and then we'll go up into the mountains and I'll show you places known only to the local peasants.'

'And who says I will come with you to this Sardegna?'

'You are going to fall in love with me. You won't be able to help yourself.'

'Such confidence,' she says. She thinks he probably means to sound dashing. She wants his lack of modesty to be only pretence.

'Can you ride a horse?' he asks, ignoring her jibe.

She giggles and shakes her head at the thought.

'Don't laugh. I'll teach you. You would have to go a long way to find another man who is as fine a horseman as I am.'

He tells her they will explore the untouched corners of the island. They will ride through the forests at the foothills of the great Mount Gennargentu. He knows a little place where they can drink local wine and eat sheep cheeses made from recipes hundreds of years old. Of course they'll stay with his aunt, the Countess Mameli, on the family estate Baddes Salighes.

She wants to know how his family came to live in Sardinia.

'It's a long story,' he tells her. 'Have you got an hour or so?' They both laugh.

'At the very end of the fourteenth century there lived a famous figure of the realm who was called Henry "Hotspur" Percy. Not Piercy, but Percy. Hotspur and his father, the first Earl of Northumberland, joined forces with Henry Bolingbroke, the Earl of Lancaster, to overthrow King Richard II. Then Hotspur and Lancaster, who had now become King Henry IV, had a falling out. Hotspur joined up with a disaffected Welshman named Owen Glendower to try to overthrow the new king. I suppose this is difficult to follow. You wouldn't have learnt any English history in Germany, would you?'

She nods her head and laughs. 'No, but do I know who all these people are. The whole story is in *Henry IV*.'

He frowns. 'You've studied Shakespeare? In German?'

'No, English of course. But go on with your tale.'

'The Piercy family sprang from the Welsh mountains where some of the original Percys had retreated after the death of Hotspur at the battle of Shewsbury. At some stage the Welsh clan added an "i" to the name to distinguish themselves from the English line. Those mountains made us tough and for centuries we proved to be a thorn in the side of the English establishment.' He chuckles at this and pauses, turning to her, making sure she understands the implication. He likes the way her eyes glow as she follows his story.

They are heading south toward the fringes of the Negev when he stops to show her the desert folding away in an endless series of barren ridges, sweeping into a distant mountain range. One moment it appears to be a sterile void of sallow rock, sand and stilted vegetation, and the next a complex vista of moving colour, an array of bronze and yellow rock, remnants of ancient cliffs stretching out to a pale horizon.

She thinks the view is magnificent. How clever he is to have found this place. He shrugs his shoulders, grinning at her enthusiasm, and kicks a small boulder over the cliff edge. Away it tumbles down the scree, flicking up tiny bursts of sand until it comes to rest with millions of others on the lunar-like floor. For a while they stand without moving, overwhelmed by the silent vastness before them. Then they turn back to one another. He breaks his gaze to look over her shoulder at something way out on the horizon. He turns her around, keeping his hands on her arms as he squints against the sun, pointing to a group of Bedouin and their camels moving slowly in a long black line through the flat basin of the desert. He turns her around further.

'And if you look out there, beyond that small line of hills, those stone structures were once the ancient city of Beersheba.'

She shades her eyes against the glare. She can just make out the outline of the ruins clinging along the ridge.

'Everybody went to Beersheba at sometime,' he says. 'Did you learn this in your religious studies? It was the water, the deep wells. They say Abraham wandered for years in this area. He was an Aramean, a nomad like the Bedouin. He dug a well in Beersheba and planted a tamarisk tree, invoking the name of God. He was on his way to sacrifice his son Isaac. Beersheba seems to have been a place to go if you wanted to get some peace.'

'How have you learnt so much already?' she asks. 'You've been in Palestine for such a short time.'

He shrugs, feigning modesty. 'But I will confess to making a fine picnic.'

He's thought of everything, she thinks, as he unpacks the car. She watches him laying out the heavy tarpaulin and the blanket stashed in the boot. He has purloined some tempting delicacies from the officers' mess, some salami, bread, cheese and pickles, and a thermos flask of real coffee, which cost him a packet in bribes, he confides to her. But, despite the thickness of the tarpaulin, the stony ground is uncomfortable and they have to make short work of their feast. She sees his discomfort at being proved wrong. 'Go on with your story,' she insists.

'Our family fortune came from railway building. The Piercy who made all the big money was my great-grandfather Benjamin, who was something of an engineering genius. By the time he was thirty-five he had single-handedly designed the entire Welsh railway system. You have to go to Wales to understand what that means. The country is mainly mountains. No one knew how to build the railway lines without having to construct hundreds of very expensive tunnels, but Benjamin worked out how it could be done. He had started out as a surveyor, and this meant he knew almost everything about the Welsh terrain. He spent all his spare time studying railway systems just so he could solve the problem. That's one thing you could say about my great-grandfather, he had a lot of determination.'

She looks at Tony and wonders about his own determination. She likes the idea of this in a man. Perhaps this is what she needs, someone who knows exactly how to make dreams a reality.

'He sounds like an impressive man,' she says.

'Impressive, yes, and fearless as well. The Welsh politicians ended up using him to lobby the houses of Parliament, where they were facing fierce opposition to building the proposed railway system. My great-grandfather was a formidable parliamentary witness. On one occasion a bill was passed after he had spent several consecutive days being cross-examined. The opposing counsel was so exasperated at being outwitted that he held his briefcase up in the air and told the committee they might as well give that to Mr Piercy as well because they had given him everything else. After this of course Benjamin was given carte blanche. He soon became very famous.'

'You must be very proud to be his great-grandson,' she says. She imagines she sees him straighten up his back.

She shivers suddenly. It is starting to get cold now. 'Winter in Palestine,' she groans. 'Why is it we can have such warm weather and then suddenly it gets cold again? They say it even snows sometimes in Jerusalem. Goodness! My mother is expecting me to be home when she gets back from work.'

He reaches out to help her up and she notices a deep scar on his palm.

'What happened to your hand?'

'Oh, that. I was shot.'

'Shot? But how?'

'Fortunes of war I suppose. We were helping the army boys get into Syria and our column got trapped behind a wadi. Made a dash for it and, whammo, straight through the middle. Took the army ambulance four hours to get me to the hospital.'

He rubs the back of his hand. 'Nearly lost it though.'

'It looks as if it were really bad.'

'It was. The young surgeon who first saw me at the hospital said he would have to amputate it. Fortunately I was still on my feet and I ran into the surgery of the senior doctor in the hospital shouting, "This stupid bastard wants to cut my hand off." The SMO got up very quietly from behind his desk and said, "Piercy, stop dripping blood all over my carpet." This brought everybody up short, and he then examined my hand and said, "You are probably right, Doctor Turner, but he is very young and I think we should have a go. I'll do it myself." It took him five hours and he saved my hand.' He holds his arm up in the air, turning his hand back and forth to show her. 'Brilliant fellow, wasn't he?'

'You were perfectly right, of course,' he says as he loads everything back into the car. 'It's not possible to have a decent picnic in this wretched wasteland.'

'I know,' she answers, 'but the coffee was delicious.'

He tells her the rest of the Piercy story as they wind their way back through the stony Judean hills towards Jerusalem.

Benjamin's reputation as a railway builder soon spread to Europe, and the king of Italy, Umberto I, invited him to help with a railway system for mountainous Sardinia. The design was so successful Benjamin was made a *commendatore* of the Crown of Italy and given the freedom of various cities of Sardinia. As part of his payment he was presented with a large tract of land in the north of the island. The Sardinians thought the land useless but Benjamin poured a huge amount of money into reclamation and turned it into an agricultural paradise, constructing beautiful gardens out of deserts and swamps and planting a forest of eucalypts. The estate became famous throughout Europe.

'I hope I'm not boring you.' Tony smiles at her.

She shakes her head. 'Not at all. It's fascinating.'

'As he grew famous, my great-grandfather came to be in huge demand. He came up with the plans for Aqua Marcia, the company that still supplies Rome with its water. He went on to build railways in France and India. He became enormously wealthy and the Piercys soon established themselves as a sort of "royal family" of Sardinia. Whenever King Umberto wanted to get away from his royal duties he came to stay at Baddes Salighes, and Garibaldi, the Italian hero, was such a close friend of Benjamin's he even asked him to be the godfather to one of his sons.'

'I've heard of Garibaldi,' Ursula says. 'Your family must have been so famous.'

'They were very well connected. Benjamin and his wife Sarah had nine children, who all married into wealth or influence. Robert's wife was an Italian countess and they had a son who married a niece of the Emperor Franz Joseph. Their daughter Ethel married Robert Buchanan-Jardine, whose uncle William Jardine founded the famous trading and banking firm Jardine Matheson to compete with the East India Company. William Jardine's aggressive trading tactics with the Chinese was the fuse that lit the opium wars. Benjamin's son-in-law eventually became the head of the company and his granddaughter, my aunt Vera, married an Italian count who was the ambassador to the Vatican. The dynasty Benjamin established is absolutely littered with lords and ladies, princes and princesses, viscounts and countesses.'

He tells her that his father Vivian is the child of Benjamin's second son Bertram.

'Vivian? I always thought that was a woman's name.'

'It can be both, that's why he hated it. Always called himself Viv. My great-uncle Menj was killed in an air crash so my grandfather, being the second in line, inherited the estate, which then went to Viv and Aunt Vera when he died.'

Ursula is amazed. 'Are you very rich?' she asks, then blushes.

'Maybe one day. If things turn out,' he says, but she gets the feeling there is more he could tell her.

'I will take you to Baddes Salighes when we are married,' Tony says, his eyes fixed on the road ahead. 'I will take you to stay with the Contessa. She will send a pony trap to meet us at the station. She will think you are beautiful.'

She throws a quick glance at him. What does he mean 'when we are married'? He hasn't even asked her, doesn't even know if she would say yes.

What he fails to say is that his father's wealth had been dissipated by Vera. In later life Tony would tell anyone who'd listen that he would have been very rich except that after his father died Vera, the sole trustee of the estate, 'borrowed' the money from the trust account. When Tony's regular annuity failed to appear from the Italian bank, he travelled to Rome only to discover the money had all gone. He visited his aunt who immediately signed him an IOU for the missing funds, but she never made good the payment.

By the time Tony met Ursula in Palestine the estate at Baddes Salighes was all but bankrupt. But long before this Viv had failed in his various attempts to make a success of himself. Unsuited to business pursuits and with an education that didn't outfit him for any particular career path, he struggled to gain his father's respect. He married an Irish woman from Limerick, Clara Eileen Roberts. Desperate to get away from Bertram's criticisms, Viv dragged his wife and small son around the world in pursuit of his own fame and fortune. In 1925, when Tony was six, the family moved to Australia where Viv, who was a fine horseman, set out to make an income as a stockrider. He won several major riding competitions in Victoria but never earnt a real living. After Australia they moved to Ceylon, now Sri Lanka, where Viv bought a tea plantation with his father's help. The business failed. For the rest of her life Eileen pined for 'her beautiful Ceylon', but Tony was always quick to remind her she wouldn't like what it had become when colonial rule ended because she could no longer afford to have servants. Viv's next venture involved the old maritime fort overlooking St Helier on Jersey in the Channel Isles. He turned the fort into a riding school. At first Tony went to the local prep school and then his grandfather Bertram paid for him to board at Viv's old school in Berkshire. However, when the time came, he refused to pay for Tony to go to upper school

'I paid to educate you,' Bertram told Viv. 'I expect you to educate your own son.'

But the profits from the riding school did not run to an expensive boarding school and Tony was forced to attend a state school on Jersey. Eventually some of his old great-aunts hatched a plan to send him out to Hong Kong to work for Jardine Matheson and learn the business. The idea terrified him. How could he possibly make good in this sort of career when he was hopeless at arithmetic? He would be a failure before he even started the job. So he ran away and joined the army. A military career sounded much more attractive. He knew that non-commissioned recruits usually joined because they were poor or were running away from a criminal life. Nevertheless, the army offered three square meals a day and a pair of boots.

Of course, with Ursula eating out of his hand, Tony tells her none of this except the part about enlisting at fifteen and managing to fool the recruiting officers by pretending to be eighteen.

'All I ever wanted was to be a soldier and serve my country. They didn't take long to notice my enthusiasm. I was only there a few weeks and they offered me an officer cadetship at Sandhurst, where officers are trained.'

Ursula has never heard of Sandhurst, but she can tell the name means a lot to Tony from the way he gives his neck a little twist upwards, as if to make himself taller when he says the word.

'I had been at Sandhurst for three months when I was recognised by an old boy from prep school. He was three years older and of course he realised I was far too young to be in the army. He informed on me and I was discharged. I was ordered to repay all the wages I had received on the grounds they were gained under false

Tony's mother Eileen Piercy

Tony's father Vivian Piercy

Tony's grandmother Daphne with her children Vivian,
Boys and Vera

Tony and Ursula

pretences. My family thought the decision most unfair. So Great-aunt Florence's husband Major Graham Rickman of the Royal Welsh Fusiliers bailed me out. Wonderful man, my Uncle Graham, like a father to me.'

Tony turns to look at Ursula. His eyes are misty.

'Killed himself, you know. Wretched government taxes virtually bankrupted his estate. Could have saved it by selling off the timber rights, but he couldn't bear the idea. Went into the stables and shot himself. Terrible, terrible business.'

Ursula leans across and puts her hand on his knee. He squeezes her elegant fingers tightly.

'I'm so glad I met you,' he says, his voice trembling slightly.

It is nearly dark when they pull up in front of Cila's little house. She is waiting by the front door. She does not speak to Ursula for the rest of the evening.

Tony comes to visit Ursula almost every day after this, and each time they see each other he tells her how much more he is in love with her. The days grow into weeks and on 4 March, barely two months after she had last seen Laurens van der Post, Ursula marries Anthony Fitz-Vivian Piercy in a civil ceremony at the British district commissioner's office in Jerusalem. Almost immediately Tony is transferred to Haifa and they move into a tiny apartment in a big block overlooking the harbour. Sometimes he is away on duty for days on end. At first this suits Ursula. She has never been on her own before. She eats and sleeps whenever she wants. There is no mother to tell her what to do, what to wear, whom she may or may not talk to or what time to be home. When he is around Tony sometimes treats her as if she is a child, so she relishes these solitary times.

But then the novelty wears off and she becomes lonely and bored. She is pregnant now and feels less like walking up and down the hills to the markets. She has read all the books she brought from home, some of them several times. When she complains to Tony, he tries to reassure her. 'One day when the war is over everything will change. You'll see, my darling. You shall live like a princess.'

Sometimes Ursula thinks of the promise he made on that desert picnic, to take her to Baddes Salighes. She imagines the Contessa floating through the hallways of the great house and introducing her to another of the house guests, the king of Italy. Ursula wonders if Italy still has a king. She also wonders why, when Tony talks about his family, it is always of his great-aunt not his father. Once when she asks where Viv is now, Tony doesn't seem to know.

'I think he's doing something in the north of England. I'm not sure what,' he says.

One morning Tony arrives back at the flat only an hour after he has left for duty.

He rushes past Ursula into the kitchen. He folds his head in his arms on the tiny kitchen table and weeps. Great waves of grief shake his shoulders. He will not tell her what is wrong, nor will he let her comfort him. Eventually he manages to gasp, 'The old boy. He's gone.'

Ursula understands he means his father is dead. 'Dead? How?'

Tony pulls a yellow sheet from his top pocket. Ursula unfolds the telegram. She looks down at her husband and then back to the message. Vivian had been working in a British military hospital in the north of England. The hospital was the target of a *Luftwaffe* bombing run and Tony's father was one of dozens killed. Ursula puts her arm around her husband's shoulders. He turns his tear-stained face to her and wraps his arms around her swollen waist. She runs her fingers through his hair.

He gets up and takes a bottle of whisky from the top of the cupboard. He half fills his glass. She watches with concern.

He has been drinking quite a bit lately and when he is drunk he often gets angry with her. On one occasion he accused her of having an affair. He pulled his lips so far down into his jaw his whole face became monstrously contorted as he screamed the hateful words. 'Why had I expected you would be any better than other women?' His face was so close to hers she could feel his spit hitting her cheeks.

She ended up shouting back at him, her heart pounding more with the injustice than with the fear. She told him how stupid he was for thinking that she would do something like that. Wasn't she his wife, after all? He grabbed her by the shoulders and shook her.

'Don't ever call me stupid.' His voice had a jagged edge to it and came from somewhere deep inside him. His eyes glittered with a malice she had not seen before. He pushed her back into the chair.

The next morning he held her tight against him and whispered he was sorry.

'My darling, I couldn't bear it if you betrayed me,' he said. 'It's just that both my parents were unfaithful to each other and it broke up the family.'

'I don't want to hear about this,' she said.

There were tears in his eyes. 'You must let me tell you. I need you to understand.'

She had turned away from him, and he took this as a sign he could continue.

'Viv had this thing with a woman called Molly. It went on for years. In the end my mother said to him, "If you don't stop seeing her I will divorce you. Tell her it's finished." And he said to Eileen, "I can't do that. If I did Molly would be finished." He just kept carrying on as usual with Molly and my mother divorced him. Not that Eileen was a saint herself. She quickly married my father's friend and business partner John. I have always suspected they were already having an affair. After this I never felt as if either of my parents really wanted me. Somehow I was always in the way.'

It was a seedy little story and she knew he would never have revealed it to her unless he was desperate, but it did its job.

Her child is growing inside her. Ursula wants to believe Tony can overcome the disappointments of his childhood. She knows all too well how deep her own scars run. Once when she and Tony were arguing she was suddenly aware of her own hysterical voice, a sound so ugly it shook her into silence. In those screaming echoes she heard a loss of control that seemed to border on madness. She wondered how she had got herself to this place.

It was her mother's voice that seemed to answer her. 'Ula, Ula, what have I done to you?'

After his father's death, Tony the charmer from the family of great wealth, Tony of such high standing in British and Italian society, becomes Tony the drunken bully. His drinking bouts are linked to the highs and lows in his life. He gets drunk when he hears the Italians are closing in on Alexandria, when the rumours spread the Germans are about to circle down through Turkey. It isn't that he is frightened of a fight, he says. It is the anticipation of the battle, a chance to face down the enemy and maybe even come out with a medal. He gets drunk again when the news comes through of the Allied victory at El Alamein. When the high commissioner for Palestine declares all British police members will be classified as military personnel for the duration of the war, he gets extremely drunk. The next day he tells Ursula he has been celebrating because at last he has rejoined the British army.

'And they can ruddy well pay my Uncle George's money back,' he announces with a flourish.

He is extremely upset when he is posted from the mounted section to the post and marine division, which is responsible for the security of the port area of Haifa and the crucial oil refinery just south of the town. 'I can't function without the feel of a horse between my legs,' he cries into his whisky. 'What can they expect from a man if they take half of what he is away from him?'

When she offers sympathy he complains no woman could ever understand. 'Not your fault. Not cut out for it. It's about strength and brains. It's the difference between a filly and a stallion. And we all know what a filly's for, don't we?' His question makes her feel sick. The next day he is seconded to duties in Hebron and her spirits lift at the thought of spending time on her own.

By the middle of each day her body is so heavy and hot she has to lie down on top of the lumpy mattress the landlady has refused to replace. Sometimes she sleeps for a while. Once she wakes up and thinks she is on a barge sailing up the Nile, but the man who is with her is neither Laurens nor Tony. She tries to fall asleep again but the dream has already slipped away.

In the afternoons she drags two of the kitchen chairs out on to the tiny balcony to catch the breeze from the Mediterranean. She sits down on one chair and rests her feet on a cushion in the other. She wishes she had something new to read. Tony brought home a pile of *Reader's Digests* he pinched from the officers' mess but she finished them all in the first week. Next time she goes to Jerusalem, whenever that will be, she will talk Mama into going to the bookshop Laurens told her about so she can buy some more English books. She wonders if her love of English novels is more special because this is something she doesn't have to share with her mother. Sometimes she even finds herself thinking in English. Her accent has almost disappeared in the time she has been with Tony, to the point where some of his friends can hardly believe she was ever a refugee. She wonders what would happen to her German if she leaves Palestine. One day she may stop thinking in German altogether.

Three British warships lie at anchor in the harbour. She hopes there will be no air raid drill today. It has been over a year since the Italians last bombed the port, but still she has to climb up and down six flights of stairs each time the sirens sound. Several times Tony has been to the commissioner's office to apply for married quarters so they can move out of this tiny flat, but to no avail. Married quarters are only available to police who were already married at the time of their commission.

✳✳✳

WHY ON EARTH did her mother choose Palestine as their new home? What would they be doing now if they had gone to London or even New York as her cousin Martin had done? All the family members who went to America seem to have prospered. She thinks about the night she left Frankfurt and how her aunt Tamara had talked to her about not wasting her talent. She wonders if she will ever see Tamara or ever be able to dance again. The paralysis from the diphtheria had only been temporary so maybe there is still a chance the damage to her hip can eventually be fixed. Perhaps the ballet dream may have only been put on hold. Ursula knows she is still young enough to start dancing again, despite what her mother says and despite the fact she is about to become a mother herself. They haven't heard from Tamara since the letter in 1941 in which she said she was going to Sarajevo. But that doesn't mean she is dead. Cila always fears the worst about everything, but how could she possibly be sure what has happened to Tamara? After all, hasn't her mother said that the Germans hold her sister in such high respect they would never kill her?

Ursula folds her hands across her stomach while she thinks about these things. She remembers somersaulting on velvet grass in a deep green park, with her mother and Tamara clapping wildly at her performance. She remembers her first attempts to learn to ice skate, and squealing at her mother for laughing when she fell over. It was half her lifetime ago, a world away from this alien world, this arid place without the old music and songs or the drip of mist from the ends of the beech branches.

There is no one here in Haifa she can talk to apart from Tony. And these days he is never interested in what she has to say. But what does she have to tell him anyway? Today it takes half an hour to wash the tiny kitchen floor because her stomach keeps getting in the way. Tomorrow she will go to the markets in Old Haifa. No wonder he cuts her off whenever she starts to tell him something. When they were first married she had assumed that once the war ended they could finally get out of this awful place and her life would really begin. Now it occurs to her that perhaps nothing is ever going to change. She may be trapped here forever having to listen to endless stories about his cleverness and his family history. He never asks her how she is feeling or what she is thinking. Until recently she has always seen the future as a brighter and happier time. But what if her future is right here and now? What if it is going to be nothing more than this life in a shabby little flat with a new baby and a man who she is beginning to realise she doesn't like much? What if when they can finally go to live in Sardinia, or in England, her life is exactly the same as it is now, just in another place with different scenery? Whenever she thinks of this she begins to cry a little for what might become of her—and for the waste of it all.

The baby swelling her belly is me. I was born in the British hospital on the slopes of Mount Carmel. My birth certificate states the day was 4 January 1943. Two months later I am christened Eileen, after Clara Eileen Roberts of Limerick. One of Tony's colleagues—Ray who is later shot by the Stern Gang—is my godfather.

Cila and Eileen

Nigel, 1943

AN INSTINCT OF THE HEART

Chapter Six

Whatever our souls are made of, his and mine are THE SAME.

—Emily Brontë, *Wuthering Heights*

Haifa, 25 November 1940

FROM THIS POINT on the peak of Mount Carmel Nigel can look across to the mountains of Galilee and beyond to where thousands of years of ferocious heat has leached the land into worthless rock and sand. Sometimes he can imagine the biblical battles that once raged for its control, hear the rallying cries of the prophets, witness the spears as they form swift clouds of deathly rain. It gives him a heavy heart to think of these conflicts continuing to rage, as if Palestine were still the most fertile land on earth. Not only Palestine but now the whole of Europe is once again engaged in a cataclysmic struggle. On his off-duty days he has taken to climbing Mount Carmel where beautiful unfinished gardens tumble down the slopes into the port of Haifa. He has been told the gardens are a memorial to a Persian poet. Nigel wonders what sort of man would inspire his admirers to build such a place of contemplation and peace in his memory. Up on the mount there is still an early morning sparkle, the rising heat has not yet reached here. Beyond the gardens sprinklings of sandstone houses are gradually filling the slopes. At the edges of these new clusters of buildings, fingers of green point into the pale pink rockiness of the wilderness. After eighteen months he is still amazed by this country where the desert dips straight down into the sea. Dusty roads snake back from the Mediterranean to places he learnt of in his mother's Sunday school lessons. Jericho, Nazareth, Bethlehem, Jerusalem, the Road to Damascus. The names roll round in his head and are as familiar as Oxford Street and Piccadilly Circus. His police duties frequently take him along these paths of the prophets. Occasionally he imagines he might be a time traveller and finds himself wishing all the signs of modern living would vanish for just a few hours so he can feel the world as it was when Abraham, Moses or Jesus Christ walked among their people. His letters to his mother and father are full of the wonders of his new experiences.

Haifa harbour is as busy today as it was yesterday when he was on duty. He gazes down on the immigrant ships lying at anchor. The flood of refugees from fascist-controlled Europe has continued unabated since the outbreak of war. Tensions are mounting on the Arab side because of the pressures of illegal Jewish immigration, Hoping to cause trouble for the British in the Middle East, Adolf Eichmann's Committee for Sending Jews Overseas allowed Jews from various parts of Europe to sail to Palestine. There is a buzz of activity around the former troop carrier *Patria* as the supply boats and coal barges zip back and forth. The ship is a large three-funnelled French passenger vessel of 12 000 tonnes, which was requisitioned by the British shortly after the invasion of France. It towers over the dark and decrepit shapes of the *Milos*, the *Atlantis* and the *Pacific*. These three small ships were chartered by Eichmann's committee to take Jews to Palestine. In September 1940 nearly four thousand men, women and children had been packed on to these dangerously overloaded, unseaworthy ships in the Romanian port of Tulcea. They sailed out of the Black Sea through the Dardenelles, past Gallipoli, and straight into the heart of the battle for the Mediterranean. Heading west, they were captured by the British navy and towed under arrest into Haifa harbour. Nigel had been there the day the ships were brought into port. Those passengers who were not overcome by heat and exhaustion were singing a Jewish song. Somebody had unfurled a banner with the words: 'Keep the gates open—we are not the last.'

He can't help admiring their courage, but the British authorities are not so impressed. The refugees' hopes are immediately dashed when, instead of being allowed to land, they are told they will be transferred to the *Patria*. The British are planning to deport them. It is rumoured their destination is to be a camp on the Mauritius islands thousands of kilometres away in the Indian Ocean.

Nigel is assigned to on-board guard duties, which means he has to prevent the refugees from trying to get ashore. While they are being transferred to the *Patria* several have jumped overboard and tried to swim for land and freedom. Of course they have been caught and dragged back to the ship. It is not the first time Nigel feels uncomfortable about the duties he has to perform. For some months he has been aware that a number of his colleagues are allowing Arab militants to smuggle in weapons but confiscating any Jewish arms they discover. He does not particularly support the Jewish position, but he feels that in the matter of confiscation of arms both sides should be treated equally in order to maintain peace. The system of British rule in Palestine is so often arbitrary and unfair. These refugees who have lost everything and whose hearts are breaking are being viewed as dangerous nuisances. Nigel has even been ordered to confiscate and destroy the letters they have written and thrown down on to barges in desperate attempts to make contact with relatives and friends already living in Palestine.

He can understand the British dilemma. But there has to be a better solution than sending now-stateless people off on the *Patria* to another uncertain fate. The Jewish Agency has been making the strongest representations to have the decision reversed. The British hold fast, using the excuse that many of the refugees are likely to be Gestapo members in disguise and consequently a threat to security. Appeal after appeal by Jewish citizens to the high commissioner in Jerusalem has failed. As the criticisms get louder and louder, the British are threatening to institute martial law if the peace is disturbed. Some of the refugees have begun to talk about going on a hunger strike. Day after day Nigel witnesses the crowded foul conditions on the ship and the despair of its passengers at being able to see their safe haven yet not be allowed ashore.

When he joined the Palestine Police he had not expected to take part in so many incidents where practical expediency takes precedence over compassion. British interests seem to be at the heart of all these decisions. Lately Nigel has begun to believe the answer to human conflict must lie outside national borders. Humankind needs to find a new way to resolve international tensions. But, he thinks, it can't be via an organisation such as the League of Nations in which individual members lobby in their own national interests instead of for the good of all. Somewhere there must be an ideology that has the peace of the world at its heart. He spends much of his time thinking about how this might be achieved. He begins to realise that such an organisation can only work if it has a spiritual basis. His own Christian faith has had a long history of generating divisiveness. He spends much time discussing his theories with Muslim and Jewish friends, but nobody has been able to convince him their particular teachings offer any more hope than his own beliefs. He is fast coming to the conclusion that there is a selfish bias inherent in all these teachings and this is always going to get in the way of any attempt to bring about universal accord.

A dull boom echoes up from the harbour and into the surrounding hills. A massive explosion blows a six square-metre hole in the superstructure of the *Patria*. Nigel watches in horror as the ship almost immediately lists to its side and begins to sink. Worn out with petitioning the British, an underground Jewish organisation planned to damage the ship so the repairs would create a delay to buy some more time for pleading the refugee case to the British. But the explosion is far bigger than the Hagannah intended and within fifteen minutes the ship is full of water. As Nigel rushes down the mountain the sounds of horns and sirens fill the air. Every boat in the harbour is headed towards the rapidly sinking vessel. He joins the rescue workers. They are using blowtorches to try and get to those trapped under the ship's iron sheets. People are being pulled naked through portholes. Several Palestine Police already on duty are taking part in the rescue. Later he discovers that one of his colleagues drowned and that another died trying to save a refugee. More than two hundred Jewish refugees and fifty crew and British officials perished. Everyone is stunned by the loss of life, not least the perpetrators. A worker who was upgrading the *Patria*'s baking oven smuggled the bomb in under the noses of the police. On the morning of 21 November Monya Mardor placed the device in a small cloth bag, which he then hid in his leather lunch bag. He made contact with Hanz Vanfel, head of the passenger committee on board the ship. That night Vanfel tried to detonate the bomb, but it didn't work. Mardor brought in a fusing system and Vanfel successfully set off the bomb on 25 November. He is among the dead.

When the sequence of events becomes known and Nigel realises that he was aboard the night the bomb failed to go off, he wonders if there is a particular reason his life has been spared. The idea he must not waste the future he has been miraculously gifted begins to grow inside him. It becomes a constant echo, especially in the face of some of his more difficult duties, those that involve the suffering of the innocent victims of the violence of the war.

Haifa, August 1942

NIGEL HEARS THAT Piercy is back in Haifa and has recently married a Jewish girl he met in Jerusalem.

'Very young and beautiful,' a colleague tells Nigel with eyebrows raised. 'I suppose it's a passport out for her. One can't imagine what's in it for him,' the man smirks.

'He's not such a bad chap when you get to know him,' Nigel protests. 'We came out together. He's a bit young still, but I'm sure he's sincere.'

When he meets the new Mrs Piercy he understands instantly why Tony must have fallen for her. She is indeed young and very beautiful, but she is also intelligent. She speaks near-perfect English with a quick wit and self-possession remarkable in someone so young. She is also pregnant.

Tony introduces Nigel as his best friend. 'This man is a champion sportsman—cricket, rugby, boxing. You name it. See that nose. Well, he wasn't born that way. Took a lot of punishment in the ring to make it that crooked.'

'That's enough, Piercy.'

'You're far too modest. If it were me I'd want the world to know—captain of the police cricket and rugby teams, Middle East forces light-heavyweight champion. All sorts of achievements and, look, he's embarrassed to even talk about them. What's the point, I say? What do you think of a man who hides his light under a bushel, my dear?'

'I would think he is quite a special person,' she answers. She sees Nigel is trying to avoid eye contact with her.

'And so he is. I want you to remember this, dear. If you are ever in any trouble and I'm not around, you can call on Nigel for help. I trust him with my life and yours.'

Ursula laughs. 'It appears my husband has set you on a pedestal, Nigel. I hope you don't fall off or you may hurt yourself.'

'Never talk about falling off to a mounted policeman,' Tony chuckles, proud of her directness.

Tony and Nigel had both applied to train with the special mounted reserve. The mounted police were primarily used to maintain order in remote areas that were difficult for the general police force to access. Under Ottoman rule, horseback riders were used to collect taxes. Later mounted troopers kept the roads safe for travellers and pilgrims. So when the British arrived they continued the mounted tradition, using both their own officers and local Palestinian policemen. This new division is an enforcement unit that can go anywhere and do anything in the harsh Palestinian terrain, a smart group of men who take great pride as they ride in their precise columns from village to village and carry with them the respect and envy of their non-mounted colleagues.

From the beginning it was Nigel's ambition to join the mounted division, but it took some months before he was transferred from general duties and sent off to a special riding school in the Jordan Valley. His journey there took him from Mount Carmel to Nazareth and on through the fertile plains of Esdraelon, or ancient Armageddon, where some of the great battles of the Old Testament had been fought. Sitting on the crossroads of Asia, Africa and Europe, this battlefield was the site of major conflicts between the Israelites and their enemies, the biblical struggles between good and evil. Here it was that the crusaders came and slaughtered the enemies of Christendom then left for the safety of their European castles. From the north came the Turkish and Assyrian invaders. On these plains David slew Goliath, Napoleon lost his dream to recreate the Roman Empire, and General Allenby defeated the Turks in the First World War then went on to take Damascus and Syria.

A few kilometres south of Nazareth the road descends sharply into the deep Jordan Valley. The training school is located in the ancient city of Beisan, south of the mountains of Galilee on the floor of the valley, more than a hundred metres below sea level. Nearly two millennia before, Alexander the Great established a Greek city-state called Scythopolis on this fertile plain. Now it is a sticky hell-hole in a barren wasteland hated by the British and local trainees alike.

It is no accident Beisan has been chosen. It provides the perfect environment to produce one of the finest mounted police sections in the world. Month in, month out, they pit themselves against the twofold dangers of rugged landscape and furious heat. In temperatures that can reach forty-five degrees Celsius in summer and rarely fall below twenty-five degrees in winter, they train on arid salt pans where mirages play havoc with directions and distances. Out here the heat is so fierce it sucks the breath from horse and rider, and leaves them faltering dangerously as they fight their way up and down the cliff faces that rise out of the desert into the surrounding mountains of Moab. Using a strain of Arab horse bred by the renowned Ruwalla of the northern Syrian deserts, they train without compromise until they are fit to face the most difficult and dangerous form of police work.

It is one exhausting day after another. There seems no end to the torturous imagination of the instructors, no moments of compromise when a stricken trainee can rest for a time. Nigel's fine skin burns and peels so often it turns to leather.

When his training is complete, he is sent out to the rural police station at Nablus. Here he spends his days combing the surrounding hills for absconders—serious criminals, murderers and robbers who have fled into this difficult terrain to escape arrest. As he criss-crosses the countryside he comes to know the Arab villagers. He is invited into their homes, drinks their coffee and shares their meals. He is impressed by their generosity and begins to catch glimpses of the richness of their spiritual lives. He rises each morning renewed by the sheer happiness of at last being in a place where he belongs, sitting astride a beautiful horse in a role that gives him a serious part to play in the scheme of things. He thinks he can see into his future.

Haifa, 1943

THERE HAS BEEN some trouble with British soldiers drinking at the hotel around the corner from where the Piercys live. Tony is called away on a two-day patrol and he asks Nigel to keep an eye on Ursula while he is gone. Nigel likes visiting this little house. They are a bright intelligent couple. Tony is a born storyteller. Sometimes his stories seem quite far-fetched but they are entertaining, and Nigel has spent many hours in their company. He hopes Ursula won't find him boring. Nigel knocks on the door just after midday. Ursula undoes the lock and peers through the crack. She sees a tall silhouette against the bright light. He seems nervous and appears slightly gangly. She throws the door open for him. He doesn't know how he should greet her. He starts to put out his hand and then drops it back to his side. He grins at his awkwardness.

She has closed all the shutters to keep out the heat. It is the first time they have been alone together. It is easy to imagine the circling that would have gone on in that little living room with a baby asleep in a cot in the room next door. The power that is drawing them together despite themselves would have made it impossible to carry on a normal conversation. They would have been desperately trying to keep to a particular subject while being sucked into a state in which the meaning of the words was irrelevant. Instead of hearing what she is saying, he would have been listening to the way her consonants occasionally fall strangely into her words, giving her sentences a rhythm he could only think of as beautiful.

She makes him tea, not in her mother's way which is weak with lemon, but in the English way she has learnt recently. After she puts the tea leaves and boiling water into the pot, she turns the teapot around three times. Nigel is watching her with a little smile of admiration. She hopes he doesn't notice how her hand is shaking. She cannot think why she is feeling so nervous.

'Milk?'

He nods and signals when to stop. She sees by the colour of the tea in his cup that

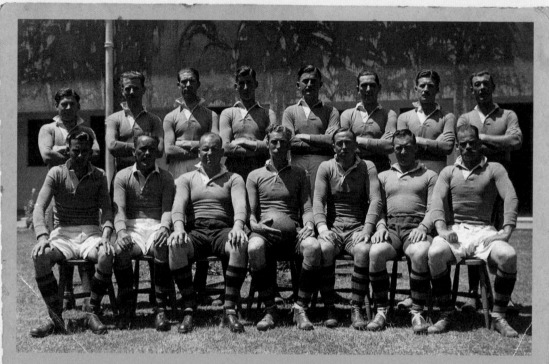

Nigel, holding ball, captain of rugby team

Nigel, captain again

it is a lot weaker than Tony would have liked it. She pushes the sugar bowl across to him and he puts three heaped teaspoons into the cup and spends a very long time stirring the mixture.

'Beautiful,' he says, after he takes the first sip. They find themselves blushing and have to look away momentarily.

His gentleness makes her feel like weeping, and she has to hold on to herself tightly to make sure she doesn't.

'You don't look happy,' he says, and a bridge is suddenly built between them. But she is still not sure how to walk across to him.

She shrugs her shoulders and asks, 'What is happiness?'

He looks at her, and waits for an answer to come to him.

'You see, even you can't describe what happiness is.'

'What do you mean, even me? I don't have any special wisdom.'

She smiles at him, and he wonders if she looks at all men this way.

'From what I have seen you are quite wise,' she says.

He blushes.

'I wish Tony were as wise and kind as you.'

His blush is fierce now.

'I'm sorry, I'm embarrassing you.'

'How long have you been married now?'

'About fifteen months.'

'You should be happy. You have a lovely baby. This house is not too bad.'

'Tony got it for us. We were in that tiny flat. It was impossible to live like that, three people in such a small space. But we weren't entitled to married quarters. Anyway he talked them into it. In the end, he said, he started to cry for his wife and child. The tears did it, he said. He was so proud of himself.'

She gets up and starts stacking the tea things. He sees she is biting her lip.

'Let me help,' he says, getting to his feet. He takes the cups from her hands and her fingers touch his. She starts to cry softly. He puts the cups down and walks around the table. He looks down at her, his hands dangling helplessly by his body. She turns away and faces the window, her arms folded tight around her chest.

'He beats me,' she says in a tiny whisper, but the words are like a lightning clap which brings the blood drumming into his ears.

'He can't. He doesn't ...' His body is rigid. His fists clench in front of him.

'He hits me all the time. He gets drunk. Then he argues. He accuses me of all sorts of things. If I argue back, then he beats me.'

They stand motionless and silent in the tiny living room with her words echoing in the dim light. 'He beats me. He beats me. He beats me.'

Finally he says, 'Then you have no choice. You have to leave him.'

'How can I leave him now? I have a child. I have no way of providing for her.'

'You can go back and live with your mother. She loves your daughter. Last week I heard you tell Tony that when he was complaining about your mother interfering.'

'That's also why I can't live with her. We argue. She drives me crazy. And now I have no hope of even getting married again.'

'What makes you think that?'

'I am tainted. Who would have me, a separated woman with a child?'

He takes a step toward her. He puts out his hands as if to reach for her, but he drops them before he does.

'I would,' he says.

She turns sharply to look at him. 'What did you say?'

'I would have you.'

She starts to cry again. She wants him to touch her. Fold her in his arms. But he doesn't. The baby cries from the next room. She looks at him and smiles even as the tears fall down her cheeks. She shrugs her shoulders and sees he is relieved there has been a distraction. She comes back with the baby, who is wrapped in a shawl and has immediately fallen back to sleep in her arms. She peels back the shawl to show him her daughter's face. He looks at Ursula's long tanned fingers stroking the tiny cheeks. He wants to hold those fingers, feel their smooth heat curling around his. He doesn't touch her fingers. Instead he strokes the soft down on the baby's head. They are bending together now, their cheeks almost touching as they peer into the little face. She thinks she hears his heart beating fast, or maybe it is her own. She knows he wants to touch her, but he doesn't. He stumbles awkwardly to the door. He says goodbye and turns quickly into the bright light.

When Tony comes home, he is drunk again. She is more gentle with him than she has been for a long time.

'You look very beautiful when you're happy,' he says, just before he falls asleep.

After she has fed the baby she stands for a long time looking out into the garden. She wonders what tomorrow will bring.

Tony discovers them one afternoon when he comes home unexpectedly with his Arab batman. He sees his wife in the arms of his best friend. He would say later he pulled out his revolver to shoot Nigel and it was only the batman leaping at his arm and deflecting the bullet that saved his friend's life.

After Nigel has gone she tells Tony she must leave him. He begs and weeps but she is unmoved. She remembers how convincing his theatrics can be. He promises to change, but she says it is too late. She knows it is nothing to do with Tony anymore. She wants to be with Nigel.

'We just fell in love' is what she says about this time. It was not what they had intended but once it happened there was nothing they could do to stop it. Nigel suffered because of it—racked by the various commandments he was breaking and by the betrayal of his friend. Despite this he could not turn away from her. On 24 August 1943 they declare their love for each other by exchanging books. She gives him a copy of *Wild Animals at Home* by Ernest Seton; he gives her Rudyard Kipling's *Sixty Poems*.

Ursula takes me, her little daughter, back to live with Cila in Jerusalem. She has no choice and of course she can do nothing right in her mother's eyes, especially when it comes to looking after her baby. My grandmother smothers me with a love she has been saving up for years. I am now the substitute baby Ursula. She buys me beautiful clothes, takes me to the same portrait photographer that she took Ursula to in Ben Yehuda Street and shows me off to all her friends. Meanwhile the battle for control rages between her and my mother. Floundering in a sea of helplessness that sweeps in with her daughter's separation from Tony, Cila attempts to reassert control over Ursula's life. Events have proved my grandmother right. Men are all to be despised as unreliable and deceitful beings with no principles. Her venom is particularly directed at Nigel. Her anger makes it impossible for him to visit the house. Instead, whenever he is able to get away from Haifa, Ursula has to use subterfuge so she can spend time with him. Of course Cila knows exactly what she is doing and this regularly raises the heat to an almost unbearable level. Cila always returns to the same solution. Ursula should go back to her husband. Her mother refuses to acknowledge the seriousness of Tony's violent behaviour.

'All people who marry argue at first. It is a natural thing,' she tells her daughter. 'I argued with your father.'

'And you left him.'

'So maybe this was a mistake.'

'Now you say this,' Ursula shouts. 'And what's so wonderful about your precious son-in-law?'

'He can make you comfortable. You won't be poor. Security is more important than this thing you call love. I would do anything to make you see this.'

On Ursula's twentieth birthday Nigel comes to the house carrying a bunch of flowers. He has managed to get a transfer and has been living in Jerusalem for nearly six months. Cila is about to leave for work at the King David Hotel. She presses her lips together as Ursula lets Nigel in. After Cila leaves he gives Ursula a little silver brooch he bought in the markets in the Old City. She pins it to her dress and waltzes round the room to show him how it looks. She sees he is trying to smile for her.

'What's the matter?' She sits down next to him and takes his hand.

'They are sending me back.'

'But you've still got months to go, and what about your re-engagement?'

'It's all over.'

'But why?'

He doesn't answer.

'It's because of me, isn't it? And of course Tony's behind this.'

He shakes his head. 'No. It is about us, but it's not Tony. It is your mother. Apparently she went to the commander.'

She jumps up. Her eyes are blazing. 'No, no!' she screams. 'What has she done? Why would she do this?'

He leans forward and takes her hand, pulling her down beside him.

'Come on, calm down. You have to see it from her point of view.'

She knows why he's taking her mother's part. It's because deep down he believes their relationship is a sin in the eyes of his god. She hates the way he sullies their love with his guilt—the very goodness she adores in him places a barrier between them. Instead of being able to revel in their love, she feels as if she is responsible for making him miserable, as if she ought to be feeling guilty as well.

'I told you it wouldn't work out coming to live here. My mother always tries to control my life.'

'She did it because she wants what's best for you.'

'She wants me to go back to Tony. She thinks I should put up with his violence because she thinks he's rich. I've tried to tell her that's probably one of his lies too, but she still won't listen to me.'

'Well, it's too late now. I went for a medical examination yesterday.'

'A medical? I don't understand.'

He had been called into police headquarters and told he had got himself into a complete mess. 'We've heard the gossip of course and turned a blind eye, but now Piercy's mother-in-law has become involved. I can't see how you can possibly stay on. Surprises me, Hall, didn't think you were the type to bring the force into disrepute.'

'Seems your faith in me was misplaced, sir.'

'I've been looking at your service record. You've passed exams in Spanish, French and Arabic. Most of our constables couldn't pass an English test. You're reliable and intelligent. You've been decorated twice and commended on one occasion. The commendation was the business with defusing the bomb under the stadium, wasn't it?'

Nigel nodded and blushed. He hated the fuss that had been made about this incident. He had only been doing his job. Any of his colleagues would have done the same thing.

'But it seems there are those who would like to make an example of you. I'll try and see what we can do to make sure you don't have a black mark on your record. I want you to see the medical examiner so we can get a report on your fitness for further service. Seems you may have a problem with your nose.'

'Nose, sir?'

'You only have one nose, the one that was broken in the boxing tournament.'

He is to be discharged as medically unfit, Nigel tells Ursula. 'They have told me to apply for repatriation because I need plastic surgery on my nose, which can only be done in England. If I go along with this it will mean they won't have to give me a dishonourable discharge.'

'I think they are crazy. You are the most honourable person I have ever met in my life.' Then she bursts into tears. 'I don't want you to go. What will I do?'

He puts his arm around her. 'It's going to take a few weeks for all this to come through.'

She wants to go with him, but he says it's still far too dangerous for them to travel. 'The way things are going the war must end soon. When it's over I'll send for you and Eileen. I promise.'

Leaving Palestine, March 1945

MY MOTHER HAS me in her arms as she and Cila argue outside the P&O ticket office. As Cila hands over the envelope of money, her face becomes pinched and her lips tremble. Ursula passes me over to her mother. I am two years old.

'I hate it when you cry,' she snaps. 'If you didn't want to give me the money, you shouldn't have agreed to do it.'

'You know very well it is against my will. If only you would be patient. Nigel has only been back in London for a few weeks.'

'I have been patient. I can't wait. I can't wait any more.'

She knows what Cila is thinking. She thinks if she keeps her in Palestine long enough, Nigel will get over his infatuation and find some pretty little unattached English girl with good manners and a genteel background. Then she can hand her daughter and granddaughter back to Tony in a neat little family package.

'Even if I don't marry Nigel, I will never go back to Tony. So your little plan to get rid of Nigel was a waste of time. I have told you enough times, if what you have done means we don't ever get married I will cut you out of my life forever.'

'That's not my reason. I am frightened for you going in the middle of the war on a ship that could be sunk at anytime. Think of your child if you refuse to think of yourself.'

'I told you, Mama, the English will have warships guarding us. We'll be in less danger than we are here from Palestinian or Jewish terrorists.'

'Even Nigel has told you it is not safe yet.'

My mother carries me on board the ship that will take us to England. Ursula can see her mother struggling to maintain her composure as we say our goodbyes at the top of the gangplank.

'Don't worry, Mama, we are going to be all right. You'll see. When the war is over you can come and visit us.'

Cila smiles, but Ursula can read the disbelief in her mother's eyes.

'Wave to Mama,' Ursula says to me as Cila heads down to the dock. '*Auf Weidersehen*, Mama. Say it, Eileen.'

But Cila does not turn round until she is far enough away so that we cannot see her tears.

We arrive in Southampton on a cold day in the early spring. Later Ursula will hardly recall any details of the voyage through the dangerous waters of the Mediterranean. Her heart sings day and night with thoughts of seeing Nigel again. Much of the time the few civilian passengers are confined below decks to their sleeping quarters. One of the few other women on the ship befriends Ursula and sometimes helps by looking after me while she takes a break. Miss Broome is a senior civil servant who is concerned about this young mother and her little girl and their uncertain future. But when Ursula talks with her about her plans it isn't like listening to Cila. She doesn't make Ursula feel as if it would break her heart if her advice were ignored. As they are disembarking Miss Broome gives Ursula her card, saying if she needs any help to call her. She is going straight up to London, she says, and will be in her office by mid-afternoon.

When it is Ursula's turn to go through immigration, the official behind the counter takes a long time to scrutinise her visa and passport.

'So you were born in Germany?'

'Yes,' she answers, trying hide the anxiety in her voice.

'England is at war with Germany. I expect you know this?'

'Of course,' she snaps, 'but I am a British citizen. I am married to an Englishman.'

'And where is your husband?'

'I don't know. He left Palestine last year. I think he is here in England.'

The official says nothing. He keeps flicking through the blank pages of her passport as if he is looking for some sort of evidence. Perhaps he suspects I'm a spy, she thinks.

'My husband, we are separated.'

'Have you come here to find him?'

She shakes her head.

'I think we have a problem here. You are actually a German national. You are a British citizen only because of your marriage, and now you are telling me your husband left you. What are we to think?'

'Actually I left him.'

The official raises his eyebrows to show her he thinks this information has made her situation worse, not better.

Then she remembers the kind civil servant. She shows the official Miss Broome's business card. He tells Ursula there is a waiting room across the hall and he will come and find us when a decision has been made.

After several agonising hours, the official finally appears. 'You are a very lucky woman,' he says. 'You have friends in very high places.'

Within a few minutes she is stepping on to English soil with me on her hip. The air is crisp and the sky is blue. She gasps with relief as she sees Nigel walking toward her. She never does find out why Miss Broome is so influential, but she never forgets her kindness.

Training camp, Nigel far right

A Palestine Police funeral

In London, 1946

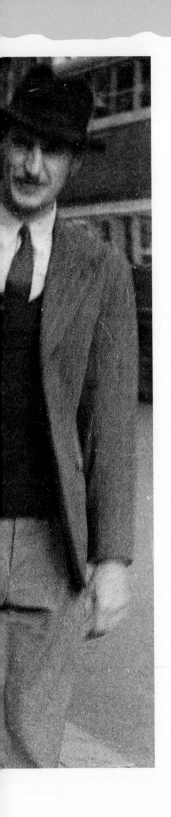

Chapter Seven

LONDON

PEACE ON EARTH
would be the end
of civilisation
as we know it

—Joseph Heller, *Picture This*

London, 1945

ELSIE HALL POURS Ursula another tea in the delicate floral cup. Nigel's father has at last taken down the heavy blackout curtains and the late afternoon sun filters into the parlour like a sigh of relief. Elsie leans across and pats the back of Ursula's hand.

'My dear, believe me, all I want is for Nigel to be happy and if that is what you can give him, then it's perfectly all right with me,' she says.

Ursula digs in her handbag for another handkerchief. She blows her nose to stop herself crying again.

'There's nothing else I can do,' she sniffles.

The older woman continues. 'This trouble between the two of you is not all his sisters' fault, you know. You also have to learn to steer your own true course. It doesn't matter what others think or say. If you believe my son is right for you, then that's all that counts.'

Ursula's eyes fill up. 'But how do I know if it is what he wants? Why isn't he here with me now? Why has he run away to Scotland?'

The thought of him fleeing from her makes her feel like wailing—and why shouldn't she if she wants to? She would if it were Mama sitting here instead of the self-contained Elsie.

'I don't think he has run away permanently. He just took this job to give himself some time to think. But I know Nigel. He's like his father. If you don't act, he'll shilly-shally forever. For your own sake you'll have to put your foot down and force him to make a decision.'

Ursula stares at this straight-backed woman with open-eyed amazement. Elsie's blue eyes, Nigel's eyes, twinkle back at her.

Ursula rubs her forehead with the back of her hand. 'Do you think it will work?' She searches Elsie's face.

'At least you will both be put out of your misery, one way or another. But if I know my son, he won't disappoint you.'

Ursula is full of wonder for this woman, for her wisdom and compassion. Still she can't help thinking whether, underneath all her charity, Elsie might be secretly despairing of her son's choice. After all, the strikes must be mounting up against her as a potential daughter-in-law. The Halls are upper middle-class, church-going Anglicans who can trace their heritage right back to the days of Elizabeth I. Ursula is very young, a foreigner, Jewish and estranged from a husband with whom she has a child. She imagines how easy it would be for Elsie to assume her son has been trapped by a go-getter out to make a new life for herself. She knows this is what his sisters think. She is sure Biddy and Joyce are constantly trying to undermine her with their younger brother. Of course they are polite to her, but not very warm. Joyce, particularly, makes little digs, which Nigel says Ursula should ignore. They probably hope his infatuation is temporary and that he'll come to his senses and move on to someone more suitable. But now Elsie has given her support, Ursula knows she doesn't need his sisters' approval. She smiles and finishes her tea.

When Nigel gets off the train at Paddington station the following Saturday, she is waiting for him. His face lights up when he sees her, and she feels some of the tension fall out of her body.

'I have something to say.' The words spill out of her mouth as soon as he is close enough to hear her.

He smiles. 'Well, go ahead. Spit it out.'

'It's not a joke.'

He puts down his suitcase. 'I'm sorry, I'm listening.'

'I want you to come back to London. I don't want us to be apart any more. I want you and I to live together.'

He looks down at his feet. They stand there silently with the other passengers milling around them. 'What's brought this on?' he says at last.

'If you really love me you will do it. If you don't come and live with me, I'll have to go back to Palestine.'

'You know I love you.'

'How can I be sure?'

He is quiet again. 'Yes, of course. You're right. I'm sorry,' he says finally. 'It's not easy for me, all this. I'm not as brave as you.' He puts his arms around her and pulls her close to him. 'I will love you forever. You can stop being afraid now.'

'Then it is done,' she says, and they both laugh as they set off towards the exit.

'There is one more thing,' she says quietly as they wait for the bus.

'Anything you want.'

'I want us to have a baby—now, our baby. I don't want to wait until after the divorce.'

***

SHE IS SMOKING the last cigarette in the packet. She stands on the porch peering into the murk of the evening, watching for the first glimpse of his shadow to turn into the gate. Dark figures appear and disappear along the footpath out of the gloom. None of them is tall enough or slim enough to be him. Every evening he begs her not to wait out in the cold, but she can't help herself. She doesn't want to miss a minute of her precious time with him. With each new set of approaching footsteps her heart jumps. She can't wait to look into his gentle eyes. This evening he'll be bringing home the wages. The money will be more than it usually is. He has done a few extra hours this week, but they haven't been able to work out whether it will be a lot of money or just a little extra. Last time he was paid overtime he bought her a bottle of sherry, but he didn't buy her cigarettes. Nearly every week he forgets the cigarettes.

Miss Sharples opens the front door. 'Oh, it's you!' she says snappily, as if she hasn't just been peering through the slit in the curtains. The landlady wrinkles her nose and sniffs at the cigarette smoke. 'Filthy habit!' she mutters, slamming the door shut.

Ursula thinks something dreadful must have happened to Miss Sharples, some great disappointment in her life, to make her so bitter. What sort of woman would be responsible for separating a mother from her child?

At least they will have the money for the weekend trip to Orpington. Just the thought of seeing her little girl fills Ursula with anxiety, because with the joy of each visit comes the agony of the leave-taking. Thank heavens Nigel is always there to help her through it. How could she manage this life without him, without the compassion that spills from him—not just for her but for everybody he meets? How easily he has slipped into the role of fatherhood. She smiles to herself when she remembers how he makes her daughter laugh.

***

WHEN THEY COME to visit me he makes all the other children laugh as well. Even some of the nuns laugh, which is an amazing sight in itself. He sits on one of the little chairs in the orphanage dining room. He is so tall he has to crouch down over the table so his ears are somewhere between his knees. My mother stands by the door watching us. Through my laughing tears I look up at her and she smiles, in that way she does with her head tilted to one side. Nigel is eating all the leftovers on the table. He is scooping up all the watery custard and bits of cold apple from the tiny bowls, slurping the dregs off the little spoon with exceedingly bad table manners. There is a little bit of custard on his moustache, and one of the boys shouts to tell him. Nigel puts out his tongue and wipes off the offending blob. When he finishes licking he looks at me and rolls his blue eyes. And we all start laughing again. He is my hero. He brings me laughter every weekend.

After the laughter they always leave. It is the same every time. I know because I have learnt to watch them carefully. They look at each other and then at me. I know the clock is beginning to tick down. When they see me watching them they look away from each other, but first I see him nod slowly to her. Then she picks up her cane handbag and holds it tight against her stomach. She is getting ready to move. Nigel is standing up now. He leans down and picks me up and carries me to her. She puts the bag down again and takes me in her arms, but then she turns her head away as if she can't bear to look at me. He pats both our backs at the same time. Soon he reduces my screams to sobs.

My mother is telling me to be patient and that I won't have to live in this place much longer. As soon as she and Nigel can find a flat where they are allowed to have children, she says, they will come and get me. I beg to go home with them, but she says Miss Sharples is very strict and won't allow children in her house. I hate Miss Sharples. I hate this St Mary's place where the toilets are outside, where the nuns shout at you when you wet the bed and the other children tease you because of it.

My mother begins to cry as I grasp hold of her coat and refuse to let her go. She is shaking, looking from Nigel to me. She does not know how to deal with my screaming. Nigel pulls me away and hugs me until I calm down, then hands me to one of the nuns. As they leave my mother looks back. I can see she is still crying.

***

IT IS HER worst nightmare, having to leave me. The pain is still as sharp when she talks about it decades later. She knew only too well how much I must have been suffering, how much she had suffered being separated from her own mother. When

I am grown up she will say it broke her heart every time. It surprises me to hear her say this because I have no memory of her ever comforting me. She says she always had absolute faith their troubles would soon be over. Even though, she will say, it might have seemed as if their position were hopeless, she never faltered in this belief. Whenever she looked at Nigel, let him take her in his arms, she knew he would care for her and she knew she could never be happy with someone else.

Nigel works all day in the plastics factory near Regent's Park. He says he doesn't mind the work, but the money is hardly enough to keep them. Ursula also looks for work, but her experience and skills are limited. She does some modelling for a while, but she is restricted by her limp and there are few jobs available in post-war London. Before she becomes pregnant again she works for several months in a high-fashion dress salon in Bond Street. Now they have to rely on his income. Many of those who served during the war get their old jobs back, but because Nigel has been discharged from the Palestine Police he doesn't even have a job to go back to. She aches for him as he goes off to the factory every day in such good spirits, as if he didn't care at all. But she knows it is a game he is playing to keep her from worrying about him.

'What have I done to you?' he asks more than once. 'This is a terrible life.'

'But you have said yourself it is only the beginning, and as long as we're together we can overcome anything.'

'But it's my fault you and Eileen are apart. If only I could find a way to make a better living.'

Then she takes his hand and holds it up to her cheek. 'We are in this together. I have faith in you,' she murmurs. 'You must trust yourself as well.'

She has news for him today. Something happened while she was out walking in Kensington Gardens. She goes there every day. It is quiet and beautiful with mothers and nannies watching as their children play underneath the old oaks and chestnut trees. She thinks of her little girl in the orphanage and the new baby growing inside her. She thinks of Nigel hard at work but nothing changing. She swallows down her fear, tries not to cry.

One morning a woman sits down on the bench beside her. Ursula has seen her in the park before. The woman's name is Beryl Kennedy. She has red hair and she is very friendly. She doesn't seem to care that my mother is a foreigner. They talk about Ursula's pregnancy while Beryl's children charge about through the manicured garden beds, trampling plants underfoot. Ursula tells Beryl about her daughter being in an orphanage. She finds herself crying when she tells the story.

Today Beryl is in the park again. Her new friend is very excited. She has a plan for my mother to bring me back to London. Since they last met, Beryl has spent a lot of time worrying about my mother's dilemma, and she has come up with an idea that she thinks might solve the problem. Her eyes dance.

'You can come and stay with us. It's a council flat and I'm not really supposed to let rooms out, but with the housing shortages nobody cares. You can have one of the children's bedrooms. It's a bit small but at least you can have your little girl. You'll have to share the kitchen and the bathroom. We can work out something reasonable for the rent.'

Ursula waits on the porch, impatient to tell Nigel her exciting news. Suddenly he is there, emerging from the gloom. She runs down the steps and throws her arms around him. 'I have something important to tell you. You will be so proud of me. We can go and fetch Eileen this weekend. We can be a family at last.'

Their new room is very small indeed. There is just space enough for a little wardrobe, a chest of drawers, a single bed for Nigel and Ursula and a cot. The Kennedys' flat is part of a grand mansion that has been acquired by the Borough of Kensington as council flats. The flat is huge and takes up two floors of the house. It is not long before my mother discovers that the rent she and Nigel are paying for their tiny room is more than the Kennedys pay for the whole flat. Now she understands the real reason Beryl was so excited.

The news of the bombing is all over the newspapers. He sees the headlines as he comes home from work: 'JEWS BLOW UP KING DAVID HOTEL'. His stomach turns at the thought Ursula's mother may have been injured or even killed. He buys a newspaper. Nearly a hundred people have died, including many British soldiers and civilians. He hopes Ursula hasn't been listening to the news on the wireless. Even though he dreads the thought of having to tell her, he would rather it came from him and not from some anonymous news announcement. She hasn't heard. She lets out a sharp gasp and her face goes white when he tells her. She grips her hands across her swollen stomach but she knows what to do.

'You must go to the post office and send two telegrams,' she tells him. 'One to Elijah, the lobby manager at the King David, and one to Mama at home. Tell them we need to know urgently. And I need some more cigarettes. Please don't forget this time.'

The next morning a telegram arrives, just after Nigel has left. He has wanted to stay home with her, but she won't let him. Her hands tremble as she opens the envelope. She looks at the sender's name first. Thank God it is her mother's. The bombing took place on Cila's day off. She is perfectly all right. A letter is following. Ursula cries for a long time when she realises her mother is safe. Then she gets into bed where Nigel finds her tear-stained and hungry when he gets home from work.

On 10 December 1946 Diana is born. Nigel and I go and visit my new sister and my mother in hospital. We stand waiting to cross a busy London street. The lights from the cars and the street lamps swirl into the evening, but I feel safe because he is holding my hand. When Diana comes home she sleeps in the bottom of the chest of drawers. There is no room for a bassinet in the already cramped room.

On fine days my mother takes us out to the park. On rainy days we go to Paddington station to watch the comings and goings. Today snow has fallen and there is not a cloud in the sky. In the park the trees are sparkling with frost and the round pond in front of Kensington Palace has frozen over. The ducks we have fed all summer are gone and in their place are dozens of people skating. The skilful ones speed and glide as if they were born to it. My mother and I laugh at the others who keep falling on their bottoms every time they try to stand up. I want to skate too but she won't let me. It's for grown-ups, she tells me. I cry so loudly she has to promise that one day she will buy me a pair of skates.

'Let's go and see Peter Pan,' she says, and I run ahead to where Peter stands on his pedestal blowing his horn. Below him are a retinue of fairies and rabbits to keep him company. I love running my hands over the soft bronze rabbits' ears. If nobody can hear me, I talk to these creatures as if they can answer me. There is one fairy low down with a perfect pair of wings. Sometimes when my mother has been angry with me I pretend to borrow the little fairy's wings and fly away. When we get home my mother wheels my sister out on to the front steps to make sure she gets plenty of fresh air. She puts a hot-water bottle in the pram to keep her warm in the middle of the bitter winter. Diana thrives. A proper English baby, they call her. My sister has blue eyes like her father's.

***

URSULA IS VERY nervous. My father Tony is due at four o'clock. It is nearly three years since she last saw him. For months now there has been a running battle over the grounds for the divorce. Finally he has agreed to meet so at least they can discuss a compromise. When he wrote last week he told her he was going to bring his fiancée. Ursula surveys their tiny room before her visitors arrive. It looks neat enough, very cosy, she thinks, with the red geranium glowing between the green curtains she ran up last week. She wishes they had proper furniture. She knows their

Diana, Ursula and Eileen, Hyde Park

Eileen and Diana

Eileen

Eileen and friend

Nigel with Diana and Eileen, Hyde Park

makeshift pieces will make Tony gloat. Nigel is drumming his fingers on the mantelpiece where the Valentine's Day card he made for her just days ago is propped up under the little mirror. He should have no reason to be nervous, but they both are. She doesn't want to talk to Tony about the divorce in front of his girlfriend. Typical, she thinks, he should bring her. He's such a show-off.

Of course they are late—that would be something Tony had planned. He is wearing a brand-new suit with the sharpest of creases in the trousers. Mary looks very glamorous too. Ursula feels frumpy in her home-made dress and she can't help noticing how Tony sizes Nigel up. She can see him suppressing a smirk as he notes the crumpled jacket, the threadbare shirt collar and the frayed pullover sleeves. Of course Tony holds the floor. He is so full of his exploits with the American army in Berlin he doesn't notice the little girl sitting on the armchair.

'It's Colonel Piercy now,' he preens.

My mother interrupts him. 'Eileen, this is your father. Come and say hello.'

'Looks just like you, Ursula. Wouldn't you agree, Mary?'

'She's a pretty child,' Mary nods.

I am standing in front of Tony now. He is as tall as Nigel. I put my hand on his trouser leg. He looks down at me and steps back. He brushes down the place where my hand was pressed, as if my fingers contained something sticky. He doesn't talk to me again, except to say goodbye.

Nigel holds my hand as I wave to my father and Mary from the porch. My mother walks out to the gate with them. She says something and Mary walks a few metres up the street, leaving them to talk. Their conversation is short but vigorous. When they are finished he leans forward to kiss her on the cheek. She pulls her head away sharply and says something before he walks off to join Mary. When my mother turns around, she is smiling.

'He's agreed to stop the adultery suit.'

'But that was going to be the quickest way to get the divorce.'

'I know, but I don't want your name dragged through the court,' she says.

'Now you're going to have to sue him on the grounds of cruelty, and you haven't got any witnesses except me, and I won't count.'

'It will be at least a year away. We'll see what happens,' she says.

Every week Ursula makes a regular visit to the local council offices to plead for our own flat. When a community nurse finally comes to inspect our present conditions, she is shocked by this family of four living in such a tiny space.

'Your wife deserves a medal,' the nurse tells Nigel.

He grins at Ursula.

Immediately we are given a lovely flat of our own near Lancaster Gate. When we move in we have almost no furniture. Ursula finds some wooden crates at the local greengrocer's and covers them with pieces of fabric to create chairs and tables and little cupboards. Nigel has left the job at the factory to sell brushes door-to-door, hoping to earn extra money with commission. But he quickly finds it is not his forte. Ursula realises he must be the world's worst salesman, but she never lets him know what she thinks. She scrimps and saves and manages to find hundreds of ways to make ends meet. Her one pair of shoes has holes in the soles, and she is wearing an old overcoat she made for herself in Jerusalem when she was fifteen. But, despite all the odds, she is now living in her own home with the man she loves and her two children. Yes, she worries continuously about making ends meet, but she is the happiest she has been in her life.

Shortly after they move into the flat they receive a visitor. Her name is Yvette, a Jewish girl who had been engaged to my godfather Ray. She has come to say that Ray has been killed. She is distraught and feels responsible for his death. A few weeks before she had been on a bus in Jerusalem when she recognised one of the other passengers as a member of the notorious Stern Gang. She passed this information on to Ray and as a result some of the gang were arrested by the British. The police commander warned Ray of the danger he and Yvette were in and arranged for them to leave Palestine immediately. Yvette left straight away, but Ray insisted on serving out the last three weeks of his official term of duty. He was shot coming out of a café on Jaffa Road in Jerusalem.

Ursula and Nigel are learning to live with each other. They are learning to live in a post-war world. Everything that was before is gone. The survivors pick up the pieces in lives that are spiritually and financially drained. Nigel keeps saying that war must never happen again. One evening they listen to Churchill railing on the wireless against the Soviets. When she looks across at Nigel, Ursula thinks she can see tears in his eyes.

She takes his hand and touches his shoulder.

'I have to do something. You agree, don't you?' he says.

She nods. So for months he treks across London to attend meetings of an organisation formed to promote the concept of world government. At rallies he listens to speakers, many of them Britain's intellectual elite, including members of Parliament. He comes home with his eyes shining, and the conviction humankind may have truly learnt its lesson, that out of the ashes of this terrible catastrophe a new world order will arise and war will finally be a thing of the past. He talks about Bertrand Russell, about the work of the newly formed United Nations. He fills Ursula's head with his passion. It doesn't matter how poor they are, how many obstacles they have to overcome. He is helping to shape a better world for her and the children, and that is more important than anything else.

But the lessons of history are not as easily learnt as this, and the glorious campaign for a new world order begins to dissolve into the petty divisions and polarisation that are the mark of most political organisations.

'They don't understand,' he tells my mother after a particularly disillusioning evening. 'It's all politics, politics, politics. They don't want to think about anything spiritual, and surely that is what's most important. Without that you have no base to work from. I can't understand how they can't see it, especially someone of Bertrand Russell's intelligence.'

He tells Ursula a story. In 1936 he attended the wedding of his cousin to the daughter of the dean of Durham Cathedral. The bishop of Durham honoured the couple by giving the address at the cathedral ceremony. To Nigel's shock and the embarrassment of the other guests, the bishop used the occasion to fulminate against divorce and the disgrace it brought upon those involved.

'I couldn't believe he could do this to Thomas and Helen. They were so admired for their Christian devotion and integrity. Of course everybody knew it was the king and Mrs Simpson he was really upset about, but that was no excuse. I was so relieved when his sermon came to an end. It was a terrible thing to do to such a lovely couple on their wedding day.'

Until that moment, he says, he had taken Christianity for granted. After this he began to question his religion and examine more closely not only his own conduct but that of the people around him, most of whom were Christians.

'And then I learnt so much in Palestine—from you, your mother, and the Arabs as well. I found out there were other perspectives on the Old Testament. I never knew the Muslims accept Christ. I never knew it wasn't Judaism the Arabs opposed but Zionism. Sometimes I think I can no longer believe my religion is the only true faith. At least I can bless the bishop for this, because without him my mind might have been closed forever.'

She thinks about this for a few days and then she asks him, 'How do you know even Jesus Christ was who he said he was?'

'It's faith,' he says.

'So if I don't believe in him, does this make me wrong in your eyes?'

'No, of course not,' he rushes in, blushing.

'Aha!' she laughs. 'You don't have all the answers, do you?'

***

IT IS A very special occasion and Diana and I are going to go with them. Elsie has given Ursula a new frock and a hat for the occasion. Nigel has had his old suit pressed and has bought a new hat.

'All dressed up and finally somewhere to go,' he says, and they both laugh with relief.

They wait a long time for the bus to come. She gets nervous because they've been told they can't be late or they will miss out altogether. The bus inches its way down Gloucester Terrace and then on to Paddington. They arrive with ten minutes to spare. Elsie is waiting for them on the steps of the registry office.

'Granny's here!' I shout. Elsie has travelled down on the train from Ledbury. She brings a present from Nigel's sister Joyce, a little serving dish. She kisses us all.

Ursula is shaking. She has waited so long for this moment that she keeps thinking something is bound to happen to stop the ceremony going ahead. The divorce took so long. Of course she had plenty of grounds, but she was supposed to produce eyewitnesses, which was impossible because anyone who could testify on her behalf was still living in Palestine or was scattered to the four winds after the war. Many years later, when the case came up in conversation, she would say, 'I had a very understanding and shrewd judge who was able to work out exactly what sort of a person Tony was.'

Now she is free to marry the one man she has truly loved. The marriage registrar becomes flustered because they only have one witness. One of the office typists is called to fill in. It is a sterile ceremony but not even this formality can dampen the occasion for Nigel and Ursula. They have no illusions about a trouble-free future, but at least in the eyes of the law and anyone else they are now bound to each other. And they truly believe only death is ever going to separate them.

Ursula and Diana, Alford, 1950

Chapter Eight

PASTORALE

the love of field and coppice,
Of green and shaded lanes,
Of ordered woods and gardens
Is running in your veins.

—Dorothea Mackellar, *My Country*

Cheshire, 1948

SHE HAS NEVER heard of a place with such a long name. 'Say it again,' she laughs.

'Weston-under-Lizard via Newcastle-under-Lyme. It's in the North Country.'

She decides she loves the name. It sounds peaceful and romantic.

'Where do names like this come from?' she asks him.

'The mists of history,' he says.

The cottage is cold and dark with low ceilings, and she laughs at him because he has to duck under all the doorways. But it is a house at last with plenty of room for their small family. She fills it with the warmth of her passion for him and the children and, poor as they still are, each time he comes home he can't believe how lucky he is.

'Let's go to the country,' she had said. 'If it's what you really want, we can make it work. You said yourself we'll get living quarters. Let's go away from this horrible hard city.'

He was reluctant. 'You don't understand. That isn't an easy life either. You've never even lived on a farm.'

'We are young. If you love it so much, I can learn to love it as well.'

'But you're frightened of animals.'

'So, I'll have to be brave.'

He reached out and stroked her hair.

'I don't think I ever met anyone as brave as you.'

The garden at the back of the cottage slopes down through the fields to the woods where we hear cuckoos for the first time. I start school and each day I brave my fear of the massive articulated lorries that pass through our village heading north in the post-war building boom with their loads of pre-fabricated houses.

Nigel brings home turnips from the fields. 'Full of vitamins,' he says. She has found out he believes in healthy eating and deep breathing.

She cooks the turnips and then she tells him, to our great relief, 'They are only fit for the cows.'

Another evening he arrives home with a scruffy black dog.

She is angry. 'As if we haven't got enough mouths to feed.'

'It's for Eileen,' he says in defence. 'Look at her, listen to her.'

My mother turns. I am standing on a kitchen chair.

'Get it away!' I scream.

'There'll always be dogs on a farm, and it's going to be a terrible life for her if she doesn't overcome her fear.'

He comes over and puts his arm around me.

'He won't hurt you, he just wants to play. He was supposed to be a working dog, catching rats, but he's so gentle he won't even chase mice. That's why the rat-catcher had to give him away.'

He pats the side of his leg. 'Whisky, come!'

I jump into his arms to get even further out of reach. He crouches down with me and clicks his fingers. The dog puts his head on Nigel's knee. We sit still like this for ages. The dog and I are watching one another.

'Now, I want you to touch his head.'

It is a long time before I reach out with my hand. The dog doesn't bite me. Instead his brown eyes twinkle at me from under his fringe. Nigel puts me down.

'One more thing, give me your hand.'

He pulls my hand toward the dog. Then before I realise what's happening he gently opens the dog's mouth and puts my hand inside. Before I have a chance to struggle I feel the wet warmth of his pink tongue and the hardness of his pointed teeth. I start to scream and Whisky licks my hand.

'See,' Nigel says, smiling at me, 'that means he loves you and he wants to be your dog.'

Our next farm is in the West Country, a few kilometres from the old walled city of Chester. Ferney Williams is a rich dairy farmer fascinated by horse racing and cockfighting. Nigel's job involves general farm labouring but his main role is as a groom responsible for looking after the steeplechasers his boss breeds and races.

The house at Alford looks out over fields to the farm buildings and the big house, and beyond that to the woods where a tramp once showed me how he did wee wee. I ran away frightened and disgusted, but I never told my mother about the tramp because she had told me hundreds of times not to go into the woods. If I upset my mother she gets bad headaches and Nigel sends me to my room. Nigel has to take her hot and cold drinks into the bedroom when she is lying down. I can hear his gentle and soothing voice as I clench my fists and face and pray she will soon drift off to sleep.

Whenever I can, I play in the fields. It is my storyland peopled by kings and queens and fairy godmothers, who whisk me away to magic places where everybody is rich and children never get into trouble. My dog Whisky comes with me everywhere. Sometimes I take my mother's doll Liselotte with me as well. She is by far the most real of all our dolls and nearly as tall as Diana. Of course I have to spirit her out of the house without anybody seeing because my mother will worry about her getting ruined out in the fields. Liselotte listens to my stories without blinking whereas Diana gets bored after just a few minutes. I like to sit on the large log in the field between our place and the big house and sing my long and complicated daydreams to the clouds. Late one afternoon some cows come to watch. They are probably looking at Whisky but I think of them as an audience. I don't mind the cows listening to me. They can't understand what I am saying so they won't think I'm silly if I decide to change my story halfway through. Cows like to stare. It's something they always do. Nigel says they are smarter than sheep, but not much smarter. The cows seem to be enjoying my performance and so I sing louder and louder. When I reach the end, the part where I gallop away on a white horse, my gold crown fixed to my head and my robe flapping behind me in the wind, I think I hear a voice calling my name. It seems as though the voice is coming from a long way off in a sort of a whisper. In fact, when I listen again, the whisper sounds quite close. It's my mother calling my name.

'Mummy, is that you?'

'Come here at once.' The whisper sounds angry.

She must be angry because I've taken Liselotte again. I push my way out through the herd. My mother has been bending down between the cows' legs calling to me. She tells me she has been there for a long time trying to get my attention, but she was too frightened of the cows to risk calling out too loudly.

'Cows aren't dangerous,' I tell her.

She doesn't know what she's going to do with me. I'm rude and cheeky. I am disobedient. I should have been home an hour ago. Now I've ruined supper and everything will be cold. She snatches Liselotte out of my arms. 'This is my doll, not yours. Look what you've done to her. I brought her with me all the way from Germany. I looked after her so carefully and now you've ruined her.' She strides ahead of me and I can see from the way her shoulders wobble she is crying.

Exactly a month after Christmas 1949 the midwife arrives through the slush and the wind, knocking on our front door so loudly we think it is the wild gale come back again. Nigel leads her upstairs to the bedroom where my mother has been moaning for hours. He takes Diana and me into the living room and reads us stories, but no matter how hard he tries to distract us, the three of us jump every time we hear another scream coming from upstairs. Eventually Diana falls asleep and he puts us both to bed. When we wake up in the morning there is a new little baby in bed with our mother. She is covered in long dark hair which the midwife says is a good omen. They call the baby Charmian Tamara—Charmian after Cleopatra's handmaiden in Shakespeare's play and Tamara after my mother's favourite aunt, the ballerina who went missing in Sarajevo.

In the garden Nigel puts up a swing and then he builds a climbing-bean summerhouse, a tall igloo-shaped structure of bamboo stakes stuck into the ground and bent to join at the top. He plants the beans at the foot of each stake, so after they sprout they wrap their tendrils around the bamboo and climb and climb and then spread out until they form a shady green arbour. In the warmer weather, my mother takes a chair into the bean summerhouse where she does her beautiful smocking. She makes all her own clothes and ours as well. She has been sewing for as long as she can remember, but her abilities never cease to amaze Nigel. She is as frugal as she is creative. She makes lampshades out of odds and ends and new pillowcases out of old sheets. She teaches herself to cook, and makes amazingly delicious meals from limited resources. Her stews become goulash, her fried food is fine fricassee. The cream he brings home from the dairy she turns into butter, working for hours it seems with nothing but a wooden paddle and a mixing bowl. In the evening she reads. We all read. Nigel reads as well, books about farming, country life and travel. But she reads at another level, as if she is reading for her life. Her books are the other part of her, all the classics, Hemingway, Conrad, Steinbeck. Books are the best presents they give each other and us. No matter how poor we are there is always something to read.

Occasionally we are visited by Nigel's relatives. His sister Biddy comes one day with her husband Percy and their three children David, Jillian and Christine. I like David. He is about my age and I show him round the farm. In return I expect him to let me read his Beano comics, but he refuses. We argue and when I start to cry Uncle Percy gives me two shillings to buy my own comics when I am next in the village.

Diana and I share a bedroom. It overlooks the road to the big house, so we can watch the comings and goings. Sometimes we watch Nigel as he canters round the field on one of the racehorses. He amazes me with the news that all horses have the same birthday. I don't like having to share a room with Diana, so I draw chalk lines on the bare floorboards and shout at her if even a toe edges on to my side of the room. My mother makes me read stories to Diana but they are all boring baby books. One day I find a pair of nail scissors on my mother's dressing table. I take them back to my bedroom and use them to cut a row of dolls out of a folded piece of paper. Diana comes in and asks to look at what I have made. I want to know if the scissors are sharp enough to cut hair. I give the paper dolls to Diana to keep her still, but just as I am about to take just the smallest snip of her hair she moves, and suddenly I am holding a large golden curl in my fingers. I run over and throw the curl out the window and the hairs spread and float down over the garden like a puff of filaments from a dandelion. Diana is dancing the dolls along the carpet, and I have to speak to her sharply to make her look up at me so I can examine the extent of the damage. I will have to cut off another curl so they won't notice how jagged her fringe looks. I only intend to cut off one more curl, but that makes her head look even more uneven so I cut another and another. Snip, snip.

This is the first time Nigel has ever smacked me. It is on my mother's instructions. She tells him he will have to do something about me because she is at her wits' end. He smacks me on my bottom with the back of the hairbrush. They don't believe me when I say I didn't cut off all Diana's curls on purpose.

***

MY MOTHER IS coming down the stairs wearing the new grey dress with the red and green patterned squares above the waist. She made the dress herself and the skirt swishes about her legs when she walks. Her beautiful deep eyes are two dark smudges above the red gash of her mouth. She has polished up her high-heeled shoes and, with her hand on the banister, treads carefully, taking one step at a time. I am sitting on the bottom stair and I have to squidge my legs around to let her pass. She is wearing her expensive scent. She smiles at me because she knows I think she is beautiful. I smile back at her because I have learnt she is never angry with me when she is wearing lipstick.

He is taking her into the village for a meal at the pub and then on to the pictures. They are celebrating a great occasion. Ferney's horse, Russian Hero, has won the most famous race in world, the Grand National. Nigel came in from the fields just to listen to the race on the radio.

'Coming up to the last jump, it's Russian Hero leading the way from Roimond,' the excited voice blared out at us.

'I knew he could. I knew it. Keep going, boy. Keep going,' Nigel shouted.

And our hero did keep going and he won. Mummy burst into tears, but she was laughing at the same time. Nigel danced her around the living room. I had never seen them dance before.

'I got sixty-six to one,' he said suddenly.

'You didn't bet?' she gasped.

He nodded 'Only a quid.'

'You didn't. How much did you win?'

'About seventy quid, but I knew he could do it.'

'Oh my God, that's nearly four months' pay.'

They danced around the table again. This spring is to be the best ever. They will buy me a brand-new red bicycle and a green tricycle for Diana. Ferney Williams, the real owner of Russian Hero, gives Nigel a rise for making sure the horse was in peak fitness for the race. Perhaps Nigel thinks his dreams might be beginning to come true, but he would never say that, not even to her. Such boasting would demonstrate a lack of humility.

My parents look very smart as they ride off on their bicycles, she in her new dress and he in his spruced-up suit. They have never been out without us before. Our next-door neighbour is going to look after us. Mrs Pridding is not beautiful like our mother, but she makes us delicious sandwiches of pork dripping and salt. She splits open chestnuts and bakes apples stuffed with sugar and cloves in the oven of her firewood stove. She has shown my mother the ways of English cooking—roasts and stews and bread-and-butter pudding. Mr Pridding is the farm butcher and when he kills the pigs all the children are sent far away into a field beyond the brook, but we creep back so we can listen to the pigs' screams of protest as they are led towards the slaughterer's knife.

Our other grandmother, Mama, arrives to help look after Charmian. She brings us lovely presents and has an endless supply of chocolates in her handbag. I was so excited when my mother told me Mama was coming. She said, 'Your grandmother really loves you. She treated you like a little princess when we lived with her in Jerusalem.' But when Mama arrives, she seems to have forgotten how much she once loved me. Charmian is the only one she cares about.

Mama has come all the way from Palestine—only it's not called that any more, she says. Now we have to call it Israel. She tells us about the siege of Jerusalem. For years there has been a lot of fighting and she was very scared most of the time. It was very hard to get food even if you had money to buy it, which most people didn't.

'Can you imagine,' she tells us over and over, 'that some people were so hungry they had to eat their cats and dogs.'

I knew I would die of starvation rather than even think about eating Whisky. My mother received many letters from Mama during that war in Palestine, but I had never heard about the cats and dogs before.

She did write once about all the dead bodies. My mother translated it for Nigel and me. '*Mien liebe* Ula, The Arabs have cut off the road from Tel Aviv. They lie in wait every hour of the day. It has become a symbol for us to keep the road open. They are calling it the Burma Road. A convoy got through a few days ago. The drivers are so very brave, and some are even young women. Many young women have joined the army and are fighting. I thank G-d you are not here. Everyone has to do his or her duty. The shelling never stops. Our doctors and nurses are so brave; they just rush to wherever they are needed with no thought for their own safety. But they cannot save everyone. They took the bodies of the dead Jews out of the city yesterday. They loaded the coffins into buses. They put signs on the sides of the buses to show they were going to the cemetery. Still the enemy fired. They had to turn around and come back into the city again. There is nowhere to bury our dead inside these walls. So they had to take the bodies of our brave young soldiers back to the morgue. They say the morgue is overflowing.'

I remember the letter made my mother cry. Ursula cries again one night when my grandmother tells her about the bombing of the Atlanta Hotel. Arab terrorists posing as British soldiers had blown up the hotel and half of Ben Yehuda Street. The walls of many buildings had tumbled into the street and huge piles of rocks and bricks were littered with the tinsel fragments from thousands of shattered windows. Advertising signs flapped aimlessly from their twisted metal stanchions. Mama had run, like hundreds of others, to stare in disbelief that the enemy could have struck so far into the heart of the city. She stood among the silent crowd at the top of Ben Yehuda Street. The smoke from the burning debris was still rising and the early

Eileen, Christleton, 1951

Elsie and Stephen Hall

Diana, Nigel and Eileen, Alford, 1949

Diana and friend, Christleton

*Charmian, Gila, Ursula and
Diana, 1950*

Ursula and Charmian, 1950

The Hall family, 1952

morning air was filled with the wails of rescue vehicles. Beside the onlookers stood a row of new ambulances, waiting to take away the dead and injured. A man and a woman ran towards them, each carrying a small child. The faces of the little family were frozen in open-mouthed panic. Behind them a rabbi and three ambulance workers ran up the street, carrying someone in a blanket. By their haste, Mama guessed their patient was still alive. Fire crews plied thin trickles of water in useless attempts to contain the damage—it was the only thing left to do. This beautiful wide new street had been totally destroyed. Gone were the striped awnings and the new cobblestones. Gone were the shoe shops and the watchmakers, gone the tobacconist where Mama had bought her cigarettes the day before, gone the photographer's studio where she had spent a fortune on studies of my mother and me. The sun's rays now caught millions of glass shards, an array of coloured fragments that spun like a kaleidoscope.

When my mother and grandmother first see each other they are so happy they hug each other all the time. They sit up every night after everyone else has long gone to sleep. They drink continuous cups of the coffee that Cila has brought with her, smoking cigarettes and telling all their old and new stories in German. One night when I wake up I hear them both crying. My mother doesn't get out of bed the next morning, and my grandmother takes her breakfast up on a tray to the bedroom. We wait at the bottom of the stairs and when she comes down we ask her if our mother is ill.

'Your mother is very sad,' she says.

'Why is she so sad?'

'Because I had to tell her some people in our family are dead.'

'Who died.'

'Her aunts—my sisters.'

'How did they die?'

'The Germans killed them in the war.'

I know about the war. The Germans killed a lot of people. Some of the boys and girls in my class had fathers who were killed in the war.

I look at Diana who is listening to us very seriously.

'Mama, are you sad your sisters died?'

'I am too busy to be sad,' she says, but I can see she is pulling her lips tightly against her cheeks like people do when they are trying not to cry.

Towards the end of the first week my mother and my grandmother have their first argument. Within a month the house is a raging war zone. One day Cila shouts at Ursula, 'What sort of a daughter are you that you could not even tell me when you were pregnant with Diana?'

And my mother screams back, 'It's your own fault. As long as I can remember all you have ever done is try to control me. Now you are doing it all over again. Go back to Jerusalem. You are driving me crazy!'

After my grandmother goes home a relative peace descends.

We're off again, this time to a new farm Mr Williams has bought. Nigel and my mother and Charmian sit in the front of the cattle float. Diana and I share the back with our furniture and the big farm bull.

We move into a new house in the village of Christleton. I have a room of my own, so now I can read by torchlight until all hours of the night without Diana telling my parents. My favourite book is *Girl of the Limberlost*. It is a story about Elanora who lives with her mother, a lonely bitter widow who doesn't understand her daughter. She is virtually adopted by a lovely childless couple, who feel sorry for her and buy her nice things and help her to make grand plans. I read the book ten times over the summer. My favourite part is the description of the leather lunch box the couple give the girl to take to school: 'Elanora slipped the strap and turned back the lid. This "showed" the knife, fork and spoon, the milk flask and the interior with the dainty sandwiches wrapped in tissue paper and the little compartments for meat, salad and the custard cup.'

I dream of running into this storybook couple who will decide to take me away and love me for myself and give me presents all the time, and especially a leather lunch box with little compartments for all the delicacies my new mother will prepare for my school lunch.

All the time I am dreaming about having another family, my real parents are making some secret plans. I am not sure what it is all about but I can tell something serious could be happening. There are long discussions way into the night—her voice sometimes raised, sometimes crying, his voice more reasonable, calming. It goes on for weeks. Some days she doesn't speak to him when he comes in from the fields rattling the milk can. He makes little jokes and we all laugh, but she doesn't. When they start talking again Whisky lies in front of the fire, his eyebrows flitting from one to the other as they speak.

A letter comes and I glimpse strange stamps. She puts the envelope in her pocket so I can't see where it is from. When Nigel comes home they go into the parlour. When they emerge they are both smiling. Something important has happened.

'Tell us!' we say, but they don't—not yet.

At the end of the summer holidays they are ready to make their grand announcement. We are going to emigrate to Australia.

'Australia?' We are incredulous.

My mother gets quickly to the point. 'It's too hard in England for your father to earn enough money to keep us. So we are going to Australia where there are many more opportunities.'

I look at my father and see he is blushing, but he's also excited.

'One day we will have our own farm,' he says, 'and Eileen, you'll have your own horse and I'll teach you to ride.'

Diana and Charmian want to learn to ride as well.

'You can't ride my horse,' I say.

We look at maps, and talk about sailing to the other side of the world on a big ship. At first it sounds exciting but then I change my mind when I realise it will probably be for ever.

When I tell my mother I want to stay in England, she says I have no option. I want to take all my books but she will only allow me three. How can I make such a choice? I cry a lot and it makes her angry. She packs up most of her own books to take to the booksellers, so how can I complain?

I have been to a Girls' Friendly Society meeting. I am sitting up at the table in the kitchen eating boiled eggs and toast soldiers for supper. Diana and Charmian are in bed. Nigel and my mother are sitting by the fire in the living room. They are talking and their voices are low. I hear my mother start to cry. I turn my head. They are not arguing, so why is she crying? What has happened? I go to the living-room door. In the dim light I can see he is kneeling beside her chair and has his arms around her. I hear him say ever so quietly, 'We'll get another dog when we get to Australia.'

I charge into the room. Whisky is not on his mat.

'Where is he?' I scream. Now it is me Nigel is having to comfort.

'We couldn't possibly take him,' he says. 'Remember how much he fretted when we went on holidays?'

Nigel had done it himself with a gun. I imagine my beautiful Whisky's soft eyes looking up at him with such trust. I can't believe Nigel is capable of such callousness. You have to do your own dirty work in life, he tries to explain. I can't believe what he is saying.

We leave England at the end of autumn. After Nigel resigns from his job at the Christleton farm, we move in with Granny and Grandfather, and Nigel and my mother spend the last few weeks on an orchard picking apples to raise a bit of extra cash for the journey ahead. At a final farewell dinner at the house in Ledbury, Grandfather Hall uncharacteristically spits prune pips into the fireplace, making us children laugh till we cry. For a few moments we forget our sadness. In the photographs taken the next day we are still smiling despite our sorrow. Our grandparents set us this brave-faced example, although they know they may never see their son or his family again.

Our ship sails from Glasgow. Pipers on the dock play 'Will E' No Come Back Again'. The kilted figures gradually disappear from view as we slip into the foggy Clyde. As the ship noses towards the North Atlantic current, all that is left to connect us to the land is a thin wailing of the final refrain from 'Auld Lang Syne'. I stay on the deck crying for my dog, and when I look up my mother is crying too. Nigel is holding her around her shoulders and rubbing his hand up and down her arm. He is telling her to think of the future, but I see his eyes are moist and red as well. I wonder why on earth we are leaving if this is how they feel.

For months they had been so excited by the prospect of this great adventure in a far-away place. They told us their decision to go to Australia had come after many months of trying to work out how they could improve our lives. Nigel loved working on the farm, but his wages were so low they knew they were going to be poor for a very long time. They decided the only way out was to leave England and go to a country where there were more opportunities. They had looked at brochures and pamphlets. Nigel had been offered a job as a teacher in South Africa, but in the end they decided to accept the Australian government's offer of an assisted passage. We even featured in a film about migration to Australia. My sisters and I dug holes in the backyard to see if we could burrow our way to the Antipodes instead of having to sail there. Our parents smiled at each other as they told us of a new life in the sun, a farming life as good as Nigel's in Chile and better than the one we had now. I never really wanted to go with them. I understood their excitement but it was their dream not mine.

The SS *Cameronia* is a converted troop ship, perfect for transporting migrants to far-off lands. The big dormitory quarters are allocated to the male passengers, and the women and their children sleep in cabins isolated at night from their husbands and fathers. We steam our way across the Bay of Biscay and on through the Mediterranean to Port Said on the Egyptian coast. The Egyptian border is only a hundred and thirty kilometres from Jerusalem where Cila lives. She has written to my mother that she would try to visit us on the ship when we docked. I wait all day for my grandmother at the top of the gangplank, but she never comes. She writes later that she had made it to the border but the Egyptian authorities would not allow her to cross over from the Israeli side.

Following the old trade routes, we pass through the Suez Canal and down the Red Sea. I try to imagine how Moses had parted this great body of water with nothing but a wooden stick. We go ashore at Aden, then on to Colombo, before the last great leg across the Indian Ocean to Fremantle on Australia's west coast. From here we hug the southern coast of the continent for four thousand kilometres before turning north to our final destination, Sydney. The trip from Glasgow takes nearly six weeks. We leave on Nigel's birthday and arrive on Ursula's. My mother loved to say they had only three shillings and nine pence in their pockets when they landed.

Nigel and Ursula with Diana, Charmian and Eileen, 1950

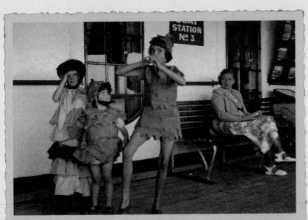

Diana, Charmian and Eileen, SS Cameronia

On the SS Cameronia

SS Cameronia sailing into Sydney, 9 November 1952

Chapter Nine

THE HOOP SNAKE

The red sun
robs their
beauty and,
in weariness
and pain,
the slow years
steal the
nameless grace
that never
comes again.

—George Essex Evans, *The Women of the West*

The Darling Downs, 1953–55

SHE BURSTS THROUGH the door, a frantic dancing silhouette framed by the blazing sun. She has flung the flyscreen back so hard it keeps on banging and banging in time with her screams. Her hair has fallen loose as she stands trembling in the doorway.

She cries, 'It chased me! It chased me!' over and over.

We stand by the kitchen table, frozen by her fear. Her breath is shallow and there are beads of sweat on her upper lip. Nigel moves toward her. He takes hold of her. He lowers her gently into a chair and strokes her hair. She is sobbing now. She clings to him until her body stops shaking. Finally she pulls herself away and looks up, her eyes staring into his.

'It chased me,' she says, but more calmly now.

'What, darling, what? Tell me. What chased you?'

'The snake. It chased me.'

He crouches down in front of her and takes her hand. 'It's gone now, darling.'

'I hate this place,' she sobs. 'I want to go back to England.'

It is little more than three months since Cila's brother, my great-uncle, David Raff and his family met us when we disembarked in the Overseas Terminal at Circular Quay in Sydney. David migrated to Australia before Hitler came to power and followed the family line by establishing a successful watchmaking business in the eastern suburbs of Sydney. It was such a comfort for Ursula to know she had family in this place at the other end of the world. What she didn't understand was that we were going to live so far from Sydney we might as well have been in another country. She would rarely see her uncle, let alone be able to lean on him in times of trouble.

We take the train from Sydney to Brisbane. The trip lasts a whole day and we spend most of the daylight hours fruitlessly trying to spot the kangaroos and koalas that feature so strongly in the Australia House immigration pamphlets. We stay for a few weeks on a little farm on the outskirts of Brisbane with an elderly couple, Les and Nell Cunnington. In 1951 they had responded to a letter Nigel had written to the Queensland newspaper, the *Courier Mail*, asking for someone to sponsor us to migrate to Australia. In Nigel's letter he had outlined his background, his time in Chile and his dream of having a farm of his own one day. Les and Nell had responded because they had spent many years in South America. It was their letter my mother had hidden from me in Christleton. The Cunningtons speak Spanish and have the same love for the land as Nigel. They not only sponsor us but also somehow manage to organise a job for him on a large property owned by the Russell family beyond the Great Dividing Range.

Les Cunnington has a huge white dent in the middle of his forehead where a horse had kicked him when he was young. The scar fascinates us. The Cunningtons quickly become our surrogate grandparents. They hold Christian church services in their living room on Sundays, a different denomination every week. They raise goats that eat the straw hats my parents bought for us in Colombo on the voyage out. Uncle Les is amazed that I am ten years old and don't know how to swim. None of us do. So he fetches some rope from the shed and takes us down to where the Brisbane River snakes along the edge of their farm. His teaching method is simple. One at a time he lowers us into the river with a rope fixed securely around our skinny bodies to stop us from being swept into the swift-flowing current. He lets the rope down slowly as we descend, hand over hand like little abseilers, until we slip into the muddy swirl, our shrieks of fearful delight piercing the afternoon. We splash and splutter until he is satisfied we have begun to understand the rudiments of swimming.

A month after we arrive in Australia, I have to go to hospital because I have developed something called mastoiditis, an acute middle ear infection that can sometimes be life-threatening. I have to spend over a week in bed while the doctors decide whether or not they will need to operate. My mother comes to visit one day.

She has had to travel from the other side of Brisbane. It takes three buses and a train to get there and she is completely worn out by the time she arrives at the hospital. She seems surprised I am feeling so much better. Surprise is not quite the right word—it is as though she is annoyed with me for wasting her time. When I try to snuggle up to her she turns away to get something out of her handbag, except I know she doesn't really need her handkerchief. It is because she doesn't want me to touch her.

'You sit at the other end of the bed,' she says. 'Then we can face each other. It's easier to talk that way.'

That night I lie for hours wondering why my mother doesn't want to touch me. The night sister comes around in her big veil and soft torchlight. She looks like an angel. When she sees I am awake she tucks the sheets around me and touches my forehead. The softness in her fingers makes me cry. 'You poor little darling,' she says. 'What's making you so sad?'

I have no words for her. She sits by my bed and holds my hand until I fall asleep.

***

UNCLE LES TELLS us children of the times when he and Nell travelled over the Rocky Mountains in a horse-drawn wagon when they were crossing North America from east to west. He tells us about the Spanish cowboys of the South American pampas at the foot of the Andes—much more beautiful, Uncle Les claims, than the Himalayas. Your father would understand what I am talking about, he says. Here was a couple who had spent their lives acting out their dreams. They are perfect mentors for this young family newly settled in the Antipodes.

Uncle Les forewarns us our life ahead might not always be easy. He says that out on the plains of the Darling Downs the winter westerly winds are so strong they blow straight through you, not around you. And we have to watch out for the hoop snake, which is known to catch up to its prey by putting its tail in its mouth and bowling along like a hoop. We never see a hoop snake although the idea, the fear, of it grips our imaginations. But we feel the iciness of the westerlies as they pierce our ribs.

The snake that chased our mother does not hoop itself—it is a big brown. It lives in the yellow grasses that cover the paddock between the big house and us.

We arrive on the Darling Downs in the middle of a harsh summer. The pastures are brown and crackling. The heat sucks the oxygen out of the air. It is a very long way from the lush green damp of a Cheshire farm, and we are not at all prepared to cope with the differences.

The chickens scratch for hours in the rock melon patch, then go to rest under the peppercorn tree, chortling in their communal dust bath. We use the roof of the chicken shed to reach across to the lower branches of the bottle tree. We have sworn to each other not to tell her how, when we climb the tree, we have to skim the redback spiders' nest that nestles in one of the deep forks in the branches. From the top of the bottle tree we can see up to the big house, across to the little church and the water tower, and down to the flat wheat fields. At certain times of the year we watch the tiny figure of our father ploughing a tractor up and down the sticky black paddocks. We steal rock melons and take them up into the tree, smashing them open so the golden flesh spills over our hands and into our mouths. The melons taste of trapped sunshine sweetened with our sin. We are running wild now in our bare feet. There have been so many arguments with her about shoes, now we just leave them on until we are out of sight of the house.

Tall weeds at the end of the garden hide goannas as big as dogs. If we disturb their sleep they leap up and smash themselves savagely against the wire-netting fence. It is hard to tell who is the more frightened, us children or the great lizards. The tracks that criss-cross the property are pocked with a series of lidded trapdoor spider holes. We investigate the depths of these holes with thick grass stalks in games of daring-do. Sometimes this is rewarded by a thick tug on the end of the stalk, at which point we drop the straw into the hole. Once I am so startled I forget to let go and a hairy black creature springs from the hole clinging to the end of my piece of grass. We all scatter screaming back to the house.

Ursula hears our yelling and meets us at the back door, her face frowning with concern. 'What's happened?' she asks.

'Nothing, we were just playing,' I answer, glaring at my sisters in case they are thinking of exposing me.

Redbacks also live in the backyard toilet, a wooden seat with a hole cut in the centre strategically placed over an open pit. The pit drains down the slope into the bush, creating a stinking run-off that attracts hordes of flies and mosquitoes. The toilet holds the biggest terror for us all. The redbacks in the bottle tree aren't really scary because we can see them, but the spiders in the dark toilet are hidden and we never know when they might jump up and bite us on our bare parts.

Our first Australian summer feels as though we have sailed into a furnace and shut the door behind us. We gasp for air, we sweat and we argue. We don't know how to be nice to one another. There is no fat in our feelings in this season of heat, no cushion for our spiny words. Midsummer days push out the boundaries of our tempers and leach the energy from our bones. Walking to school or hanging out the washing is a torturous exercise requiring stamina our bodies simply do not have. The fierce heat and the mosquitos ravage our European skins. We are sunburnt and covered in great reactive red weals from bites that we scratch incessantly until they turn septic. We have exchanged English chilblains for Australian boils.

We aren't prepared for our first winter either. For weeks it is so cold we have to wear two jumpers at once and send away for thick woollen gloves which make all the outside chores cack-handed. The tractor ruts are frozen solid and the ridges spike at our feet through our thin city shoes. We have to walk beside the tracks because it is more comfortable than trudging through the soldier grass. Some days the winds are so strong the smoke from the kitchen stove blows at right angles from the chimney. Gums toss wildly, raggedly, and our noses are tipped with blue. We warm our hands on the outside of the wood stove and snuggle into old blankets on chairs in the kitchen.

Kingy Robinson comes to visit us. He is a house painter by trade and a legendary wandering nomad, and has been with the Russell family since the turn of the century. He has turned the interior walls of the water tower into a gallery of his self-portraits with titles like *Kingy at the Somme* and *Kingy on the Road 1932*. Kingy admires the new furniture that has just been delivered from Dalby. He stays for several cups of tea and recounts his friendship with old Mr Russell. 'He was a good 'un,' he jerks his thumb in the direction of the big house, 'but this one'd get rid of me if he could, but he can't. It's in the old boy's will—a place for life.' His main complaint about Charlie Russell is the limited ration of rum he has instructed the cook to dispense to Kingy each evening. There is a set mark on the glass that Kingy surreptitiously edges up until the cook discovers the subterfuge.

Several weeks later my parents come back from a bus trip into town to discover that Kingy has let himself into our house and, in an act of friendship, has decorated the brand-new kitchen table and chairs and dresser with a fake wood-grained pattern. The method he proudly demonstrates to them involves laying down a coat of brown paint and then coming back over it with a narrow strip of leather coated in white paint. Our kitchen setting looks like a camouflage design for zebras. My mother's initial reaction is fury and even Nigel's ears turn red, but they never say anything to Kingy, and the ghastly decorations are not painted over for a long time for fear of hurting the old man's feelings.

The beginning of our second year on the Darling Downs brings a distinct change to our family fortunes. Charlie Russell offers Nigel the management of the dairy

Meeting Uncle David at the Overseas Passenger Terminal, Sydney, 1952

Eileen, Nigel, Stephen, Charmian and Diana at Timbour

At Timbour House

Stephen and Eileen

farm. It is a promotion and a chance to establish himself in his own right. It will be a share-farming arrangement and my parents are excited at the prospect of a big improvement in our financial circumstances. Still Nigel has a very hard job ahead of him. The previous dairy managers, a pair of brothers who managed the farm for years, have left after a falling-out with Russell. This is sheep and grazing country. The terrain and the climate are so unsuited to Jersey cattle it is unlikely the dairy would stand as an entity if it had to sit outside the support structures of the larger property. The most serious problem Nigel faces is the lack of good workers to help run the farm. A series of young men come and go, keen at first for the work, but they are eventually driven away by boredom and the need for company of their own age. There are many occasions when Nigel has to get me to help him with the milking.

Stephen Charles Hall is born on 17 November 1954, just after we move into the dairy house, a sprawling dwelling which, at some stage, had been extended to house the two previous families. The explorer Ludwig Leichhardt stayed in this house while he was preparing for his fateful trip into North Queensland. The house is a warren of tiny dark rooms. There is no dining room so during the warmer months we eat on a wide-open verandah under a giant net that keeps out the flies during the day and the mosquitoes, moths and flying ants after dark. Every afternoon water has to be heated in the wood-fuelled washing copper in the backyard and carried through the house in buckets for our baths.

The big Jimbour House where the boss and his family live was built of sandstone by convicts in the nineteenth century. It is set in the midst of spectacular gardens containing a large pool where, as part of the local school curriculum, we complete our formal swimming training. Most parts of the house are off limits to the workers and their families. Although I am allowed to play with the boss's daughter Margaret-Ann, who is a similar age to me, my boundaries are strictly drawn. Margaret-Ann's bedroom opens on to a wide verandah. I can play in her bedroom and on her verandah, but nowhere else in the house. Her father, on the other hand, places no such restrictions on his access to his employees' homes. When we first arrive we are housed in a cottage that lies between the main house and the garage and stables. Instead of going around the cottage like everybody else, Charlie simply takes a shortcut through our living room whenever he chooses. My mother is furious and she argues with Nigel, who refuses to confront his boss for fear of losing his job.

One day I arrive home from school to find Nigel waiting on the verandah holding my little brother, who is only a few weeks old. I cannot understand why Nigel is at the house at this time of day. My mother is ill, very ill, he tells me, as he hands

Stephen over to me. He has to take her to the hospital in Dalby. He helps her down the steps. Her face is yellow and covered in perspiration. She can hardly walk, she is shaking so much. She doesn't even notice I am standing there watching. She has trouble getting into the passenger side of the station manager's little black ute. She whimpers. So he picks her up and they appear to be doing an awkward little dance as he tries to manoeuvre her on to the seat. He touches her hair when she is finally settled. He shuts the door on the skirt of her dress but I don't say anything.

He tells me to look after the others, tells me to be very careful and not to do anything stupid. I can see by the way his forehead puckers he would not leave me with this responsibility if he had any other choice.

When I go inside I try to make my sisters tidy up their toys. I am desperate to get the right tone, her tone, but they ignore me, so obviously I haven't got it right. I try raising my voice to a scream, but they giggle and run away to hide. I get bored with playing mother so I go into the real mother's bedroom with Stephen on my hip. I scrabble through her forbidden jewellery box trying on necklaces and brooches. My sisters sneak in and catch me out. They're going to tell. So I have to bribe them by getting down the jellybeans from their hiding place at the top of the pantry cupboard. Nigel comes back without Ursula. She has a severe case of blood poisoning, caused by a reaction to a mosquito bite that has become septic. He tells me she will be in hospital for several days and I will have to stay home from school until he organises someone to help out. I am so overjoyed at the prospect I cannot begin to understand his dream is starting to unravel.

For days I stay home from school to look after Stephen. A bleak wind blows in from central Australia, dumping leaf litter on the verandahs. The latch has come undone on the nursery door and the windows rattle and bang. I am reading so I hear nothing until the baby's screams finally jolt me into alertness. Stephen is screaming in his cot, his face red and soaked with tears. I don't know long he has been waiting there like this, crying for me. He is cold and wet. His nappy is dirty. I change him into warm dry clothes. He is still sobbing and I pick him up and hold him. He leans his head against my shoulder, taking his breaths in little tiny gulps. I wriggle my finger in front of him and he grips it with his little fist. I swing his arm out and we do a little twirl around the room. He smiles, reluctantly at first, then laughs out loud.

Outside the wind is trying to batter through the ancient weatherboards. Inside my baby brother and I waltz and laugh until we are dizzy with our love. I am charged with the warmth of his forgiveness.

Margaret-Ann is sent away to boarding school. She wants me to take care of her pony Daphne. I had learnt to ride on a much quieter Shetland called Tommy. The first rule Nigel taught me was that I couldn't go for a ride unless I had caught and saddled the horse myself. Catching Tommy was easy. He could spot a piece of bread from a hundred metres away. Daphne is too skitty and smart to be taken in by a mere morsel, and catching her can sometimes take up to half an hour. I use Daphne to escape from the chaos of the house, but it is an alien countryside I set out to explore. They say the landscape in which a child grows up forms the prism through which the future world will be viewed. I long for the sight of English woods the colour of broccoli, for the structure of small square fields and for the wildflowers that grow between neat hedgerows and ditches. I ache to lie down on a sponge of bright green grass and spend hours watching the passing parade of clouds. In this new country everything is harsh and drained of colour. There is no apparent order here, just great yellow and brown tracts of inhospitable flats and rocky hillocks. Cattle and sheep graze around stony knobs tearing at stringy yellow grasses. There is not a spot to lie down on without getting bitten by something painful and dangerous. The Australian landscape hasn't been cleared of all the toe-stubbing, knee-grazing bits of flinty stone that lie in wait for the unprepared.

Sometimes Daphne stumbles slightly as we make our way downhill. I let the reins fall and pat her neck. 'You pick the way,' I whisper, and she does, her dainty toes testing the ground like a soldier navigating a minefield. When we reach the level ground my heartbeat slows. Sweat seeps from her neck and little thrills of excited achievement tremble down the length of her body. I burrow my nose in her mane and drink in her horsy perfume. I imagine stealing Daphne and sailing away on a ship back to England, where we could wander the countryside in safety.

I don't ever think about what sort of life my mother might be longing for. I am too self-absorbed in my own homesickness, in my love for my new baby brother and my resentment at the perceived injustices my parents visit on me. I am twelve but Ursula is barely thirty. It never occurs to me that she is also grieving, that her hip has started to hurt because the cartilage in her bones is gradually being eaten away, that it must be becoming clear to her by now that Australia is unlikely to be the Utopia Nigel has painted for her. There are no Chilean servants to do the dirty work, to chop the wood, carry the buckets of water, pluck the chicken feathers, light the wood stove and clean out the stinking toilet with carbolic. No local libraries she can just drop into to select her precious books to read on the hot sleepless nights. I am too selfish to imagine a pain worse than my own, to understand she too probably lies awake at night thinking of her own places—thinking of the German city she talks about so often, or the biblical land where she and Nigel fell in love. What would have been her choice if she had not followed his dream, the dream that has led only to the same old poverty in a different guise? I don't bother to guess at what her dreams might have been, what she might have given up for her family—things she will never breathe, even to him. She loves him so much, no matter how unhappy she becomes, she will not offer up her secret longings for fear of wounding him with his guilt.

When he tells her things will improve she tries to believe him, but she has been ambushed too many times by disappointment. Now, after she comes home from hospital, she begins the habit of taking to her bed on her bleak days. Sometimes she drifts for days in and out of a deep, seemingly endless despair that she has stopped trying to hide. On the worst days I stay home from school to look after Stephen.

A woman with her daughter, English immigrants like ourselves, comes to help in the house. It doesn't work out. In the meantime someone must have written to Cila in Israel because one day she simply turns up to take over the household. Immediately she wrestles me for control of my baby brother and we peck at one another constantly. We hardly understand each other's language but we know how to get under each other's skin. I am no longer the favoured grandchild, the one who has replaced my mother in my grandmother's affections. I am a rival for her grandson's love.

When you are twelve you are not supposed to be on the same eye level as your grandmother. You shouldn't be able to see the way her dark irises flash with disappointment and anger. You shouldn't be able to smell the tobacco on her breath. You shouldn't be able to look into her mouth and see her nicotine-stained teeth, or the way the tragedies in her life have dug deep grooves which frame this mouth.

She confronts me, her shoulders pulled back, her chest puffed out. She and I circle the room like two hens in the chook yard.

'Don't be so sheeky,' she hisses. 'You are joost a child.'

She struggles to get out her English words and I am cheered by her discomfort.

'You look like a grinning tiger,' she shrieks at me.

Ursula and Cila fight as well, over other things—over my grandmother's criticisms of the state of the house, the wildness of her grandchildren and her son-in-law's failure to provide properly for his family. The battles rage endlessly.

Late one day Nigel appears through a deep blue dusk to find the three of us in the backyard engaged in one of our endless confrontations. We turn to him to arbitrate.

He tries to listen but we shriek over one another accusations and protestations of our own innocence. He is powerless to stop us for long enough to make any sense. In the end he says, 'Jewish women, you all drive me crazy.' I am devastated. I can't possibly be one of them, like these two shrieking banshees. I am not even a woman yet. I am not one them. Am I?

Shortly after this latest row, Cila goes to live in Sydney. There she will be closer to her brother David. She gets a job working for the catering division of Qantas.

Often when we are between hired dairy hands we work together, my stepfather and I. I love this so much more than being down at the house with my mother. I am a quick learner and I know it pleases him, but no matter how hard I work the lion's share of the labour is his. He is up before sunrise to round up the herd, do the milking, the scouring of the equipment and sheds, deliver the cans to the pick-up station, feed the pigs and the poddy calves, muck out the dairy yard and the sties, and then he starts all over again in the mid-afternoon.

I hate the cows that kick when you try to attach the milking machine. There are half a dozen in the herd. The younger cows are particularly quick and vicious and seem to know exactly where to aim to do the most damage. I try to make myself busy at the other end of the milking shed when one of these temperamental creatures is brought up from the cow yard, but none of my dodging gets past Nigel. I hear him calling, 'Eileen, this one needs a leg rope.'

He is training me to face my fears. His desire to bring his children up to his Kiplingesque standards is bound to be thwarted by the weakness of our natures, but it is part of his life's goal and he never misses an opportunity to try and shape us into highly moral beings. He constantly exhorts us to be on guard against the temptation of taking the course of least resistance.

We might have made it except for the pigs. I love the pigs best. They are the smartest, and the cleanest. Sheep have little tiny brains which they use for nothing else but running round paddocks like shoals of fish in rock pools. Cows are only a little bit cleverer. At least they recognise me when I come to separate them from their calves. The cantankerous ones chase me to the top railing of the cow yard. But we never have a minute's grief from a pig until Nigel lends Charlie Russell's prize boar to the local butcher to sire his sows. It is an act of friendship and generosity that will change the course of his life. The boar returns having caught a virulent strain of swine fever that decimates the population of the piggery. The pigs, after all, still belong to Charlie Russell. It takes some days for my parents to realise this is the end of the grand dream.

Charmian, Margaret-Ann and David Russell,
Diana and Eileen

Diana and Charmian, Moggill

Ursula, Stephen, Charmian, Diana and Eileen, Dalby, 1955

At Nambour, 1957

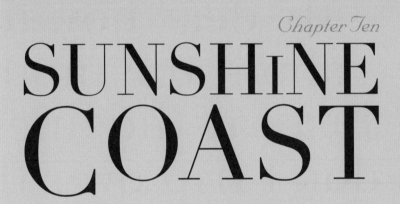

Chapter Ten

SUNSHINE COAST

My dear boy, forget about the motivation. Just say the lines and don't trip over the furniture.

—Noel Coward, to an actor in his *Nude with a Violin* on Broadway, 1957

Eileen, standing, in 'Hay Fever', 1958

Dalby, 1955

NIGEL HAS SENT me to my bedroom again. It's not actually my bedroom. I share it with Stephen, who wakes up whenever I try to put the light on to read at night. I love my little brother but I don't think I should have to share my room with a baby now that I am nearly thirteen. It is the beginning of the school holidays and the evening is hot and muggy. Nigel has caught my mother and me shouting at each other again. Our arguments have been getting worse since we moved into Dalby from Jimbour. My mother has been spending a lot of time sitting in her chair in the living room smoking cigarettes. Every time we argue she says that if I knew the pressures she is under I would never behave like I do. Then she cries and says she doesn't know what is going to become of us all. I am trying to help, I tell her. I do lots of things like the hoovering and washing up and peeling the vegetables for dinner and looking after Stephen. What more does she expect from me, I yell at her. Then she shouts at me that I should have more respect for my elders, and to stop answering back every single time she tries to tell me something.

   This time we are arguing because my new friend Pat has asked me to go around to her house the next day. I like Pat because she talks to me about the grown-up things that have started to interest me, things like the way my body is changing, things I would be too embarrassed to talk about with my mother. I am especially concerned about the idea of getting breasts. I don't really have any at the moment, but I know this is about to change. Pat has breasts already and they are quite big even though we are the same age. I am grateful Pat at least has warned me to be careful because of what happened to her. One day while she was sitting in class one side just blew up like a balloon. One minute she was completely flat like me and the next there was a whole breast on her left side. She said if it happened it would make me feel all lopsided and unbalanced. So the best thing would be to tell the teacher I was feeling ill so I could go home and wait for the other side to blow up to get my balance back again. My mother doesn't like Pat because she thinks she is coarse. My mother doesn't understand how hard it has been for me to make a friend in my new school. So I cry and tell her she only wants me to stay home to help in the house.

Neither of us hear Nigel come in through the back door. He has walked home from Carberry's, where he sells spare parts for cars. I've heard him tell my mother he knows nothing about cars. Engines and mechanical things have always been a mystery to him. He worries if he doesn't get the hang of it soon he mightn't even be able to keep his job.

'What's this?' he calls out over the top of our screaming. He is trying to make his voice sound bright, except it comes out all thin and tired.

She turns to him. 'I can't stand it any more. You will have to deal with her.'

So he sends me to my room. I'm lying kicking my feet on the bed and weeping for my mother's selfishness. Eventually I get sick of crying and get up and put my ear against the bedroom door. I can hear him trying to pacify her. It makes me so mad. Why doesn't anyone ever believe me? Why doesn't he come and talk to me like that, gently and sympathetically? Then he knocks on my door. He has a book in his hand and one of his fingers is holding it open at a particular page.

'Your behaviour towards your mother is totally unacceptable,' he begins.

'But ...' I try to interrupt. I want him to hear my side. No one ever listens to me, I think. No wonder I lose my temper all the time.

'No buts. You have to learn self-discipline. You'll stay in your room until you can recite this poem by heart.' He hands me the open book.

It is Kipling's *Sixty Poems*. On the inside cover there is an inscription: 'To Ursula, with love, Nigel, 24th Aug. 1943'. I work out I was eight months and twenty days old when he gave her the book. I turn back to the page. The poem has a one-word, one-syllable title, 'If'. Fifty years later I can still recite most of it. The first lines are: 'If you can keep your head when all about you / Are losing theirs and blaming it on you'. If I had been mature enough to understand the message Nigel was trying to send me I could possibly have saved myself a lot of heartache in the future.

Brisbane, 1956

WE HAVE MOVED again, this time to Brisbane. Nigel has a new job working for the McNiven Company delivering sweets to shopkeepers. Halfway up the street lives my mother's new friend who sleeps with a pet carpet snake in her bed. Faith Denton spotted Ursula as soon as we moved into our new house in the suburb of Inala on Brisbane's western outskirts. My mother hates the fact that all the trees in Inala have been chopped down to make way for the housing commission estate. The trees have been replaced with rotary clothes lines, which have spread like a fungus, spinning the washing round and round on windy days and small children and yelping dogs on others. The bushland has been replanted with pretty little weatherboard houses and squares of green grass, but the dry winds of poverty blow up and down the arid gutters and rattle the doors.

Aunty Faith, as she insists we call her, has a house full of dogs and birds and cats. There was a Mr Denton when we first arrived but he left shortly after, not because of the terrible smell in the house but because he was sick of having to share his bed with a snake. Aunty Faith ekes out a living as a piano teacher and a psychic. She gives me music lessons for a few weeks, but my ear is poor and I have no sense of rhythm so we don't get very far. Faith holds regular séances in her living room. Nigel doesn't approve of dabbling in the occult but my mother goes anyway. She comes home one night to tell us Aunty Faith had seen my godfather Ray, the one who was killed by the Stern Gang. 'Uncle' Ray was apparently standing behind my mother's chair. He spoke to Faith and told her to tell my mother that he was watching over me. I find the idea of someone watching me all the time quite unnerving. Sometimes I think my mother made it up just to try and make me behave myself when she can't see what I am doing.

We have to walk through Italian market gardens to get to our new school, where I have fallen in love with the gentle Miss Paterson, who is pretty and kind and tells me I am good at English. When the inspector comes to the school and Miss Paterson chooses me to read John Drinkwater's 'Moonlit Apples', my love for her knows no bounds. To impress Miss Paterson I join the Brisbane Children's Theatre and once a week I have to travel into the city by bus and train for rehearsals, which makes me feel very grown up. My mother sews me a beautiful costume for my part as the evil princess in *The Young Crusaders*.

As I get off the bus in the dark one evening after rehearsals I hear loud voices that seem to be coming from our house. My heart starts beating very fast. It is less than a block to our place, but I am always relieved to get inside the front door. I'm especially scared of walking past our next-door neighbours' house. Mr Jorgensen and his son are alcoholics. Mrs Jorgensen used to be an alcoholic but she turned over a new leaf and stopped drinking. That was when the housing commission gave them the house next to us and a whole lot of new furniture, including a beautiful china cabinet which Mrs Jorgensen spends all day polishing. Mr Jorgensen and his son have wild arguments that usually end up with them hitting each other. My mother is always worried when my father is away on his country deliveries because sometimes when they are very drunk the Jorgensens shout and swear at us as well.

As I creep past their house, I can hear Mr Jorgensen shouting. From the light in their kitchen I can see his silhouette pressed up against our fence. He is shaking his hand and shouting in the direction of our house.

'Do you hear me, you stuck-up bitch. I'm coming over to burn your house down.'

I am too scared to go in the front gate. Instead I climb over the far-side fence and go round to the back door. My mother has been waiting for me to come home. She has switched off all the lights and she gathers us together to make a run for it to Aunty Faith's, which is where we went last time Mr Jorgensen started threatening us. Suddenly the police arrive next door. Mr Jorgensen tries to get away over his back fence, but he falls down and the police catch him and take him inside the house. We can hear lots of banging and yelling.

Mrs Jorgensen shouts, 'Take me husband. He's the troublemaker.'

Then we hear the son yell at the police, ' So youse want a fight too.'

'Mind me china cabinet!' shouts Mrs Jorgensen.

There's more banging and then the sound of glass breaking. Mrs Jorgensen wails pitifully, 'Officer, officer, take me son too.'

Nambour, mid-1950s

WE ARE ALL thankful when at the end of the year Nigel gets a better job as manager of the Paul's Ice Cream depot on the North Coast, and we are once again on the move. This time it is to Nambour, north of Brisbane, where I get a bedroom to myself with a view over a lush green garden shaded by an enormous old mango tree. In his new job Nigel has to deliver the company's ice cream products to all the little beach townships and villages between Gympie in the north and Landsborough in the south. The sugar cane and banana plantations spread out from the Glasshouse Mountains all the way up the coast. Driving through the heart of Nambour, traffic on one of Australia's main highways is regularly forced to a halt as the little cane train chugs across the main street to the sugar mill. The lines of motorists are forced to drink in the sweet perfume of molasses as they wait to get going again. This is long before the North Coast is renamed the Sunshine Coast, and before the village of Noosa, which is a little stop on Nigel's ice cream run, becomes a millionaire's paradise. It is a time when most people prefer to live away from the sea's edge because of the damage the salt air does to their cars. It is a quarter of a century before Nambour achieves national recognition by building the tourist attraction The Big Banana.

Starting the job at the height of summer, Nigel is thrown straight into the deep end. His deliveries begin early in the day and he works really late most evenings. There's the huge van to be stacked, paperwork to be done, reports to be prepared, money to be banked, the truck to be washed and polished. I am nearly fourteen and Diana is now ten. We often have to help to stack the van. I am not sure what makes my stomach turn now whenever I catch the smell of a paddlepop. It might be because it reminds me of the long hours in the freezer room repacking broken boxes, or eating too much damaged product at one sitting, or because my nickname at my new school becomes 'Paddlepop' because of my skinny legs and Nigel's occupation. At fourteen you don't see the funny side of teasing when it is directed at you.

Often I sit high up in the mango tree and cry. I take out my misery on the parrots that come to feast on the golden fruit. Sometimes I feel so angry I chase the birds away by yelling at them and shaking branches. They fly off in a rush of indignant squawking and fluttering. But as soon as I am quiet again they return to their feasting. I wish my mother would forgive me as quickly. From the mango tree I can see the washing on the line, which seems to be the single piece of order in the chaos of our household. She loves hanging out washing and takes great pride in making sure items are grouped together. 'A neat line shows a neat mind' goes one of her mottoes. She quotes this to us sometimes as she leans with one shoulder against the frame of the laundry door, a cigarette wobbling damply between her forefingers. 'Socks with socks and frocks with frocks,' she puffs at us. I wish she would pay as much attention to the rest of the household chores as she does to the washing. She leaves the rest mainly for Nigel and me to do. I want her to be like all the other mothers, especially Estelle McKewen's, who irons her daughter's school uniform and makes little cakes to put in the neat lunch box she packs for her everyday. I don't

Ursula, November 1957

Lunchtime at Nambour, 1957

Diana, Charmian and Stephen, 1958

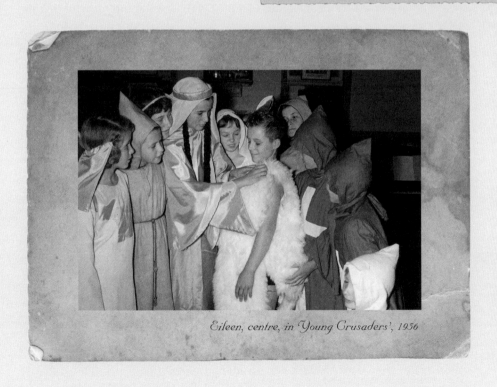

Eileen, centre, in 'Young Crusaders', 1956

care that my parents are interesting and articulate, and talk about books and religion and listen to classical music. I want parents who maintain an orderly house and mow the lawn more than just occasionally. I want to come home from school to fresh lemonade and lamingtons, to a quiet place with a desk where I can do my homework. I want there to be enough money to buy a proper pair of shoes so the kids at school will stop teasing me about the ones I have to wear. I want to go to a real hairdresser to have my hair cut, not the barber's shop. On top of all this I wish my mother weren't Jewish.

The boys next door have been spreading rumours about me at school. They say they have seen me bending down to pray to Allah. Little matter I am a Sunday school teacher at the local Church of England church, and Yahweh is the god of the Jews not Allah, and Arabs not Jews prostrate themselves in prayer. In my bones I know my mother is to blame. The rumours about me are given credence by our family's difference, by her difference especially. Her dark beauty, which has been an asset in another time and place, is now a liability. It brands her as an alien, a Jewess, and marks me as the daughter of a Jewess in a community fearful that the careful balance of their lives might be easily tipped by us, the intruders. In the playground the boys jab their hard fingers into my arms and demand, 'Are you reffo like your mother?' Spluttering with laughter, they bob up and down while looking around to see who is going to acknowledge their bravery. I scream at them until my voice is hoarse and my eyes are puffed and red with crying. The girls in the schoolyard watch without sympathy, then giggle and link arms. In the classroom the same boys flick blotting-paper ink balls at the back of the white school blouse that my mother had made so many sacrifices to buy. When she sees the indelible marks she reacts as if it were my fault, as if I had offered my tormenters an open invitation to ruin my new clothes.

My friend Shayna understands. She is the daughter of my parents' friends Naomi and Simon Bracegirdle. Naomi is also Jewish and she and her husband are both communists. I feel even sorrier for Shayna than I do for myself—at least my family aren't reds. Shayna came home from school once in tears because she had been accused of having a father who was a Russian spy.

Our parents meet through the Nambour Amateur Theatrical Society. Simon is the director when I successfully audition for the part of Jackie Coryton in Noel Coward's *Hay Fever*. Later I took part in other productions and Simon roped in Nigel to use his experience in the Metropolitan Police to play the part of Chief Inspector Hubbard in *Dial M for Murder*.

Through the Bracegirdles, my parents are drawn into a social group of intellectuals, including the folk music historian and composer John Manifold and the playwright George Dann, who makes an anti-Semitic comment to Ursula and Naomi without realising they are Jewish. The two women turn on George and give him what Simon later describes as a well-earned lesson on the dangers of racism. Simon forms a musical society. My parents invest in a beautiful polished wood radiogram. I am allowed to stay up when it is our turn to host the regular evening gathering. I am very proud that two of my teachers are among the guests. Over my parents' protestations, my geography teacher John Denhamer insists on pouring me half a glass of sherry . My world takes a sudden shift into adult territory. I feel alive and confident. As the needle winds its way through the first bars of Ravel's *Bolero*, I demonstrate my new confidence by simulating a conductor's actions with my hands, my head bobbing and nodding to the music as it rises and falls. I am in heaven until I look up and see my mother glaring like thunder at me. My hands drop immediately to my lap, my head to my chest. I am a child again.

When my grandmother comes for a visit from Sydney we have a tidy house for a while, although the old battles pick up where they last left off. I have to share my room with her and she fills it with the smell of face cream and cigarettes. She makes the face cream herself and has spent years trying to get someone interested in helping her market it as a product. She calls it 'Charmian' after my little sister and tells us once people realise what a wonderful cream it is we will all become rich.

Cila brings news that the German government is offering compensation to Jewish citizens who were forced to flee the Nazi regime. She has employed a lawyer in Berlin to negotiate her case. The lawyer thinks Ursula is entitled to compensation as well because the problems with her hip were caused by the diphtheria she caught in the Palestine refugee camp. There is much talk about how much this money is likely to be. Maybe it will be enough for a deposit on our own home. It takes a few years but the lawyer eventually claims that he has managed to obtain a substantial sum for both my mother and my grandmother. However we never know the truth of it because he skips off to Brazil with all his clients' money and is never seen or heard of again.

It is about this time that my mother receives a letter from her father Solomon, who she hasn't heard of since she waved goodbye to him on the station at Frankfurt in 1933. Somehow Cila has tracked him down as part of her research for the compensation case. I would have been very excited if I had got a letter from my father Tony, but Ursula doesn't seem particularly interested. She tells us that it wasn't as if he had ever been a proper father to her and, if it hadn't been for Cila, Solomon would probably never have bothered to look for her. He wrote that he had survived the Holocaust by escaping across the border to Switzerland and had gone back to live in Frankfurt when the war was over.

There is a constant stream of discussion at our dinner table about the problems besetting the world. Why are children in China and Africa starving? Why are there still wars? How did dictators like Hitler and Stalin rise to power and kill millions just so they could retain that power? What can we do to change the world? Is it possible to create a world full of love instead of hate? For as long as we can remember our parents have been searching for a religious belief that offers a solution to these questions. They investigate the Quakers, Christian Science and theosophy. Theories are raised, discussed and compared, but for the most part set aside. For a time my mother becomes a Rosicrucian, my grandmother as well. The Rosicrucians believe in reincarnation. I find the idea of having lots of different lives fascinating too. I have recently read the bestseller *The Search for Bridey Murphy*, the story of an American housewife who it is said regressed under hypnosis to a previous life as a nineteenth-century Irishwoman from Cork. I like the idea of living forever, especially if it means you can have several goes at it. I assume my next life will be better than the one I am having at the moment.

Because of Nigel's experience in London with the movement for world government, my parents deliberately avoid examining any ideology that is even vaguely politically based. So much so that I grow up with barely any understanding of the world of politics. But their friends Naomi and Simon believe the answer has to be political. Simon particularly hates the idea of religion and thinks people who have religious beliefs are fools who are not to be tolerated. He makes an exception in Nigel's case. Nigel is still a committed Anglican. I see him occasionally kneeling beside his bed in prayer before he goes to sleep. His focus at the moment is on a centre for world peace and government. Recently he has met an architect who agrees to draw up a design for building such a centre. Despite their differences, the Bracegirdles and my parents develop a friendship that will last for more than forty years. What draws them together is respect for each other's intelligence and the common desire to save humanity by ridding the world of selfishness and greed.

With all the religious talk in our household, I announce one day I have decided to become a missionary when I leave school. My decision is not so much a calling as a desire to impress my parents with my piety. My announcement scarcely raises an eyebrow, although I do catch a look that passes between Ursula and Nigel, but by the way my mother is rolling her eyes I realise it is not pride they are feeling. In a way their lack of enthusiasm is actually a bit of a relief because I had been worried about having to spend the rest of my life attending boring church services.

I have fallen in love with Michael Johnstone, the boy who lives over the back fence. He, in turn, is in love with Judy Vacher, my best friend. Michael has one dance with me at every school dance because his mother has made him promise he will, and this saves me the ignominy of being a total wallflower. When Mrs Johnstone did her scholarship exam she won the Lilley Medal for the best mark in the state. Whenever I visit her house she tells me not to waste my potential, but I do because I spend too much time dreaming about her son when I should be studying. I talk to my mother one day about boys. Judy had told me that Warren Bentley had told her that just the other day he had seen me at the swimming pool in a bathing costume and he was quite surprised. Could it be true a boy might think I looked pretty, me with my flat chest, skinny legs and big nose? What he actually said to Judy was, I didn't look too bad. I pluck up the courage to ask my mother what she thinks, although I am not sure how to bring up the subject. My parents, especially Nigel, disapprove of talk of boys and hair and clothes. Such interest in one's appearance demonstrates a lack of humility, and in our family true humility is generally equated with sainthood, a state that will stay beyond me for the rest of my life. So I spend the afternoon being especially good and helpful. I take the washing in off the line, folding it ever so neatly to her exacting standards. I do the washing and drying up in the kitchen and put all the dishes away. Then I peel the vegetables for dinner.

She is sitting in the living room doing the crossword when I blurt out my question. I ask if she thinks I'm beautiful. I can see she is surprised by my question. She puts down her paper and lights a cigarette while she thinks about her answer.

'You're not beautiful,' she says at last. 'You're quite attractive though.'

That will do, I think. My expectations haven't been very high anyway. At least now I can be sure I am not ugly. But if my looks aren't the problem, there must be some other reason nobody wants me as a girlfriend. What is it the other girls have that I don't?

I see how the men hover about my mother whenever friends come to visit. She fascinates them with her deep dark eyes and her talk of books and the state of the world. She doesn't even have to flirt like the popular girls at school do. She is just herself. If I were her I could have any man in the world. I could have Michael Johnstone, or go back to England and marry Nigel's nephew David Mead even if he had refused to let me read his comics. I think about finding myself a vet who wears a tweed jacket with leather elbow patches until I read *Bonjour Tristesse* by Françoise Sagan, the young French novelist who gained the attention of the world with this first novel written at the age of nineteen. I decide I will become a novelist and then I will look for an intellectual Frenchman with a beret who will call me *ma chérie* because he appreciates me for my mind not my body. On the radiogram the Everley Brothers sing 'All I Have to do is Dream' and Pat Boone croons 'April Love' just for me. I am yearning for a love so deep it will break my heart. One Saturday morning my sisters and I are bopping in the living room to the latest hit, a song about a witch doctor who can tell you how to make a spell so powerful someone will fall in love with you instantly.

'Yeah!' we shout and giggle, then sing along to the crescendo. 'Ooh eee ooh ah ah, ting tang, walla walla bing bang.'

'So sexy!' I squeal.

From nowhere, Nigel's hand comes smack up against the side of my face. The blow is so hard I spin sideways. I am too shocked to even cry. I have absolutely no idea why he has slapped me. Not since he smacked my bottom when I was six years old had he hit me, not even when they caught me stealing money out of the drawer in their bedroom or when I called my mother a selfish old witch. Now his face is red and the veins in his forehead are bulging. 'You will never ever use such language in this house. Get to your room now. You are to stay there for the rest of the day.'

One Sunday morning several months later I decide I will get up early and make my parents breakfast in bed. I tiptoe down the hall and open their bedroom door quietly. They are making love. Their shocked faces flash up at me before I can close the door. I stand in the hallway unable to move, doing something I have always done to overcome embarrassment: I stand there for ages clenching my jaw up into my ears, creating a drumming noise that blocks out thoughts as well as sounds. What really overwhelms me is that his embarrassment must be worse than mine. Somehow I know my intrusion hasn't been as humiliating for my mother.

Apart from the battles I have with my parents, and the usual constant shortage of money, the two years we live in this town is a relatively settled period. My mother loves her little weatherboard home on stilts set up high to catch whatever breezes might pass through in summer. It is light and airy, with neighbours who nearly all mind their own business and never seem to shout or get drunk. It is a place my parents can be proud to invite friends home to. They buy a dining-room suite and a carpenter friend makes them two beautiful bookcases. Using a second-hand sewing machine, Ursula makes new curtains and cushion covers for the lounge suite. She makes dresses for us all, cutting out the paper patterns on the new dining table. Sometimes we hear the sewing machine whirring late into the night. She starts to draw as well. She paints portraits of the family. We are amazed by the likenesses.

She still reads voraciously, indiscriminately: Woolf and Steinbeck, Wordsworth, Shelley and Shakespeare, *Don Quixote* and Agatha Christie. She subscribes to *Reader's Digest*. I follow her reading path but our mutual passion doesn't draw us any closer. Someone gives her an old Olivetti typewriter and she writes poems about each of her children. I can only remember mine was all about my temper tantrums, with a saving-grace line at the end: 'but she really loves her little brother'. She goes to work on a crime thriller. She tells us she has worked out a perfect murder weapon, a piece of hard ice which the killer has shaven into a knife-like blade so sharp he can slit his victim's throat with it. Once the ice melted, there would be no evidence to tie the weapon back to the murderer. We are all very impressed with her ingenuity. With George Dann's encouragement, she writes a play which is broadcast on ABC Radio a couple of years later. It is a story about a little plane that crashes on a desert island. Nobody now can remember the substance of the plot, but the family can still recall how impressed everyone was with this creative achievement.

'Amazing talent from a person who left school at fourteen and whose native language was not English,' someone was heard to say.

When school finishes at the end of 1958 I get a job in a café serving tea and coffee to tourists and truck drivers. With my first week's wages I buy my mother two classical music records, Richard Tauber's *Love Songs* and Ravel's *Bolero*. The second week I buy myself a circular skirt with a bright orange and blue Hawaiian pattern. My mother turns up her nose when she sees it, but I don't care. I am thrilled to have my own money at last and I am also looking forward to getting my last two years of school finished so I can go to university.

Nigel and Ursula, 1961

NINE
GATES
Chapter Eleven

I am the royal Falcon on the arm of the Almighty. I unfold the drooping wings of every broken bird and start it on its flight.

—Baha'u'llah, *Tablet to Manikji Sahib*

Brisbane, 1959

I AM HAPPY when I find out we are going to move back to Brisbane because I'd flirted with a boy from there who came into the café where I worked in the school holidays. He flirted back, not like the Nambour boys who all ignore me. I hate this country town, but for my parents it is a wrench. In the weeks leading up to us leaving I can hear them talking into the night. There is an urgency in their lowered voices which tells me something is quite wrong, but I can't find out what it is. Maybe something has happened with Nigel's job again. Then we move back to Brisbane, renting a house in the industrial suburb of Rocklea. The house is set just off the main road, across the street from a pub.

When my parents sit me down and explain that, because of their financial difficulties, I will have to leave school and get a job so I can contribute to the family income, part of me is thrilled at the idea of going to work. Just before the junior exam my class had undertaken a vocational guidance test. Ever eager to impress, I had ticked those boxes I thought made me sound clever. So the report that was sent home to my parents suggested my chosen career should be in the field of science. At the time they registered some surprise. Undaunted by the unsound basis for my choice, I successfully apply for a job as a laboratory assistant in the pathology department of Brisbane General Hospital.

Just after I start work my mother goes to Sydney to have an operation on her hip. Over the last two years the pain she has suffered since she was a little girl has become much worse. Cila, who is still working in the Qantas catering department, has organised for Ursula to see a specialist she has found. The surgery he recommends will be complicated and her recovery long and difficult. Diana travels down to Sydney with Ursula to stay with Cila. Charmian and Stephen are sent to stay with friends in Nambour. I remain in the Rocklea house with Nigel.

Hospital in Glebe, Sydney, 1959

THE NURSE COMES in with the coffee and biscuits. On the tray is a letter. Ursula likes this nurse. She is rough and sometimes swears a bit, but she seems to really care. Most of the other nursing staff are unfeeling. They don't understand what she is going through. They don't care about her pain, don't care she feels trapped here so far away from her family.'You are lucky,' the nurse says, handing her the envelope. 'It seems like he writes every day.'

'Every day,' my mother nods.

'My word, you must have something going for you. The postage must be costing him a fortune. How long have you been here now?'

'Four months. Dr Scougall thinks I'll be ready to go to the convalescent home in a couple of weeks.'

'And you haven't seen your hubby in all that time?'

'He came once, just after the operation, but he can't afford to take the time off work, and the fare costs too much.'

'You must miss him and your kids.'

Ursula's lips tremble. 'They are with friends, all good people, but it's not the same. I worry about them all the time, especially my little boy. He's only five. But one of my girls is down here. Diana. You've seen her. She's staying with my mother in Mascot.'

The nurse has tidied her up. Brushed her hair and helped her put on a bit of lipstick. 'It will make you feel better, dear.' She straightens up the things on the bedside table, the library books Cila has brought, the handkerchiefs, the cards and letters. She empties the ashtray. 'You'll be glad to get out of this bed,

I expect. It'd be too bloody long if it was me. Don't know how you have the patience.'

Ursula nods. The nurse's sympathy makes her want to cry. 'At least you understand.' She raises her voice slightly, glancing around in the hope the uncaring nurses can hear her.

From the nurses' station come the sound of telephones and the persistent tinkle of bells. They never answer her bell straight away. Sometimes they wait until the third or fourth time she rings. They seem to act as if she were just an ordinary patient. They must have some comprehension of what she is going through. Don't they read her clinical notes? Her operation has been groundbreaking. Dr Scougall is the best orthopaedic surgeon in Australia. He found that osteoarthritis has eaten away at her bones. The operation he performs involves removing the diseased bone and grafting new bone from her right shin. He inserts stainless steel pins into the new and old bones to ensure the graft holds together while the bones are knitting. The medical expenses are costing Cila a fortune.

They will come to get her soon for her physiotherapy session. The thought of it makes her light a cigarette. Her hand shakes even as she opens the matchbox.

She wouldn't wish this pain on anyone. At every session there comes a point when she longs to faint away. Sometimes she does, and she hears their echoing voices calling, 'Here she goes, catch her, catch her,' as she slides out of her agony.

On the worst days she remembers dancing. The memories cause more pain than the physical torture. She remembers coming home from ballet classes, Cila putting on the *Swan Lake* record and pushing all the furniture away to clear a space in the centre of the room. 'Show me. What did you learn today?'

She danced for her mother, but she was really dancing for herself. The music entered her body and she felt like a magical being. She didn't have to remember the steps, the precision and the order. Her body was choreographing itself.

She hasn't danced for a quarter of a century, and it is only now she realises she has never really let that dream go. The very first time they put on the heavy body cast after the diphtheria she should have admitted to herself she would never dance again. What miracle has she been expecting to mend her crumbling bones and send her off in Tamara's footsteps to dance with the Bolshoi? Her dream hadn't shattered as it should have done. It has simply slipped away without her realising—until now.

Cleveland Point, 1959—60

I AM STANDING on the stone wall that separates our garden from the sea. The tide is almost out and the great shallow expanse of Moreton Bay is beaten silver beneath a cloudless sky. I am home for the weekend to the little house Nigel has rented on Cleveland Point while they wait for their housing commission application to be processed. We moved here after my mother came home from hospital because the rent is cheap. It takes nearly two hours on the train from the city. Cila thinks it is a terrible place, but I love it. I could stand here for hours just watching the gulls wheel and shriek across the wet sand as thousands upon thousands of shelled creatures plip and plop in and out of their tiny hidey holes. I can hear my grandmother calling me to help her. I pretend not to hear her at first. It's what I have been doing lately whenever anyone calls me.

My grandmother has moved up to Brisbane and is working at Lennon's Hotel. She has really come to take care of my mother while she recuperates. Cila wants me to help her unpack boxes in the front room. She opens a box of photographs and rifles through them. She makes her disgust sound. Paahhg!

'What is it?' I ask curiously.

'You know this man?' She flashes a photograph at me.

I nod. It is my father Tony with my mother. She really was beautiful, I think, but there is something creepy about him—like the villain in a Hollywood film, the bad one who is after the heroine but loses out to the hero.

Cila tells me she should have taken Ursula to America not to Palestine. New York should have been her destiny. All of my grandmother's relatives who went to America have become successful. My mother might have been a famous fashion model or even a lawyer. At the very least she would have had the opportunity to marry someone who is successful. I know she is implying that Nigel is a hopeless provider. I hate the fact we are always poor, but I don't like it when my grandmother makes these comments, especially when he's always so nice to her. At least he treats her with more respect and kindness than her own daughter does.

'Eileen, listen to me,' my grandmother says. 'If you want to be really happy then you must never marry just because of love. You see what it has done to your mother? She could have had anything. She had such intelligence, such beauty. Instead she married your stepfather and all she has is children and money problems.'

It is as if she knows I spend my waking moments looking for someone who will love me.

'I think I should throw away this picture,' she says, but I snatch it from her and take the box of photographs into the safety of my mother's bedroom.

I am sixteen and I have a new skirt, in a sweet cotton fabric of pale grey paisley dotted with pink roses on a white background, and I have made it myself. Me, fumble-fingered, impatient, untidy, I have hand-sewn this skirt, little stitch by little stitch, all neat and even. It is my triumph. Matron showed me how to make it. She manages the Girls' Friendly Society hostel where I stay during the week because I am attending evening classes four nights a week. The other girls at the hostel tease me about going to 'school' while they are out at parties and dances, but Matron looks after me. She keeps my dinner warm on college nights, a privilege that makes the other girls jealous. Matron and Nigel had a long talk when I arrived at the hostel. I suspect he asked her to keep an eye on me. I think he thinks I am wayward, which is why he lectures me all the way into the city about keeping my attention on my studies and not on boys and such things.

He says, 'Don't even think about getting married until you're twenty-five.'

I am silent. What on earth does he mean? Who is he to decide what I will or won't do when I am grown up? I don't ask him if he realises in order to get married you have to be engaged first. Since the closest I have ever come to having a boyfriend is one sloppy kiss with a boy I hardly know while watching the fireworks at the Nambour Show, where does he get this idea I am about to fall off the rails? He talks on and on about focusing on my education and my career. As usual he edges around the realities without ever asking me what I am thinking. Many years later, after I have given up on my education and then on my career and am dug down into married life with four children, his words come ringing back.

In the middle of the year my parents move back to Inala and the housing commission estate, this time to a new brick house. I go back home as well. Inala is closer to the city than Cleveland but I still don't get home from classes until after ten-thirty at night.

One Saturday morning, just after I returned from living at the hostel, my mother confronts me. She is disappointed in me, she says. Again, I think. What have I done this time? She has been sorting through my suitcase so she can do my washing and has found my new skirt.

'You are so irresponsible when it comes to managing your money,' she says, dangling the skirt out in front of her.

I don't understand what she is talking about. Besides, I'm thinking, when does she ever do my washing? It is just her excuse to poke around in my things.

'It was for the party,' I say lamely.

'Yes, but you could have saved a lot of money by making it yourself.'

'But I did. I made it myself,' I insist.

She holds the skirt up. She doesn't say anything, but I can see she doesn't believe me. I snatch it away from her and turn the waistband over to show the tiny stitches I have painstakingly sewn. She shrugs her shoulders and walks off. She doesn't apologise. She doesn't say anything. She doesn't have to. I have scored a victory and that is enough for me.

I have made the skirt to wear to a friend's eighteenth birthday party. I met Jan Whelan at evening classes when we both enrolled in English as part of our matriculation course. The classrooms are in an old building near South Brisbane railway station. We gather for the first time on a humid midsummer's evening, noisy with the loud whirring of old ceiling fans and trams rattling up and down Grey Street. We sit next to each other. It is the beginning of a lifelong friendship. We are an unlikely pairing. Jan is neat, well-dressed, organised, self-confident and mature. I am untidy, scatty, insecure and naive. What draws us together is our love of literature and an early confession about our mutual aspiration to become writers.

Sometimes on the weekend Jan and I visit each other's homes. I love going to her house. She has two sisters and a brother. In the rumpus room that Jan's bank-manager father has built under the house we play *Ray Connif Meets Billy Butterfield* and Peggy Lee's *Fever*, read copies of *Seventeen* magazine and experiment with hairstyles and make-up. Weekends at 158 Grovely Terrace are always full of fun and belly laughs.

The atmosphere is completely different in my house. Although my mother is almost recovered from her hip operation she has a new affliction. It is 1960 and no one talks about clinical depression, not even the parade of doctors she visits to treat her headaches, insomnia, palpitations and tiredness. She spends many of her days in bed. As the eldest, much of the responsibility for the household chores falls on my shoulders, especially on the weekends.

In the cause of pursuing my totally unsuitable career in science, I now have a job at the University of Queensland in the Geology Department. My grandmother had once offered to pay for me to go to university and study law. I had an obvious talent for argument, she had said, and I should put it to some practical use. But I thought law sounded very boring. I left my job at the hospital because the university allows its employees six hours off a week for external study courses. But as it turns out my new boss is a tyrant who point-blank refuses to give me the time off I'm entitled to. Now my days are spent painting numbers on rock specimens and entering the details in a large leather-bound ledger. I get up early in the morning and get home late four nights a week after classes. On Friday, my night off, I have to do the washing up, 'because everybody else has to do it when you're not here.'

'Your mother's not so bad,' Jan tells me after the first time she spends a weekend at our house. 'I suppose not,' I say out of loyalty, but Jan doesn't have to put up with what I do. She doesn't get woken up before six every morning by her mother calling her name over and over. I know Ursula only wakes me up to make sure I have time to bring her coffee and toast in bed before I leave for work. Jan doesn't have to spend all her weekends doing her mother's shopping and washing and the other housework that builds up through the week while she's at work. Jan's mother Daisy doesn't expect her to change her books when she goes to the library and she wouldn't pull faces if Jan brought back the wrong ones. Jan doesn't have to keep her brothers and sisters quiet while her mother sleeps. More than forty years later Jan says to me, 'You know why I loved coming to your place then? It was because your house was full of books.'

One weekend when the rest of the family has gone out to visit friends, Jan and I decide to teach ourselves to smoke. My mother has left me with a mound of ironing. We have gone halves in a packet of Craven A unfiltered cigarettes. We take it in turns—one of us irons while the other smokes. At the end of the day the ironing basket is empty and so is the cigarette packet, and we are both feeling ill.

'I think you are too hard on her,' Jan says, shaking out the sleeve of Nigel's shirt. 'How old is she, thirty-five? She's still so young. No wonder she resents you. How would you like to be stuck in the house all day with all those little kids? Maybe she'd like to go out occasionally and have a good time, maybe go to a nightclub.'

I think this is an odd way to talk about my mother. I have never thought of her as being young, and certainly can't imagine her ever wanting to go to a nightclub.

My mother would often say, 'If I could sleep through just one night I would be a happy woman.' She does sleep, only it is in the daytime, with the curtains firmly drawn, surrounded by her potions and books, her glasses of water, her empty coffee cups and her ashtray full of crushed-out cigarettes. My mother lies in her bed for days on end. 'Is she going to die?' the younger children sometimes ask. She lies in the dark room with the dim light glowing behind the red shade of the bedside lamp, her eyes grown dark and her face a flaccid white. 'I cannot live like this anymore,' she moans. Sometimes she gets up in the late afternoon.

Ursula and Naomi, Inala

Naomi and Eileen, Inala

*Diana, Cila, Charmian and, front, Stephen,
Inala, 1961*

Diana, Stephen and Charmian, Inala, 1961

Charmian, Eileen and Stephen, Inala, 1959

We hurry to please with coffee and sandwiches. 'Would you like some water?' I ask when I am feeling generous. Sometimes she does not bother to reply, except she lets me see her hand is trembling.

Sometimes, as she does for the rest of her life, my mother tries to escape from us for good. She uses pills and potions and deep gulps of gas from the oven.

'I will leave you all because you don't care,' she tells us whenever we are not taking enough notice of her. Sometimes we watch her framed in the door, trembling at the bathroom cupboard, hair fallen forward, scrabbling in bottles. Sometimes we even find her stretched out on the floor, and then there is a great commotion, a high drama. Squeals of panic ring around the house, frantic calls are made on the neighbour's telephone to the ambulance, to the doctor, to Nigel at work. We wait, hearts beating, watching her shallow breath, the blue curl of her lips and the ashen pallor of her skin. Someone props a pillow under her head and tucks the crocheted blanket from the armchair around her inert body. The little ones wail in tune with the sirens. I always suspect underneath it all she is choreographing the drama. I am sure she does it to get a reaction, to test us, to make sure our love is not wanting. Perhaps she peeks between her eyelashes to assess the weight of our fear. Once though, when they lift her on to the stretcher, I see a wet patch on the carpet and my heart thumps at the thought that she might have gone too far this time. When she is tucked up in her clean white hospital bed in the crinkly white sterile gown demanding water and cursing the inattentive nurses, we lose interest and go home to relish the peace her absence creates.

Often I ask myself which one of us my mother loves—or if she loves any of us at all. Sometimes her friends tell her she must love children because of the size of our family. She tells them she planned us all.

At the end of 1960 Australia is hit by a severe drought, which causes a fall in wool production and rising prices. Harold Holt, the Liberal treasurer, introduces a credit squeeze to contain inflation. As a result of 'Holt's Jolt' unemployment rises to the highest rates in thirty years. Because of the 'last in, first out' principle Nigel loses his job as a salesman for Neon Signs, where he has been selling this new form of outdoor advertising. Not long after this he gets very drunk, a matter of some amazement to us children. Our parents are hardly even social drinkers. There is generally a bottle of sherry in the house, but it is only brought out on special occasions or when we have visitors. Not only does Nigel get drunk but, as he is getting off the bus, he falls over and breaks his false teeth. My mother is angry enough with him to confide in me what has happened. In turn I am angry with her for revealing Nigel's fall from the pedestal on which I have always held him.

Shortly after this something happens that changes the course of my parents' lives. My mother is friendly with Vi Horne, who lives two doors away from us. One day Vi tells my mother she is a member of the Baha'i faith. There are fewer than two hundred Baha'is in Australia in 1960. The central theme of the Baha'i message, Vi says, is that humanity is one single race and it will not be long before the world will be unified into one global society. The following week Vi invites my parents to a Friday night 'fireside' meeting at the home of Geoff and Viva Rodwell so they can find out more about the teachings. Initially they are cautious. They have been down this path on numerous occasions and they have no reason to believe this will not result in the same old disappointments once they begin to dig down into the facts.

After they come home from the meeting, my parents talk far into the night. They seem very excited. When we get up in the morning they are both up and out of bed. It's a long time since I've seen my mother having breakfast at the kitchen table. They are reading some pamphlets. My mother hands one to me. She smiles as she says I'll find it very interesting. It has a list of things Baha'is believe. One of them is equality of men and women. I like that one. I'm paid a lot less than the boys I work with. The others include the abandonment of all forms of prejudice, the elimination of the extremes of poverty and wealth, universal education and a global commonwealth of nations. Nigel is very excited about this last item. None of the other religions they have examined has dealt specifically with world unity.

Another pamphlet is about the history of the religion. Its founder Baha'u'llah was born in Persia, now Iran, in 1817. In 1863 he announced he was the messenger from God. He said he was part of a long line of prophets stretching back beyond recorded time, including Abraham, Moses, Buddha, Zoroaster, Christ and Muhammad. God, at a different time and a different place, had sent each of them. Baha'u'llah was the prophet for this day and age and brought with him a blueprint for the future, which he claimed would usher in a period of time called 'The Most Great Peace'.

Nigel takes only two weeks to decide he must become a Baha'i. My mother takes a little longer. She has two obstacles to overcome. The first is her acceptance of Christianity. Having been brought up in the Jewish faith she has never accepted Jesus Christ as a prophet from God. Just after she married Nigel, she had been baptised into the Church of England, not so much because she had become a Christian believer but to please her mother-in-law Elsie, whom she held in such high regard. In order to become a Baha'i she first had to accept that Jesus was part of a 'progressive revelation'. This led eventually to Baha'u'llah, who had written, 'And when Thou didst purpose to make Thyself know unto men, Thou didst successively reveal the Manifestations of Thy Cause, and ordained each to be a sign of Thy Revelation among Thy people ... and the Day-Spring of Thine invisible Self amidst Thy creatures.'

This troubles Ursula for some time, as does the question of reincarnation, which she has come to believe as part of the Rosicrucian creed. The Baha'i teachings do not support the theory of reincarnation. However, one of the Baha'i tenets especially appeals to her. It states that each individual is expected to search for the truth independently. She borrows a pile of books from the Rodwells, and reads and reads until she finally comes to a decision. Even though she finds nothing to actually convince her that Jesus was who he said he was, or even proof there is no such thing as reincarnation, the more she reads the writings of Baha'u'llah the more convinced she becomes that the Persian was who he claimed to be. His writings were so luminous, so concerned with the world at hand. She reads, 'The earth is but one country and mankind its citizens' and 'the well-being of mankind, its peace and security, are unattainable unless its unity is firmly established.' But the quotation that she comes back to over and over again is 'the best beloved of all things in My sight is justice.'

She becomes deeply committed to Baha'u'llah and the validity of his revelation. Over time, she said, she gained such clear insight and understanding of his writings that she was readily able to surrender her previous convictions and accept all he revealed, on an intellectual as well as an emotional level, with a total conviction of their truth and validity. Soon I make a similar declaration, of course, and so does Cila. Eventually my commitment to Baha'i fades as I become distracted by other things. But my grandmother remains a member of the faith. I have often wondered if, like me, Cila chose to follow Ursula's path because she hoped it might bring her closer to her daughter.

It's the end of my first year of evening classes. Nigel is unhappy with me. I have done badly in my exams, failing one subject and barely passing the others. He takes me into the kitchen to give me one of his lectures. I sit at the table and he stands in front of the stove. It's what I've been expecting. I'm going to get a good talking to. I expect he will understand how difficult it is to study with the limited time I have available. I expect he will say, despite this, I need to apply myself more. I need to be focused and knuckle down. He will talk about guts. He always mentions guts somewhere along the way—intestinal fortitude. Difficulties are just challenges to be overcome.

He says some of these things, but he also starts to talk about the time I am spending with my friends from tech. He thinks I am being led astray. By what he says I think he believes I have a boyfriend. I wish, I think. If he knew how hard it is even to get a boy to look at me. It's not hard for Pam Beale, my pretty friend with the high heels, blonde curls and big breasts. Nigel should see what the boys do when she walks down the street with us. All those wolf whistles—they are never for me. Once one of the boys in our class, who was in the army and had been transferred to Woomera, came back to Brisbane for a weekend. He rang up and asked me out. We went to the pictures and at the end of the evening he asked me to marry him because he was lonely on the isolated army base. His name was Norman. He only wanted me because he couldn't get anybody else.

All the time Nigel is lecturing me about the dangers I could get myself into, I'm thinking, fat chance. I'm half laughing inside, and somehow he must have guessed. I probably have that when-is-this-all-going-to-be-over sort of look on my face.

Then he raises his voice to a new intensity. 'The way you are going you could end up as a prostitute.'

I know the word represents something dirty and immoral, but I don't actually know what a prostitute does. So I have no idea how this possibly relates to my own behaviour. He must have seen the bewilderment on my face.

'I'm only telling you for your own good.' His face is quite red now.

I can't speak. I don't know how to defend myself. I feel like crying.

'You have to understand God is always testing us. We are all tested. In my life I have been guilty of breaking some of God's commandments. That's how much I have been tested. Do you understand?'

I nod because I know he expects it. Besides trying to work out what he thinks I have been doing, I am trying to work out which commandments he could have possibly broken.

I get another little sister when Naomi Joyce Hall is born the following August.

And I finally get my first boyfriend. His name is Greg Vickers. He is a sweet boy with a lovely smile. We meet on the train going home from evening classes. In two weeks Greg and I are going to a New Year's Eve party at Jan's house. As usual I am broke. I want to wear something special to the party. Jan has offered to help me make a new dress, but it means going over to her place for the weekend. I hate telling my mother I am going to Jan's. Even when she doesn't say anything, she pulls a face or sighs, which is her way of telling me she thinks I'm selfish and inconsiderate. I always put off telling her things like this. If I tell her too soon, she has longer to wear me down with her dark and thunderous moods. If I leave it too late, she will produce all sorts of tasks that I have to do for her before I go.

This time I tell her well ahead of time because I expect she will be impressed I am making my own dress. But it doesn't work.

'I haven't been well,' she says, her voice trembling as she lights a cigarette. She always lights a cigarette when she is angry.

'I was hoping this weekend you would be able to give me some help with the baby.'

Oh no, I think, don't do this to me. Not this time.

'I'm really sorry,' I say. 'Normally I would stay home, but if I don't do it this weekend I ...' I hear my voice trailing away. She's not even listening to me. She's looking out of the window.

Suddenly she turns, stabbing the cigarette into the ashtray.

'You really are one of the most selfish people I have ever known in my life.'

'I'm not,' I begin to whimper. 'You know I'm always helping, always staying home on the weekends because you are sick.'

'I pray you don't have one-tenth of the suffering I have had in my lifetime.'

She's cornering me again, as she always does, but this time I am thinking of the white dress with the big flared skirt, and I come out fighting.

'Not the suffering again!' I am suddenly screaming. 'I'm sick of hearing about it.' And then the torrent breaks. I'm sure every neighbour in the street must have heard us. At the end I storm off to my room.

'And I'm going to Jan's whether you think I'm selfish or not.'

We don't speak for two days. It is my mother who breaks the silence, asking me to sit down because she has something to say to me.

'I think you and I just can't live under the same roof any more,' she says. 'It's about time you moved out.'

I can't believe what I am hearing. Move out. I want to hug her, except I know this is not the reaction she might have expected. Instead I nod and tell her I understand. She picks up her book. The conversation is over. I have wanted to run away from home many times but for some reason I have never actually thought of just getting up and going.

A week later I have found myself a share flat in Paddington near the centre of Brisbane. I will be moving out on the weekend. I am terrified my mother will have changed her mind, so I don't tell her I'm leaving until my suitcase is packed and I am about to walk out the door. She is genuinely shocked, and this simply confirms what I suspected, that she never thought I'd take her seriously. So it was just another one of her dramatic gestures. She tries to talk me out of leaving. Her voice is gentler than I can ever remember. I feel myself wavering.

'It's too late,' I argue. 'I've paid my rent in advance.'

Of course we both know this is an excuse and that it's really because I can't wait to get away from her. I can't believe I had never even thought of leaving home before she had made the suggestion. She's begging me not to go. How can I leave like this? How will she manage without my help? I want to tell her it's her fault. She was the one who opened the door. I'm just walking through it. The bus isn't due for another half an hour, but if I wait at the house I will be sure to cave in.

'I have to go now' is all I say. She looks distraught and for a minute I want to go up to her and put my arms around her. But it would be a dangerous thing for me to do. I am shaking so much now. I hardly have the strength to pick up my suitcase. I have to pass the front of the house on my way to the bus stop. She is standing by the living-room window. Before I force myself to look away I see she is weeping, but I don't know if her tears are for herself or for me.

May Ball with Ursula, 1963

THE
SHADOW

Chapter Twelve

Between the idea
And the reality
Between the motion
And the act
Falls the SHADOW

—T.S. Eliot, *The Hollow Men*

Leaving Brisbane, November 1963

DIANA WATCHES THE jacarandas dancing in the heat on the far side of the hospital car park. She turns back to look at her mother, as a nurse pushes through the curtain.

Ursula's face is puffy with too much sleep. Her cheeks are criss-crossed with pillow lines. Her mouth has slid down to the left side of her chin.

'Mrs Hall, wake up!' the nurse shouts. She sounds like Diana's PE teacher. Ursula moans and turns away from them.

Diana has expected the hospital treatment to bring her mother back to her normal self, but Ursula has slipped further away. Even her spirit seems to have left her. Her body is lifeless inside its sack of yellow skin. Her limbs flop and she groans every time the nurses try to move her.

Diana wants to restore her mother's dignity—brush her matted hair, wipe the spittle from her face with a cool cloth, button up her gown to cover the parts of her that are exposed—but she is only sixteen and doesn't know how to push through all the hospital bureaucracy.

An older nurse comes up and pats her shoulder. 'Don't worry, darling. It's just the drugs. She'll be right as rain in a couple of days.'

Two days. She feels giddy with panic. She goes outside to find Mr Rodwell.

'They can't wake her up,' she tells him.

'She'll be all right once we get her on the train. The nurse is very confident she'll just sleep.'

Diana feels her cheeks begin to quiver. He puts his arm around her shoulders. 'She needs to be with your father now. They're both relying on you.'

'I know, but can't we wait until she wakes up properly?'

No one had discussed the plans with her, except to say she should go to the hospital with Mr Rodwell to pick up her mother and then take her by train to Newcastle over eight hundred kilometres away. She has no idea who has paid for the tickets, sorted out arrangements for her brothers and sisters or talked to her father. She wants to ask Mr Rodwell more questions, but she can see he is as bewildered as she is. Who will be in charge of their lives once they get to Newcastle? She is becoming very frightened this role may fall on her by default.

The nurses have taken her mother's old house dress and shoes out of the locker. This is what she was wearing when the ambulance brought her to hospital weeks before. They prop her up into a sitting position and push her arms through the sleeves as if she is a rag doll. They bully her with experienced kindness. Diana remembers her mother getting ready for other outings. She remembers her looking alert as well as beautiful, remembers her boasting about the smart outfit and the silk purse she had made of a sow's ear, remembers her black hair shining, remembers the ruby lips and the expensive perfume saved for special occasions. She would never want to be seen in public in this shabby dress and scuffed shoes, with all her beauty dissipated by drugs.

Mr Rodwell has hired a wheelchair from the hospital, but Ursula is too heavy for the pair of them to carry it up the steps at Roma Street station. Her head keeps falling whichever way the wheelchair tips. Train commuters stare as the young girl and the middle-aged man try to manoeuvre the semi-conscious woman slumped forward with her mouth open. Mr Rodwell goes off to find a porter to help them.

Diana refuses to look at the stickybeaks on the platform craning their necks to get a better view. Instead she rearranges the clothes over her mother's fleshy parts as the men heave her out of the chair, all the time attempting to keep her in a sitting position. Whenever they stagger her mother groans. Diana keeps stroking Ursula's hand even though she is not sure it is making any real difference. Their seats are at the back of a third-class carriage at the rear of the train. They edge her into the seat next to the window. She wakes up for a moment before her head falls against the glass. Mr Rodwell rushes off to his car to get a cushion and picnic blanket. Between them they try to make her comfortable. He hopes Diana is going to be able to manage. She'll be all right, she tells him, and wonders how she has found the words to give him this assurance.

***

RARELY DOES A family fall apart all at once or just because of one terrible disaster. Breakdown often happens so gradually no one even notices. When you look back everyone can see the signs so clearly—the strange flickers in the eyes, the voices rising and falling in the middle of the night, the doors that slam, the unattended refrigerator with its limp and slimy vegetables, the sadness falling in layers over the dusty furniture. By the time anyone begins to take notice it is almost too late to bring things back under control.

The worst moment had come the day her mother started screaming, but that wasn't the beginning of it. Maybe it was the moment when Diana realised there was something different about her father—a kind of excitement appeared to have taken over his whole body. She had never seen him so happy before, but when his eyes shone they looked out into a distance at something he could see but she couldn't. Maybe it all started before this, when they had moved to the horrible old house in Morningside. It went with the new job Mr Rodwell had organised for her father as a nightwatchman in the factory across the road.

'Look, Nigel,' her mother had complained, 'not a lick of paint. Look at the windows, they're filthy. How am I supposed to clean them in my condition?'

She was pregnant again.

'I'll do them, dear, as soon as we unpack.' But he quickly forgot.

He wasn't very good at domestic things, Ursula would say about her husband. She said it as if it were awarding him some sort of badge of honour. She joked about his hopelessness as if to say, don't think he is all perfect. She sent him off one day to buy white cotton to cover the bassinet. He came back proudly with a bargain-price piece of gaudy yellow seersucker. She laughed because she should have known he would get it wrong. Instead she made the seersucker into a skirt for Diana to wear to a Hawaiian end-of-school party.

He never finished anything around the house. One day he mowed a cricket pitch into the long grass in the garden.

'Why don't you finish the job?' Ursula had called from the kitchen window, but Stephen was already putting the stumps in and they pretended they hadn't heard her. They all played into the gathering night, taking turns at batting, bowling and wicketkeeping. They hunted down the ball in the long grass as the fruit bats flew overhead. Diana thought cricket was a silly game, but she kept playing because it was something sane and normal that pulled them in close to each other without the need for words.

Suddenly it seemed Nigel couldn't wait to get to work every evening. He said he never got lonely because the silence gave him time for contemplation and reading. In fact, he said, he had never felt more clear-headed in his life. He practised his deep breathing exercises, which made him feel fitter and stronger. At home during the day he appeared to need very little sleep.

One evening at the dinner table he began a long lecture on people's moral responsibility to those less fortunate.

'I cried because I had no shoes,' he ended, 'until I saw a man who had no feet.'

Diana saw there were tears in his eyes. She looked at Charmian and Stephen to see if they had noticed. They were looking down at their plates, their mouths twisted with giggling dismay, not for his words but for his sentimentality.

Day and night he prayed for God's guidance. As his heart began to blaze, he became more and more frustrated with his own lack of action. One day he made a big announcement. The tiny Baha'i community in Newcastle in New South Wales needed help to bring the message of the faith to the local community. Nigel had decided they would move there. The family was going to become Baha'i pioneers.

'Where's Newcastle?' the children asked with dismay.

'It's just north of Sydney,' their mother answered for her husband. 'I saw it from the train once. It's a horrible place, full of soot from the steel factories, and the tallest television aerials I've ever seen. It's the last place in Australia I want to live.'

Besides, she said to him, there are five children to be considered and a job for him and a place to live. She was sick of having to lug her family round the country.

But he would hear no argument. His current job was badly paid and, as she frequently pointed out, the house was awful. Once she agreed to go he would apply for a job with BHP, the mining company.

'Of all the gifts of God, the greatest is the gift of Teaching,' he quoted her from a Baha'i text.

Her cheeks were burning. She puffed one cigarette after another furiously. 'The Baha'is are important. I understand this just as much as you do, but no one would expect you to sacrifice your family.'

He blushed hard. It was an unfair blow, but he held his ground. His stake this time was very high and, because she was not used to such obstruction, a compromise was a long time coming. For weeks they held on to their positions with more childishness than logic. Some nights the children lay staring into the cracks in the ceiling listening to their loving fury as it rose and fell, to her high-pitched trembling and his low murmuring protests. A compromise was finally reached. She would agree to go as long as he didn't rush the process. He had to secure a job and a place for them to live before they would move. While he took the time to make his plans, an uneasy peace settled over the unpainted weatherboards.

In autumn another brother arrived. They called him Michael Daniel, and he brought with him a distracting energy that lasted only a few weeks. Even though all thoughts of pioneering seemed to have been put in limbo, Ursula still slid into a dark post-natal depression. Then late in winter she was hospitalised with pneumonia. Diana stayed home from school to look after Naomi and Michael while her father tried to sleep. When Ursula came home from the hospital she was hardly well enough to look after herself, let alone her children. All day she sat around, staring into space as if she were looking for something she had lost.

Once Diana managed to escape to a friend's house. Her friend's mother cooked dinner while the two girls lay around in the living room watching *Bandstand* on television. Afterwards they ate Golden Circle canned pineapple with ice cream while the mother washed up. Diana couldn't help thinking she had never watched television while her mother washed the dishes. A few weeks later Diana brought the same friend home after school. Ursula was still lying on her bed in her nightie. 'You'll have to peel the potatoes. I'm too ill,' she said.

It gradually dawned on Diana that her father was hardly aware of what was happening in the family and she could no longer look to him for support with her mother. He had been caught up with something that had evolved during the long hours of meditation and prayer. Slowly he had begun to relinquish his hold on practical matters. Children don't understand their parents. She did not realise he was being swept up in a wave of discovery. His whole being throbbed with a joyous energy. His work kept him awake all night and he found sleep almost impossible during the day. But he did not seem to need sleep. His answer to Ursula's melancholy was to exhort her to join him, but she had no energy for the journey, and the more he held out his hand to her the further away she drifted.

***

URSULA IS SITTING on a chair in the kitchen in Brisbane wearing her blue dressing gown. Diana has just put Michael down in his cot.

'He's asleep,' Diana tells her mother, but Ursula doesn't answer. She is staring at the grimy linoleum tiles. She clutches a packet of cigarettes in her right hand. Diana notices this hand is trembling.

'Have you seen Daddy?' Diana asks.

Her mother still doesn't respond. Diana hears a clattering outside. When she turns around she sees her father is on a ladder cleaning the dining-room windows. He waves the cleaning cloth through the glass and smiles. He is always smiling these days, she thinks. So why isn't her mother happy as well? When Diana turns back to say something to her mother, she is sitting bolt upright staring through the kitchen door at her husband. Her eyes have widened as if she has seen something utterly shocking. She puts her hand up to her head and starts pulling at the roots of her hair, and then she lets out the most terrible howling sound Diana has ever heard. On and on the screams come like the wails of some caged and tortured animal.

Diana looks back at her father to see his reaction. There is no reaction. He continues to clean the panes as if nothing in the world has changed. She runs across and taps frantically on the glass.

'Daddy,' she says, pointing to where her mother is now bent double in her anguish. 'Quick, there's something wrong.'

He smiles at her and goes on rubbing the window. 'Don't worry, darling. Everything's going to be all right.'

Events kaleidoscope over the next few days. People come and go—friends, doctors, Cila. Somehow Ursula has gathered herself enough to get some help. Months later she tells Diana she threatened to leave her father if he didn't go to see a psychiatrist. He is not ill, he argues, he has simply gained enlightenment and is truly happy for the first time in his life. Finally he agrees to be admitted to hospital but only after he realises he will be sectioned if he doesn't. In those days the answer to manic episodes was electro-shock therapy. He doesn't know this before he agrees to whatever treatment will be judged necessary.

Diana does not visit her father in hospital. She is frightened of what she might find. She feels ill herself when she thinks he might be lost to her permanently. The nights are the worst time because she cannot distract herself from imagining the consequences if he fails to recover. She tries to imagine him as he had been just weeks before. Once he had ridden down to the tram stop at Bulimba and doubled her home on his bicycle after her evening sewing class. Lately, though, he has done nothing. He has stopped playing cricket and has even stopped cracking those dumb jokes Diana always finds so embarrassing. Now she wants all that back, but she cannot get rid of the image of him cleaning the windows with emptiness in his eyes.

I go and visit Nigel in the hospital. I can't see what all the fuss is about. He looks fine, although unusually flushed, and his eyes are particularly shiny. He gives me a letter to post. It is addressed to a Hollywood couple, Dinah Shore and George Montgomery. He has read in the newspaper they are about to divorce and has written pleading with them to reconsider their decision and to properly consider the sanctity of marriage. It seems he thinks the whole world is his to save.

One morning Cila arrives at the house and shortly after calls an ambulance. Ursula is packed off to hospital too. There are now five children at home with no parent to care for them. Cila, who has to keep going to work, hires a housekeeper, a horrible woman who is cruel to the children. Eventually my grandmother takes the heart-rending decision that Stephen, Naomi and baby Michael will have to be placed in temporary care in a children's home.

On the weekends Cila and I visit them. Stephen and Naomi always stand at the gate to wave goodbye to us. The gate is a high wire-mesh contraption that makes the place look like a prison. They twist their little fingers through the wire. They look bewildered but they don't cry. I have never seen my grandmother cry before, but she does as soon as we are out of sight.

'How can you explain this thing to such small children?' she asks.

I have no answer for her. Perhaps I could take time off from my job to look after them.

'No!' Cila insists. 'Some people in this family need to earn some money.'

Charmian goes to stay with a Baha'i friend and Diana with the Bracegirdles, who have moved to Kelvin Grove. There is a lot of blame in the air, about how hopeless her parents are, and Diana has to listen to it all without knowing how to put up a defence, even though she is sure there is one. She waits until bedtime so she can cry into her pillow. She will not let anyone see how angry she is. She cries for the pieces of her life that are being plucked away one after the other.

Ursula looks weak and washed out when I see her in hospital.

'I don't know how to cope any more,' she says, and holds out her hands. They are trembling. Why has it always got to be about you, I am thinking. It seems as if she is trying to compete with Nigel, to prove she is in a worse state than he is. She takes a letter out of her handbag to give to Nigel. It is from the Broken Hill Propriety Company in Newcastle. She has never opened a letter of his before.

'Give this to him, 'she says to me. 'It's not the job offer he was expecting. They just say if he is ever in Newcastle at anytime he could come and talk to them. At least it's something positive to look forward to. It will make him feel better.'

A few days after I give him the letter I get on a tram in the middle of Brisbane and there he is sitting opposite me.

'I've finished with all that,' he says. 'I'm perfectly all right.'

I am still worried, but he sounds like my father again and who am I to argue with him? He tells me he has bought a ticket for the evening train to Newcastle. He is going home to collect some things.

'I want my family to be together again,' he says.

✳✳✳

IT IS A MONTH since Nigel booked himself out of the hospital and left for Newcastle. He has a job as a works guide at BHP and has rented a couple of temporary rooms while he looks round for something bigger. Now he has sent for Ursula to join him.

As the train ploughs through the night Diana hears a noise that makes her heart sink. Her mother has begun snorting like a pig. Some passengers are talking loudly, others are murmuring, a baby is whimpering, a little group of children is running up and down the length of the aisle. High above all this rises the terrible sound of snoring. Several people turn to look at them. Diana tries to change her mother's position, adjusting the pillow under her head, but this only seems to make matters worse. The snores have now grown louder and have broken down into a series of guttural vibrations that reverberate from one end of the carriage to the other. Her fingers grip her mother's wrist.

'Stop snoring!' she begs, tears scalding her eyes. 'Please.'

Her mother pulls her hand away and grumbles through her stupor. Her head falls back towards the window and the snorting starts again. Diana bites her lip and stares out the window. The train clatters over a long bridge. She glimpses a sign that indicates they have crossed over the state border. She looks at her mother's watch—sixteen hours to go.

The air in the carriage is stifling and all the windows have been flung open to catch the breeze the train's passage is creating as it plunges through the heat of the late afternoon. The wisp of air that reaches the passengers is loaded with grit and smoke from the engine's funnel. Soon everyone is reaching for their handkerchiefs to clean out their eyes and wipe down the seats. This will be the longest of journeys.

Occasionally her mother wakes up and asks for a drink of water. They have brought nothing with them. A few well-organised passengers, mostly middle-aged couples, have come prepared with flasks of hot drinks and sandwiches in neatly folded greaseproof paper. Mr Rodwell had given Diana five pounds for the expenses on the journey, but the dining car is three carriages away and she is so worried about leaving her mother on her own that she only manages to get herself food a couple of times during the whole journey. The water dispenser is in the small alcove at the end of the carriage, but the plastic cups are so tiny she has to make a dozen trips each time her mother asks for a drink.

At Casino more people board the train and once again Diana has to endure the covert stares and whispers until the new passengers adjust to her mother's rhythmic sawing.

Nigel has a taxi waiting when the train gets into Newcastle. His beaming smile turns to concern when he sees the state Ursula is in.

'How long?' he asks.

'Since we got on the train,' Diana whispers.

The taxi heads east toward the cliff tops. They pull up in front of a terrace house in Beach Street.

'I've got two rooms for a few weeks,' he tells her. 'It's not perfect but it's only temporary until I buy a house.'

He must be mad still, she thinks. How can he be thinking of buying a house when there's not enough money to buy school shoes?

When they get inside, Diana has to take a deep breath. The house reeks of alcohol and stale fat odours. They have to half-drag, half-carry her mother up the narrow staircase to their rooms. From the upstairs window Diana looks out over the ocean. A storm is blowing up from the south. The waves look dangerous and wild. She thinks about stories of people who just walk into the sea and drown. She thinks she hears her father call her. She clenches her fists. She wants to lie down and sleep. She doesn't know how to tell him she can't do it any more. Finally he knocks on her door and asks her to get her mother a cup of coffee from the kitchen downstairs.

'I'm sorry,' he says, 'you must be really tired.'

'I'm ok,' she says, but her heart is as leaden as her legs as she treads her way down the staircase.

Mr and Mrs Love, the owners of the house, are in the living room watching television. The kitchen is full of dirty dishes and empty drink bottles.

'Help yourself,' they call out to her.

Nigel and Ursula, Morningside, 1963

Eileen, Diana and Charmian, 1965

The Hall family, 1965

Naomi and Cila, 1963

Nigel working as a BHP guide, 1963

'Would you like a beer?' Mr Love shouts.

She comes to the living-room door and shakes her head.

'One of Mum's sherries?'

'Shut up, Dad, she's just a kid.'

'Don't tell me to shut up. Just watch your mouth.'

Mr and Mrs Love's daughter Sheila comes into the kitchen.

'They're just joking,' she says, but Diana can read her embarrassment in the awkward way she throws her head to one side to prove she isn't lying.

Sheila is fourteen. After a time she asks Diana if she would like to go the beach in the morning. Diana explains her mother is very sick and she has to look after her while her father is at work.

'Where's he work?'

'BHP. He's training to be a visitor guide.'

'My dad used to work at BHP, in the coke ovens. He's on compo on account of his lungs. Maybe you can come to the beach on the weekend when your dad's home.'

Sometimes on the weekends she gets to go to the beach. Occasionally, if her mother is buoyant enough to sit up and read for a while, Diana escapes for a couple of hours.

Most evenings the Loves fight liked trapped animals, snarling and striking out at each other with increasing ferociousness as the evening's alcohol rations are gradually consumed. Frequently Mrs Love calls on Nigel to adjudicate on the affray.

'Mr Hall! Mr Hall! Quick!'

Using his best London police manner, Nigel always manages to stay Mr Love's raised hand before any real injury is caused.

One evening when Diana and her father are watching the television news in the Loves' living room, her mother falls out of bed. The sound of her body hitting the floor above their heads is awful in its suddenness. Nigel races upstairs and comes back down less than a minute later.

He stands in the doorway, his face stretched white.

'Diana, I'm going to say something, and if you dare pull a face I'll knock your block off. Call an ambulance as fast as you can.'

In an emergency situation it makes no difference to the medical staff whether someone has overdosed by accident or design. They are not interested whether the patient woke up befuddled and confused and took an extra dose of something or other. Or whether she just thought, I've had enough of this dark room with its drawn curtains, its stifling heat and the heavy shadows it casts over my heart, I just want to get out of here and never come back. Or whether the patient decided, I am sick of lying here on my own all day, I want someone to show me they care about my pain. All the doctors want to know is the amount and type of drugs that have been ingested. In any event, they usually err on the side of safety and pump the patient's stomach out, while her daughter and husband sit in silence in the waiting room listening to her vomit herself back into life.

***

WEEKS LATER DIANA begins to see her mother's attention shift slightly from herself—to the room, to downstairs and then to the outside world. She sees her father growing happy in his new job, sees his self-respect returning. BHP wants him to do some translations of Spanish and French scientific papers. Already his popularity is rising among his new colleagues and friends.

Somehow he finds the money for a deposit for a house, an old weatherboard in the outer suburb of Waratah. With four large bedrooms, it has more room than any other house they have lived in. As soon as the bank settlement comes through Cila takes the long journey from Brisbane to reunite the rest of the children with their parents. Diana guesses the deposit for the house must have come from her grandmother.

One day she hears Ursula say to Nigel, 'Do you remember being ill?'

The tips of his ears go red and he says, 'I wasn't ill.'

The subject is never referred to again.

The house they move into in Prince Street is empty, and they have to wait for the removalists to bring their furniture from Brisbane. Ursula wanders from room to room, shaking her head. She opens the back door and goes out on to the verandah. The railway line runs past the bottom of their garden and beyond that is the smoky Comsteel factory (hiss and boom). She is thirty-nine with five children to care for and no reason to believe her future will be an improvement on her past. There is a knock at the front door. A woman, a stranger, is standing on the doorstep. Behind her, parked in the street, is an old car and trailer. Tied down to the trailer are two big armchairs. The woman introduces herself. Her name is May Ball. She has heard through a mutual friend, a Baha'i, about this family from Queensland with all these children who have just moved into an empty house. She has six children herself and is horrified at Ursula's predicament. So she and her husband Russ, who is undoing the ties on the chairs, drive straight over with their contribution. Ursula invites them in.

The two women have much in common. May is intelligent and well read. It is May who brings Ursula back to life and encourages her to start living again. It is May who finds a way to pull her up each time she falls into one of her black holes. Who else has the daring to talk Ursula into being a volunteer visitor at the very psychiatric centre where she has been a patient? They are the founding members of the Stockton Grannies, which becomes a legendary volunteer organisation.

Slowly, very slowly, Ursula's life begins to turn around. She and May form a women's discussion group. She takes WEA courses in Spanish, shorthand, astronomy and quantum physics. Because of his popularity, Nigel is promoted to a position in the personnel department at BHP. In time she too gets a job, as a secretary at the BHP works research section. Their financial situation becomes more stable. Through their efforts, the Baha'i community begins to grow and their lives take on new meaning and purpose.

Sydney, August 1966

I AM IN a taxi with my parents on the way to the registry office. I am wearing a yellow skirt and jacket that is a copy of the one Audrey Hepburn wore in *How to Steal a Million*. I'm not sure now if the outfit suits me or not. I've told everybody I'm glad I am having a wedding with no fuss or frills, but secretly that's not true. I wish we were going to a church and I were wearing a long white dress and a veil. I wish we had flowers and candles. Still, we can't afford a traditional wedding, and it wouldn't really be appropriate for me to be wearing white considering how long we've been living together.

I met David at a party in Brisbane shortly after my parents moved to Newcastle. He didn't seem to mind my skinny legs and flat chest. He told me later he liked my eyes. I liked his smile and the way he seemed really comfortable with himself. The first night we were together we couldn't wait to tell each other our life stories. One of the first things I told him was that I was Jewish and then he said his father was Jewish as well. It was as if we had given each other a seal of approval. Later he told me he had never admitted having Jewish blood to anyone before. He'd grown up in East London using his fists to prove he wasn't a 'dirty Yid'.

'You made me realise I shouldn't feel ashamed,' he confessed. He said it in a way that made me feel special.

The next day we went on a picnic and he brought lots of olives and salami that were hard to get in Brisbane in those days. We were both so excited when he found this was my favourite sort of food. That night he leapt over a two-metre wall so he could get in and open the door to his friend's studio. He wanted to play me a Joan Baez record because he couldn't believe I had never heard her music. A few weeks later we cried together when we heard John Kennedy had been assassinated. David had separated from his first wife and was living with his mother and little girl. His wife, who was pregnant with their second child, had gone home to live with her parents. Now, nearly three years later, David has just got his divorce and custody of his two children.

I keep looking out the back of the taxi hoping to see David and his mother following in our car. He works as an illustrator and had to deliver a job in the city first thing this morning. He promises me faithfully he won't be late like he always is. I'm sitting in the front seat and I steal a glance over my shoulder. My mother smiles at me but it's Nigel I'm really concerned about. It will be such a relief to have the ceremony over so I can stop feeling guilty about living in sin.

When we first moved to Sydney I was the one who decided we wouldn't tell people we weren't married. And we wouldn't tell my parents we were living together. David thought all this was very funny at first, but after a few visits to my parents he got fed up with the fabrications and having to be on his toes in case he let something slip. Eventually he said either I would tell them or he would. I was so worried about their reaction I couldn't tell them face to face. I wrote them a letter, and I suggested to David it would be his fault if Nigel had a heart attack. He laughed, telling me not to be so ridiculous, that my father was as healthy as a mallee bull. The first time I saw Ursula after I had sent the letter, she told me she and Nigel had lived together for several years while she was waiting for her divorce. I got the feeling she had been dying to tell someone this dark secret. She told me not tell anyone else in the family. 'Bloody hell!' I thought. 'What a pair of old hypocrites.'

It is only three days since the decree nisi has become valid. In the taxi behind ours is David's grandmother, his sister Valerie and his two children, six-year-old Suzanne and Peter who is two. The registry office is in a new building on the Pacific Highway opposite the bowling alley in St Leonards. We pile out of the taxis, into the lift and up to the fifth floor. Suzanne has the day off school and I'm terrified she will tell her teacher tomorrow she was away because she had to go to her parents' wedding. Twenty minutes go by and still no sign of David, then it's half an hour. He arrives nearly forty minutes late. His mother tells me the sleeves on his new shirt were too long and she had to find a clean old shirt and iron it. Again I wish we were having a church wedding. The registrar speeds through the ceremony because he is running so late. It is all a bit of a blur except for the part when he says, 'Don't throw confetti on the footpath.' No one's even thought of confetti, I think. This wedding is more about me making good with Nigel than it is about anything else.

Our first baby arrives nine months later. We call him Nigel. Two and half years later I have Toby. Charmian, Diana and I are married in the same year and it is not long before my parents have several grandchildren. It is Ursula who first recognises that her oldest grandchild, Charmian's first child David, is profoundly deaf. Eventually there will be nineteen grandchildren, including my stepchildren Suzanne and Peter, and so far nineteen great-grandchildren.

Nigel and Ursula, 1965

Nigel and Ursula, Baha'i Temple, Haifa, 1976

Chapter Thirteen

RETURN TO MOUNT CARMEL

Give ear unto ... the resplendent Light of God ... that, ye may be guided aright to the ways of peace.

—The Bab, *The Qayyumu'l-Asma*

Hall family with Baha'i friends

Haifa, 1976

AT BREAKFAST IN the hotel Ursula feels so heady she can hardly eat. Even before Nigel has time to finish his coffee she is hurrying ahead of him through the foyer, her walking stick echoing on the cool tiles. In the taxi they zigzag their way up Mount Carmel to the Baha'i pilgrims' entrance. Even Nigel is showing his excitement. They chat to the Arab taxi driver, asking questions about this place and that, as their memories come flooding back. Then she falls quiet. She is thinking about the times more than thirty years ago when she had to climb this hill. She can't believe how she managed it then, weighed down with her pregnancy and never having any money to get a bus, let alone a taxi. After they pay the fare they walk down through the gardens. She stops in the middle of the path and turns to Nigel, taking hold of his hand. 'Who could have ever believed this?' she says.

She realises that up to now her images of Haifa have always been the bleached black-and-white versions from an old war story, not the glossy colour images from the Baha'i brochures. The colours come cascading around her, a soft breeze sweeps up from the bay. The air is filled with the perfume of flowers and birdsong. She feels dizzy. From every terrace they can see a different view of the Shrine of the Bab and, beyond this, the Arc. They come around a corner and the Bay of Haifa stretches out into the Mediterranean. She trembles a little as she remembers the view from the tiny flat she shared with Tony.

She shakes her head and turns to Nigel. 'We had no idea back then, did we? We thought this was going to be a memorial to a Persian poet. How did we miss it?'

'But isn't Baha'u'llah the greatest poet of all?' He smiles at her.

'Do you remember what he said about the gardens?' she asks him.

He nods. 'This will be the avenue of the kings and rulers of the world, and they will ascend and walk around the Shrine of the Bab.'

'Ah, but now when their time comes,' she smiles, her voice shaking, 'those kings and rulers will have to follow in our footsteps.'

Nine days of this, she thinks, nine days of heaven. She writes some of her memories down. She is afraid of forgetting even the most trivial details. They arrive at the Pilgrim House at nine-fifteen. They are in Group D, which will gather at half past two. They pass some of the waiting hours in the library. In a photograph album she finds a picture of Cila on her pilgrimage a few years earlier. It is easy to spot her mother. She is the tiniest figure among the assembled pilgrims, standing awkwardly with a group of tall Russians, Americans and Congolese. One wall of the library is lined with framed drawings of Baha'u'llah's son Abdul Baha.

At three o'clock their small group is led inside the shrine dedicated to the Bab, the messenger of God whose mission was to prepare the world for the coming of Baha'u'llah. Someone brings Ursula a chair to sit on. Nigel kneels next to her, his head bowed, his hands hanging loosely by his side with his fingers slightly curled just above the floor. At first she is so overwhelmed she cannot begin to even think, let alone pray. The air is still except for the candles flickering in time with the breath of the pilgrims. She wonders if the others can feel the Bab's presence. She wonders if they are remembering the words he said as he paved the way for the new messiah.

'It is all about that resplendent light because the Baha'i faith is a beacon shining on a world that has been shrouded in darkness up to now—it is our only lamp of hope.'

She remembers one of his followers had said after meeting the Bab, 'Awake for, lo! The Morning Light has broken.'

She knows the light in the Bab's tomb is not just the glow from the lamps and the candles, but an illumination of spirit that is already beginning to fill the darkness in her mind. Her heart pounds as she asks herself how she could possibly deserve a gift of such incredible bounty.

When they are taken next to the Shrine of the Master, Abdul Baha, she is unable to describe what she feels, except that she is too overwhelmed to pray. She asks God to especially take care of Charmian and her little David.

On the third day she writes: 'Today we visited the Shrine of Baha'u'llah for the first time. It was indescribable and I pray to God that I shall never forget this experience. We had a wonderful opportunity to pray at the Holy Threshold for quite a long time. We prayed for our children and their families, our friends, communities. I beseeched God to assist me to become selfless and enable me to serve His Cause and do the utmost.'

Prince Street, Waratah, 1979

BEFORE URSULA CLOSES her eyes all she sees is the thin line of light straining through the narrow slit at the edge of the curtain. Just one hour of sleep, she thinks, and waits for the dark space to embrace her. She knows she could pray for relief. She tries now and then, but it takes too much effort. How long is it since she prayed at the Shrine of Baha'ullah? Three years? She sighs softly as from deep in the back of the house comes the muffled burr of a radio. The pain in her hip is agonising and she stretches out her left leg looking for some relief. Even another painkiller probably won't help. Anyway Nigel has taken them out of the bedroom. He's scared she'll get muddled and take too many. Misery has overtaken her. It rises up from under her ribs. She remembers something Ernest Hemingway wrote: 'I love sleep. My life has the tendency to fall apart when I'm awake.'

The sound of a door slamming wakes her, and she hears feet scuffling down the hall. It's Michael home from cricket. He's a good boy, she thinks, but at sixteen he sometimes forgets to be considerate. She can hear his father giving him a quiet telling off. After a while Nigel inches open the bedroom door.

'Sorry, darling. I suppose you are awake now? How does your hip feel?' he asks, as he leans across to kiss her forehead.

She turns her face to look at him but does not answer. Secretly he'll be pleased she hasn't slept very long. Every now and again he tries to lecture her about not sleeping in the day.

'You never need to sleep in the day when you go to work, do you?' he says sometimes, trying to be gentle with her.

'You've never had depression. How would you know what's best for me?'

'What harm would it be to try?' he replies, but he knows that his argument is already lost.

Whatever anyone thinks, she really does want to go back to work. They need her wages and working makes her feel important. It's another form of distraction, like sleep. She is now a senior secretary in BHP's works research department. She had started out as a typist, but because she was so fast and had excellent shorthand she was soon promoted and given more and more interesting work to do. She knows her bosses think she's really smart. She's proud of what she's achieved, working in the same job for eight years. The last time she had a proper job was for a few weeks in London when she was in her twenties. Her wages make such a difference to the family finances and at fifty-four she should have had several more years of work. Now everything seems ruined.

***

THE FIRST SURGEON had wanted to do an operation to freeze the bones in her hip permanently. He explained the reason she was in such pain was that the osteoarthritis had done so much damage in the last twenty years, but the damage was now so extensive she was not a suitable candidate for a hip replacement. The only procedure he would recommend would eliminate all motion in the hip. The idea of fusing the hip was terrifying. Even though she was in constant pain at least her limp was still flexible. Once the hip joint was frozen her left side would be permanently stiff. She would never be able to sit properly in a chair again. What worried her most was the thought of not being able to go back to work. She consulted a second surgeon, who was the brother of a colleague at her office and claimed he could perform a hip replacement successfully. He was so convinced it could be done he had even telephoned her at work to talk her into it. Making the final decision nearly drove her crazy, and discussing it with Nigel and her friends didn't seem to help. How could it? They weren't in her body. It was a horrible lonely place to be. If the second surgeon had been right, the operation would have changed her life. Of course it hadn't worked. It was only weeks before the replacement hip began to fall apart. The teaching trip was ruined.

For nearly twenty years they had been planning this trip. Their inspiration had been Mr and Mrs Hyde Dunn, who had introduced the Baha'i faith to Australia in the 1920s. Nigel and Ursula planned to visit Baha'i communities in every state of Australia. The tour would focus on the role integrity played in human relationships. They wanted to show how important it was for Baha'is to exemplify this quality in their everyday lives. They titled their talks 'The Dynamic Force of Example'.

As they set off on their trans-Australia journey, Ursula's hip felt better than it had since her childhood accident. The operation had been such a success. Everybody commented that her limp had practically disappeared. It wasn't until they arrived in Brisbane that she had an inkling that something was starting to go wrong.

By the time they reached Alice Springs she knew she was in trouble. Finally in Perth she had to be hospitalised, fortunately, as it turned out, at one of the finest orthopaedic centres in the country. Their assessment confirmed her first surgeon's diagnosis. The amount of bone loss and damage meant a hip replacement should never have been attempted. She was forced to spend four months in hospital in Perth while the surgeons attempted to repair the damage from the previous operation as best they could. She still refused to have the hip seized.

Now, back home in Newcastle, she wants all these memories to stop going round and round in her head. She knows there are some people who think she's a malingerer, even some of her children. What would they know? Those who really matter understand—Nigel, May and her good friends Joy Voradsky and Gita. The doorbell rings. She hears voices. Nigel comes to tell her May has arrived. He's starting to call in the troops, she thinks. Yesterday it was Diana who tried to talk to her about pulling herself together for the sake of Nigel and Michael. May's the one to bring her out of it, he's thought.

'I'll get up,' she says. She doesn't want May to see her in bed like this. She'll get dressed. She puts on an overhead light and blinks in its brightness.

Sydney, 1968

URSULA CAN'T STAND being in our house, a strange house to her, another minute longer. The room David and I have given her is too bright, too open. A large bird squawks in the bushes outside the curtainless windows. She likes birds, but not when they wake her up at five o'clock in the morning. She can't even make herself a cup of coffee because everyone is asleep and she doesn't have a clue where anything is kept in the strange kitchen that doesn't even have a salt cellar. For an hour at least, she has been lying here thinking about what we said last night when she told us she wanted to go home. We had pressured her to stay on at least until the weekend.

The Hall family at Michael and Jenny's wedding

*Nigel and Ursula with Suzanne and Eileen, and, in front,
grandsons Nigel, Toby and Peter*

*Martin Kupferberg and family with Gila in
New York, 1979*

Ursula with granddaughter Jess

They were trying to sound as if all they cared about was her happiness, she thinks. It was obviously a performance. What would they know about what made her happy? They made it sound like some sort of holiday. It wasn't her idea of a holiday, more like a punishment for misbehaviour. That's not how they had put it, of course, but that's what they meant when they said Nigel needed some time on his own. Things had started to get on top of him, they said. He worried about her constantly, which is why he always came home from work in his lunch break to check on her. She told them she never expected him to have to come home in the middle of the day. She had tried to tell him it wasn't necessary, but he had insisted. He even said he enjoyed it because he missed her when he was at work. What did they think she was going to do anyway? Did they know, she had asked them, that the arrangements to come and stay with them were made without even consulting her? Did everybody think she was incapable of making any decisions? She was having a bad bout of depression, and who wouldn't be depressed if they had her life, but she hadn't lost her mind.

'Just a break for you, darling,' he had said, but in her heart she knew it was meant to be a break for him. She had only agreed because May thought it a good idea as well.

She wonders what he is doing at home right now. He will be sitting at the kitchen table in Prince Street eating boiled eggs and drinking coffee. He will have finished his obligatory prayer. His prayer books will be stacked in a neat pile beside his plate. When he finishes his eggs he will reach for the marmalade for his toast. It will be quiet in the house. If she were at home he would be getting up in a minute to make her a coffee and toast. He would bring it into the bedroom and smile at her as he asked how she was feeling. Why had he never complained to her about feeling overwhelmed and tired? He had never so much as hinted she was a burden. She thinks perhaps she should ring him, but for some reason the thought of talking to him makes her feel nervous. How ridiculous, she tells herself, he loves her still. Doesn't he tell her every day? Before he drove away on Sunday he touched her hair and told her to take good care. She smiles when she thinks of him tooting and waving all the way up Eileen's long drive. But what if it has all been a subterfuge, a plot? What if he is fed up with her altogether? What if he doesn't know how to tell her he's finally sick of her illnesses, sick of her depression, sick of having to look after her, sick of the fact she has lost her looks? What if he never wants her back again?

She sits up and puts her feet on the floor. Her hands are shaking and she can hear her heart thumping. She tries to stand up but feels faint and has to sit down again. It takes her only a few minutes to decide what she is going to do. She takes her address book out of her handbag. She will ring May and ask her to come and get her. There's a phone in the dining room near the kitchen. May takes her time to answer.

At this point I come into the kitchen and find my mother on the telephone. I realise she is crying.

'I'm sorry to wake you,' she is saying. 'I didn't know who to turn to. I am in terrible trouble. Nigel doesn't want me any more, and David and Eileen are keeping me prisoner.'

'No, we are not!' I say. 'Who is it? Who are you talking to?'

'It's May. She's the only one who cares about me.'

'Don't be ridiculous. Let me talk to May.' I snatch the phone out of her hands.

'It's all right,' I say to May. 'She's just upset. I'll calm her down. Nigel just needed a break for a few days. He's coming down to get her on Saturday.'

'I want to go home now,' Ursula cries after I put the phone down.

'Please go to your room. You're waking everybody up,' I say. My voice echoes back at me—imperious, as if I am talking to a naughty child. When she obeys me I feel unexpectedly powerful.

I make my mother a cup of coffee and take it into her bedroom. She's sitting on the edge of her bed going through her handbag.

'I'm sorry we upset you. We were doing what we thought best,' I say, putting the coffee on the bedside table.

'That's typical of you, Eileen. You always think you are right about everything.' She has regained something of her composure. Now it's her voice that rings with parental authority.

I am set on trying to get her to see the sense in staying on until the weekend. She is set on doing exactly the opposite. I so much want this to be successful because I know Nigel must have been pushed to his limits to even contemplate sending my mother away for a break, especially to me. If she goes home now it will be another failure on my part. This is my chance to do something for him at last, to show him that at thirty-six I have finally grown out of the hysterics of my childhood, that I am wise enough to handle the most difficult of situations.

I try gentle questioning, but she won't play the game. She's not suddenly going to tell me her innermost fears.

'Eileen, I want you to understand. I have to go home today.'

I stall for time. I call Diana. We have a long talk about the pressure Nigel is under. Ursula is so demanding of his time and his patience she has exhausted him. Even while she was working she expected him to look after most of the housework and the cooking. She especially resents the time he spends on anybody else, and because he is so generous and giving this is a constant source of conflict. She has suffered so much over the years with her hip and other illnesses, but what we find difficult is the way she uses these problems to manipulate us all, especially Nigel. No one has the courage, I say to Diana, to tell Ursula what she is doing to him.

My mother is sitting on the bed trying to pack, pushing things into her bag one minute and pulling them out the next. I sit down next to her.

'Please stay. If not for yourself, for Nigel.'

'What about me? What about what I want?'

'Don't you think for once you could think about someone other than yourself?'

She starts to shake. I tell her not to start that business. It isn't going to wash with me.

'How dare you talk to me that way,' her voice quavers.

She wants this to end in a fight to give herself more ammunition to go home. Don't fall for that, I tell myself, but don't cave in either.

'I'm sorry,' I say gently. 'I just want you to see it from his point of view.'

'Don't you dare discuss my relationship with my husband. You don't know what you're talking about.'

I am stung badly. She has put me on the outside again.

'It's the drugs, isn't it?' I snap.

She pretends to be puzzled.

'You know what I mean. You're addicted. We all know it. It's why Nigel sent you down here—he's worried you will overdose. You came down with a week's supply and I bet they're all gone. Now you want to go home to get some more.'

She scrabbles in her handbag and triumphantly produces two little white tablets.

'Two pills left, five days to go. Doesn't add up, does it?' I can hear triumph in my voice.

She doesn't answer. Someone ought to tell her about the havoc she has created all her life with her self-indulgence and attention-seeking. Torrents of memory begin to swell in my mouth. I hold them back. If I let them out now they will become a flood. She looks thin and frail, and there is a bead of sweat above her upper lip. I take a big swallow and offer up a thin little platitude, which she treats with derision. Perhaps I should kneel down and put my arms around her as I would with one of my children. Then I remember wanting her to hold me. I want to ask why she has never held me in her arms, not even when I was in hospital.

Instead I say, 'I'm right. It's the tablets, isn't it?'

She looks up at me, her face full of contempt. 'I never thought I would say this, Eileen, but you are actually quite a cruel person.'

'Cruel?' the word bursts out of me. 'You can talk about cruel.'

'And you have never been wrong in your life, have you, Eileen?'

And so it goes, backwards and forwards. Little drops of poison seeping into the heat of the day until the air is humid with hurt and blame. Finally Ursula calls a friend who lives near us to come and collect her. It will be forty minutes before the friend arrives, but she walks up to the end of the drive to wait by the gate. I follow her as she uses her walking stick to pick her way along the bumps and ruts of the driveway. She is breathless when I catch up with her. She doesn't realise she is standing on the edge of a large ants' nest.

'Mind the ants,' I warn.

She moves a few steps. I can see she is trying to conserve her dignity.

'It's too hot to be standing up here. At least come and wait inside.'

'Over my dead body,' she snaps. 'And don't try to pretend you care.'

'Of course I care about you. I love you.'

She turns her back and hobbles closer to the edge of the road away from me.

'You should have thought of that before you started. Now I just want to be left alone.'

And then the floodgates open. I dance around in front of her so she has to look at me.

'What would you know about love? Have you ever really loved anyone in your life? I know you love Nigel, but anyone else? Even when I was in hospital, you couldn't even hug me, your own little girl. How old was I—ten? What about the time Diana lost her baby? You took two days off work, but not to support her. No, you went home to bed because you were too upset to work. You did the same thing when the Granville train disaster happened and you didn't know one single person hurt in that crash. You just wanted the attention for yourself.'

She is shaking badly now and peering up and down the road looking for her friend. But I am past sympathy.

'What about the time I rang to tell you David was in hospital after the car accident? You know what you said when I told you what had happened? You handed the phone to Nigel and said, "You have to talk to Eileen." You have never been able to deal with anybody else's pain because you are always too busy with your own and working out how you can use it as a weapon to suck everybody dry.'

I have lost my battle to get her to stay and I have made everything worse for Nigel. So I decide to exact the full amount of revenge.

'It's always like this. You've been manipulating your family all your life. What about you doing something for someone for a change. What about you making Nigel a cup of coffee, or having his dinner ready when he comes home from work? What about loving us? What about loving me?'

When she doesn't answer, my fury continues with another list of litanies. I count them off on my fingers. They pour out as if I have been rehearsing them for a long time. Finally, my anger spent, I walk back down the driveway and go into the house. In the months, days, years, that follow one image of her is fixed forever in my memory. It is my mother's face ashen with the horror of my tirade. Her eyes are filled with shock, her cheeks and chin crumpling like a child's. I had longed for her love, but all she had been able to offer me was her power. When I took that away there was nothing left, and now I was overwhelmed with shame.

It was nearly a year before I saw my mother again. It was at Cila's funeral. The rest of the family was on tenterhooks, but nothing happened. My mother refused to even look at me. It was another two years before she asked Charmian to tell me she would like to hear from me.

Cila, 1979

NOT LONG BEFORE she died, Cila was reunited with her cousin Martin whom she had last seen on the street in Frankfurt in 1933. For forty-five years she did not know whether he had managed to reach America or if he too had perished under Nazi rule. She found him by advertising in a German-language Jewish newspaper published in New York. Cila visited Martin and his wife shortly after he replied to her advertisement.

It was joyful time for her because there were so few of her family left. Most of those who had survived the Holocaust had since died. Of her immediate family, only her sister Nina in Tel Aviv was still alive. Many times in their letters she and Nina had discussed the possibility of Cila going to live in Israel. But the cost of even the tiniest apartment would have been prohibitive, so it had never happened. After her retirement Cila had bought a little cottage a few blocks from Ursula's house in Waratah. She was in her late seventies but several days a week she walked around to Prince Street to clean the house and run errands. Despite the unhappiness her relationship with Ursula caused her, she knew she was still useful to her daughter and as long as she was needed to fetch and carry she could not leave. Her visit to Martin was the one bright spot in the last months of her life. Diana and Cila shared the same local doctor, who confided to Diana that her grandmother was suffering from a serious heart condition and knew that the trip to New York could easily trigger a fatal attack.

Martin and his wife Hildegard showed Cila the sights of New York. They walked everywhere, as most New Yorkers do, and Cila found it hard to keep up with them. They went to Martin's favourite restaurant, on the sixth floor of a city building.

'And so Cila,' Martin asked his cousin, 'you never found yourself another man after Solomon?'

Cila shrugged. 'I had my chances. But my daughter was more important to me than my own life. And thank G-d for that—without me I don't know how she and her family would have survived.'

They talked that night of those they had lost.

Martin said, 'My whole family perished—my parents, my teenage brothers and two sisters. That tragedy lives with me day and night. My parents as well as the remaining families in Eastern Europe were Chassidic Menchen, who only lived for G-d and for their children. During the terrible Holocaust their tears were not seen, their cries were not heard.'

He took hold of her hand when he saw she had tears in her eyes. 'Ah,' he said, 'but we must count our blessings. For G-d has given us our families, given you your beautiful daughter, given us something else to live for.'

***

MICHAEL ANSWERS THE telephone to his grandmother, who wants to speak to Ursula. He says his mother is asleep, but he will go and wake her if it's important.

'No, don't worry,' she says. 'Tell her to ring me when she wakes up.'

Cila puts the phone down and goes into her bedroom. She turns down the covers of the bed and climbs in carefully so her body does not disturb the geometry of the folds and triangles, which she had arranged earlier that day. The ritual of bedmaking has always been important, and even now the gold-covered goose-down quilt that she carried with her from Frankfurt lies folded in its neat rectangle on the chair beside the bed. She lies straight as a ramrod. Her closed eyelids are flickering, sheer ivory threaded with tiny mauve veins.

The walls of her little cottage tremble as a fully laden coal truck thunders over the bridge on its way to the city. From her garden comes the scent of a lemon tree. The radio, turned down low, is broadcasting a Verdi opera. Cila's pulse is a fading echo in the dim afternoon light. Her heart is beginning to close down. She breathes in shallow gasps. Somewhere beyond her immediate consciousness great draughts of pain are grasping at her chest.

'Papa,' she says. She sees her father, the watchmaker of Dynów. She is back in her village, the place she has not seen for close to sixty years.

She turns her attention to the living. She hopes to G-d Ursula will let Nina know what has happened. Maybe she should get up and write a note, but she knows this is not possible. They should write to Martin as well, in New York. How wonderful it was to see him. It was the happiest she had felt for years. She knows she will not set eyes on her daughter again, or her grandchildren. She pictures each of them—the boys, Stephen and Michael, and the girls, Diana, Charmian, Eileen and precious little Naomi.

She has been ready and waiting for months. She told me this only a week before.

'Mama, how are you feeling?' I had asked when I called.

'I am waiting to die,' she said in a way that required no response.

At five, the grandfather clock chimes softly and she sits up on her elbows and looks to the open door. Her eyes are brightly lit and focused. Soft shafts of afternoon sun fall on the polished hallway furniture. 'Ah, they are coming,' she says. Through the door come first the men in their simply cut cloth and their pointed beards, her father Hirsch of Dynów and then her uncles, David of Bardejov, Lieb of Bukowsk, Michael of Radomyschl, who perished in the Holocaust along with her aunt Nechuma. Her brothers David and Abraham follow her uncles—such successes they had made of themselves. Then comes her mother Ethel and her sisters, Nina, sweet Miriam who was cut down in the Warsaw ghetto and the beautiful vivacious Tamara who was lost in Sarajevo. Her heart is being squeezed.

'Ula,' she whispers. The telephone rings urgently, on and on. She does not hear it.

Tony and Eileen, Congleton, 1986

Chapter Fourteen

FINDING A
FATHER

'Wot's in a name?'
she sez ...
An' then she sighs.

—C.J. Dennis, *The Songs of a Sentimental Bloke*

The Train to Sydney, 1963

I CARRY AN image of a father around with me, or of what it would feel like to have a father of my very own to love me.

My forehead is pressed against the passenger window. A sign flashes out from a building set back from the road. For eight hours the station wagon has been eating up the miles between Brisbane and Sydney. We are travelling along the fast inland route down the New England Highway that cuts it way through the heartland of the great pastoral estates on the New South Wales plains. The country towns along the highway look like the marks that represent them on the map: busy red circles of activity linked by long straight stretches of emptiness spinning off into the horizon. Spreading out from the towns the wheat farms are followed by sheep and then by cattle stations. Sometimes I see an unfamiliar breed, but I am no longer interested in rural things. I am a city girl now, done with farms, and I am easily lulled into sleep by the monotonous landscape and the sun streaming into the car. The other girls have been talking and giggling all day, about make-up and fashion and boys. I am too self-absorbed to take part.

I am twenty and my head is full of the world waiting for me at the end of the road. Indiscretions, failures, relationships gone wrong—all these things I have finally left behind. I am imagining myself sauntering around the streets of Sydney, full of confidence, full of hope. The first real love of my life has just married someone else, and I've quit my library job at the *Courier Mail* newspaper to join a travelling sales group selling magazine subscriptions to hapless small business owners. This job is just my passport to freedom. Something to get me going until I find real work.

Maybe one day when I'm successful I'll go back. I expect by then I will have been to London and New York. I will have made a name for myself, though at this stage I am not sure what sort of name it will be, or even what path I intend to follow. I imagine my future self as so elegant, accomplished and articulate that even my mother will be impressed. She might acknowledge me because I have finally made something of myself. Her predictions about me were always wrong.

I am thinking about her, about the way we always fight, when I see the sign. It says 'Piercy's Café'. My heart is thumping in my chest, my hands are perspiring. Piercy is my father's name, it's my name, it's the one I have never used except when I had to. The Department of Education made me sit for my junior examination under this name. Every Queensland schoolchild had to produce a birth certificate to be allowed to sit the state exam. Mine was given back to me in an envelope on which the Nambour High School headmaster had scrawled 'Eileen Ursula Fitz-Vivian Piercy, commonly known as Hall'. Fitz-Vivian was my father's middle name, but somehow it had been tacked on the front of my surname, effectively giving me a triple-barrelled name. Even when I was quite young I thought it was stupid, a silly English affectation that made me sound like a character out of a British comedy. To avoid being teased I hid my name away until I was old enough to legally change it to Hall.

I still have the envelope the birth certificate came in, and even now when I look at it I always feel as if I am supposed to make some sort of decision about who I am. Am I a Hall or a Piercy? I know everything about Hall and almost nothing about Piercy. Even so, I can never become a real Hall or know what it means to be a Piercy. So in truth I am neither. I adore Nigel, but he has never been truly mine. He belongs to them, to my five sisters and brothers. I am the family interloper, a piece of flotsam from my mother's broken past. I might have been accepted and cared for, loved even, but I am greedy for the one thing I can never really have—for Nigel to be my real father.

It seems that I have lived most of my life like this, being only half of something, feeling like a shadow in other people's lives. No matter that my parents never actually say it, I always feel like Tony's daughter. The daughter of that man, the one who had been so terrible to my mother that she had to leave him. I hate the thought of his blood running in my veins. As I grow older I imagine my mother looking at me and seeing him, listening to me and hearing him. I want to be the daughter of a good man, I want to be Nigel's daughter.

I am trying to work out exactly where Piercy's Café is—what town we are passing through. I will come back here, I swear to myself. Piercy is an unusual name. The owners might even be relatives or, and the thought struck me so hard I found it difficult to breathe, it could even be him. My mother once told me that Tony lived in Melbourne as a little boy. Perhaps he had decided to come back and live in Australia. This is the first time I have ever considered the possibility of meeting him. Then I wonder why I would even bother. He is supposed to be a horrible person, but then, I think, what if this isn't true. My mother has always been prone to massive exaggerations. Goodness knows, she has driven me wild millions of times with her blown-up distortions of my behaviour. Maybe this is what happened to their marriage. Maybe she drove him crazy, which is why he hit her. Maybe, after all, he is an ordinary man who once had a lapse. Maybe he would welcome me with open arms, maybe he is even looking for me. It will be more than twenty years before I find out.

England, 1986

THE PLANE'S ENGINES are making a different sound now. 'Thrust' is a word that comes to me. I have always hated the going up and the coming down parts of flying. When that nose points up or down my body becomes rigid with fear. I refuse to watch the pre-flight safety demonstrations because they fill me with trepidation. Later I panic because I haven't got a clue how the face masks drop down, how to brace myself or where the exits are in case of an emergency. The Qantas flight is lumbering down through the clouds on to the tarmac at Heathrow. My hands are clenched on the arms of the seat. So much fear to be dealt with in life. And meeting my father is one of them. Of course the landing part of the journey is trouble-free.

It's early morning London time and I am feeling a bit disoriented, perhaps because of the red wine I drank with the last airline dinner. The cold bites the back of my neck.

All through the flight I have been picturing Tony as he might look. My mother had kept just two photographs of him for me. One was a family shot with Ursula and me as a newborn. None of us look particularly happy. My father is handsome in a sleazy sort of way. There had been other photographs, but my grandmother had found and destroyed them to protect my mother from unpleasant memories. He was twenty-three when I was born so I have worked out he must be sixty-six now. I hope he is still alive. I have a shadow of an image of him from when I was a child. I was four the time he came to visit us in that tiny flat in Kensington in London.

My youngest sister Naomi is waiting for me. She looks lovely. She is twenty-five and just married. We don't know each other very well. She was just a baby when I left home and she began travelling as soon as she was eighteen. She was only five when I got married, the same age as my stepdaughter Suzanne. They are more like cousins. So that makes Naomi more a niece than a sister. She and Martin live in a lovely apartment in Abbey Road in St John's Wood. She seems to be thriving in her new environment and has adopted a posh English accent that brings back memories of the accent I had to lose quickly when I first immigrated to Australia. Now when I talk to my sister and her new English husband I can hear my voice sounding twangy and coarse.

'Do I sound really Australian?' I ask her with concern.

'Of course not,' she replies, but I know she is just being polite.

We discuss my plan of attack. Years before I had tried to trace my father through the Red Cross. They tracked him down to an address he had left only six months earlier, and I cursed myself for procrastinating. I have allowed time for a couple of weeks of research. In the morning I set out for St Catherine's House where all British birth, death and marriage records are kept. On the way I get a bit lost and, using my best English diction, ask a friendly newspaper vendor for directions.

'How yer going? How's Bondi Beach?' he responds in mock Aussie before pointing out the way. I am mortified.

Within an hour I find both my father's birth certificate and my parents' marriage certificate. This research stuff is easy. The next day I track down the Palestine Police Old Comrades Association. A pukka voice on the other end of the line says, 'Piercy, Piercy? There's someone up the West Country with that name, a Colonel Piercy if I remember correctly.'

Now I am imagining a well-to-do father, probably someone wealthy and sophisticated. Suddenly a new thought enters my head. Perhaps he will resent an intrusion into his settled life.

'Tell him I just want to catch up with him,' I say, worried he will think I am some sort of money-grubber.

'It might take me a few days,' the association's secretary says.

Naomi and I go down to the pub to celebrate my first research breakthrough. When we get back to her flat, my brother-in-law has a message for me. 'Your father rang,' he says.

Alarm bells go off in my head. What is Nigel doing calling me at this time? Why to speak to me and not to Naomi? There must be a serious problem. Perhaps my mother is ill.

'He left a telephone number,' Martin says.

'Telephone number? Oh my god! That father.'

***

TONY MEETS ME at Congleton station. I have caught a morning train from King's Cross. I change trains at Stafford where I endeavour to ask platform directions from a porter. His accent is so thick it is like another language. After several indecipherable attempts, I realise he is asking me if I am from New York.

The train pulls into Congleton at twelve-thirty. Of course I recognise Tony straight away, as he recognises me.

'My dear,' he says. 'My dear!'

He stands high over everybody else on the platform. He is completely grey but still handsome, still with the same neatly trimmed moustache he wore in the family photograph. He is neat in the way men who have had a military career are neat. He is wearing a blue blazer with shiny silver buttons. He is very thin. He grins widely as soon as he sees me. He catches me against him in a bear hug. As I fight gently to disengage myself, I smell whisky on his breath. I hadn't thought of this, that he would be as nervous as I am.

He leads me to a battered Triumph convertible which he has parked in a space reserved for disabled drivers. As he puts my suitcase in the boot he catches me looking up at the sign and raises his hands in a gesture of admission. 'Couldn't keep my daughter waiting. Could I?'

We turn out of the station car park into the high street that climbs away from the railway line. The signs along the way read 'Tesco', 'Lloyds Bank', 'Devonshire Tea All Day', 'Reschs'. Crooked Tudor architecture is wedged up against concrete boxes, each made the uglier by juxtaposition with its neighbour. As we drive he tells me he has been married for fifteen years to Ingrid, a German woman he met when he lived in North Africa. Ingrid is much younger than my father and works as an engineer in the Siemens factory, which is the lifeblood of the town. She can walk to work from their house. We circle the park, with its garden clock fashioned from flowers. The street

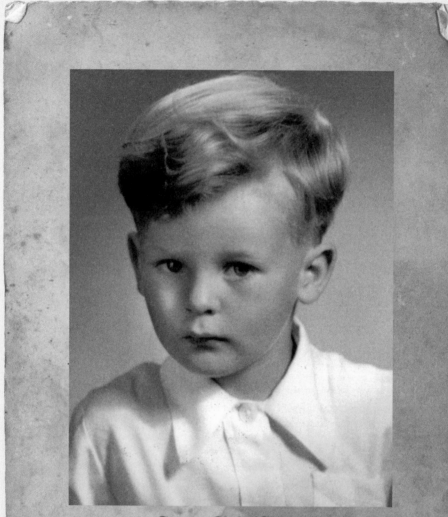

Tony's son Michael Piercy, who died too young

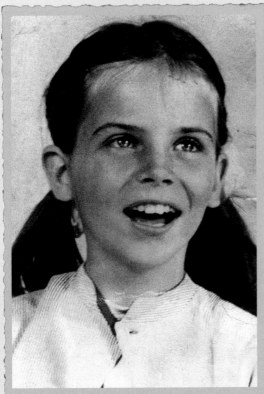

Tony's daughter Pamela Piercy

Tony's daughter Diana Piercy

opens out to a wider avenue and there are glimpses of large old mansions with tall manicured hedgerows, then where the road narrows smaller houses with lower unkempt hedges, and finally open ground lined by a cluster of motley factories. We enter a satellite village, zigzagging through narrow streets past rows of small double-storey terraces. He points to a window box full of red geraniums and parks in front of it.

When he opens the door to the house I smell roast lamb. I sniff and grin appreciatively.

'You will find out your father is an excellent cook, my dear.'

Ingrid is due home for lunch. Tony does all the cooking now because she is the main breadwinner. He has a part-time job as a private detective. He points to the small logo on his blazer. I wonder why a private detective would wear a uniform that advertises his profession. Later I work out he is actually a small-claims debt collector.

He offers me a drink, and when I refuse pours a whisky for himself.

'I would have thought you would be more like your mother,' he says suddenly as if somehow I have disappointed him, but I don't know if it is my looks or my refusal to have a drink. If it is the latter, he would be disappointed in her as well. As for the former, I have always been a plain shadow of my mother. There has never been a time in my life when people have not talked about her beauty, and then sometimes they talk about how much alike we are. I expect they are thinking, well, in colouring at least. Whenever I look in the mirror I can hardly believe how badly I have been put together. It seems to me fate has always teased me for what might have been by allowing me to inherit only the raw pieces of my mother's looks. In the mirror I see the unevenness in my face with its nose sitting off at an angle. I am stretched out like a brown stick with knobs instead of curves. I expect this is what my father sees.

He shows me his garden, a narrow strip at the back of the house, a riot of colour in the grey concrete landscape running down to the canal. The canal is full of bottles, plastic bags and human rubbish. I think I can make out the shape of a dead cat floating under a sodden cardboard box. Tony is oblivious to the canal. He shows me the fish pond that he built the previous summer. In winter the pond had frozen over, nearly suffocating the fish. He and Ingrid had to punch a hole in the ice and grope around in the muck to find the survivors. They kept the fish in a bucket of water in the laundry until spring. When it was warm enough and they put them back in the pond, the fish swam round and round the pond in little bucket-sized circles for two weeks, unable to cope with their liberation. He chuckles loudly as he describes the fish actions. He points out his foxgloves and then some lupins he has grown from seeds stolen from Balmoral Castle. He wrote a letter to the Queen Mother confessing his crime and telling her how beautiful her lupins look in his garden. He received a polite reply from her secretary. He takes me inside to show me the letter in its frame over the living-room mantelpiece.

We sit in the tiny airless living room with its nicotine-coloured ceiling and walls. He wants to tell me several stories about his past. They are romantic sagas about Assyrians and Arabs, a cross between Rudyard Kipling and T.E. Lawrence. He asks me nothing about my own life or my children—his grandchildren. He is on to his third whisky when Ingrid arrives home. We shake hands shyly as if neither knows what to expect.

'Have you shown Eileen to her bedroom?' she asks Tony.

He takes my suitcase up the steep narrow staircase, bumping it against the walls all the way. He puts it down in a guest room on the right at the top of the stairs, telling me that he and Ingrid bought the house five years ago. It is what is known as a 'two-up, two-down'. Quite a bargain, he adds.

He points to the room on the other side of the landing. 'That's our bedroom. The bathroom's through there, unfortunately, so if you need to go in the middle of the night ... well, don't worry, we won't mind.'

Maybe I am imagining it, but something about his tone makes me feel uncomfortable. For a moment I have a picture of him thinking of me taking down my pyjama pants.

In the bedroom I freshen up my make-up and take off my jacket. He watches me as I come down the narrow staircase.

'So glad to see you've got the Piercy tits,' he says and then he sniggers.

Ingrid appears behind him. I hope she hasn't heard what he just said. Suddenly I remember Nigel slapping my face for saying the word 'sexy'. Now the memory of that slap seems like an ever-so-gentle admonishment.

'I suppose your father has been boring you with his stories as usual,' Ingrid says, touching Tony gently on his arm. Her English is good, but stilted and formal with a pronounced German accent.

'My wife likes to tease, don't you, my dear?' His tone is English jolly, but it has a nasty undercurrent I wish I hadn't heard.

'My, lunch smells wonderful. I am a very lucky woman to have someone like your father looking after me.'

We eat in the little dining alcove off the kitchen. Lunch is truly a feast. We wash it down with a bottle of Australian red I have brought as a gift. Ingrid offers up constant praises—to Tony for the lamb, the potatoes, the gravy, the home-made mint sauce, and to me, several times, for the wine, declaring it to be the best she has ever tasted.

They met in Tunisia where Tony was working as a guide taking tourists on trips into the Sahara Desert. Ingrid was thirty-nine, but not yet a woman of the world, as Tony explains at length. Not a great beauty, he says, but with a sweet smile. She was a shy engineer on holiday from her job in an electronics factory in Nuremberg.

Ingrid interrupts him to say, 'He was the most interesting man I had ever met in my life. German men, ugh!' She throws up her hands in disgust.

There had been another woman, a rich widow, a great beauty, who was also pursuing him, he tells me. But Ingrid was such a vulnerable little thing, he was quite taken with the need to protect her. They were found in bed together by the widow and things turned very ugly. Of course, the widow put up a fight but little Ingrid won his heart.

Ingrid smokes several cigarettes, punctuating her husband's monologue with regular chuckles and nods. I recognise there is a routine that goes with this story.

At the end of the meal I take out photographs of David and the children. Ingrid is excited by the idea of Tony's grandchildren.

'Such handsome young men. You must be very proud. See, Tony, here are your grandsons.'

He leans across and takes the photographs from her and looks at them for a moment.

'Tall chaps, eh? Do you think they look like their grandmother?' He looks up to ask me, 'How is Ursula these days, still as beautiful as ever, or is she getting old?'

He puts the photographs down on the table so he can get up to pour another drink. When he sits down again I pick up the photograph of my eldest son Nigel.

'He's been racing push bikes in France,' I say with pride, offering it to him again. He takes it from my hand and studies it for a moment before he gives it back.

'You called him Nigel, eh? Well, it doesn't surprise me. That man was one of the best. I loved him. Then he betrayed me. I would have killed him you know, except for my batman. He grabbed the gun off me.' He gets up to pour himself another drink. He teeters a little as he navigates the bottle over his glass.

I don't want to hear him talking about them like this. I am humiliated for them. I am angry with Tony. Doesn't he understand I am their child still? Why is he throwing this at me? Of course, it is to justify himself, but he should go and tell someone else, not me. I am supposed to be his daughter, her daughter, your daughter.

Why is it no one ever behaves as I want them to behave?

I take another photograph out of my handbag. It is not one I had intended to show him, but now I want to make him pay for what he has just done to me and for being so disinterested in his grandsons. I hadn't expected him to fall in love with us, but at the least I had expected curiosity. When he sits down again I hand him the photograph of Ursula and Nigel with all their children and grandchildren at a family reunion the year before. I show it to him. He stares at it for a long time.

'She was a very beautiful woman, your mother—once,' he says, and covers Ingrid's hand with his. She smiles back at him, but I can see nothing in my father that would make a woman love him.

He is drunk now and he is chortling. I am thinking it is a very English thing to do, snorting and chuckling at the same time. He is chortling about my mother and looking across at Ingrid for encouragement. I can see she knows the story well. She is smiling at him but not with her eyes, and I realise she has guessed how I am feeling.

'When I met your mother she was a damned attractive woman,' he says.

He tips back in his chair, puffing a chain of smoke into the yellowed ceiling. He leans forward again and looks at us both. We have nothing to say.

'A very fine filly indeed.' He smiles and nods his head.

I realise the old bugger is still in love with her, or at least his memory of her. I almost feel pity for him but there is something about the way he draws his lips back over his teeth that disgusts me.

I want to change the subject so I pick up the photograph of my youngest son Toby.

He looks at the picture for a couple of seconds before putting it back on the table. 'He's tall, like you.' I think I might be beginning to sound angry. I don't know why I can't leave this alone.

'Well, your mother certainly went for the tall ones, didn't she?' He's chortling and showing me his teeth again.

He stands up and weaves his way out through the kitchen to the toilet. Ingrid looks at me with concern. 'You have to forgive him. It has been such a shock, you turning up on his doormat like this.'

'It's ok,' I say, patting her hand. But I am lying to her.

After Ingrid leaves for work the next morning, Tony and I set out for an appointment he has made with the local newspaper to tell the story of our reunion. He leaves the Triumph at home. I realise later it's because he wants to spend the afternoon in the pub. The pathway to the town centre meanders along the dirty canal. On the way he points out the artistic endeavours of the municipal gardeners. He insists that we walk arm in arm, but the back of his knuckles keeps grazing my breast. I find it hard to disengage without giving offence so when I do pull away to admire a bed of tulips shaped like a bell, or violets spelling out the name of the town, he quickly comes back to claim me. I am too timid to stop this game, and we play a parody of father and daughter all the way along the stagnant canal.

Over a beer in the pub he tells me about his second family. Just after he divorced my mother he married Mary, who he had brought to visit us in London in 1947 when we lived in the flat in Kensington. They had three children, the oldest a boy named Michael and two daughters, Pamela and Diana. I am amazed, I tell him, because I already have a half-brother and -sister called Michael and Diana. I ask him where they live and tell him I would love to meet them.

'You won't be able to see Michael because he is dead,' he says without emotion. 'A shooting accident when he was fifteen, stupid little blighter.'

When he goes to get himself another drink, I think about what he has just told me. I have an overpowering intuition this was no accident, that my brother's death was suicide and that my father was somehow responsible. I am so certain I may as well have been given conclusive evidence.

When Tony sits down again he tells me he doesn't know where my sisters are. He has lost all contact with them. They turned against him years ago. He gives me examples of the troubles between them, their disobedience and running away, the awful things they have done and said to him. But what I really hear is the terrible anger these two girls have for their father. He relates an incident about collecting one of them from a police station after she had run away. On the way home in a taxi, his daughter had taken off her shoe, leant forward to where he was sitting in the front seat and begun smashing the point of the stiletto into the back of his head. He is impressed by my obvious shock. He doesn't know it is because I am wondering what he must have done to her to bring on this awful rage. Of course he doesn't give me any clues about where to find them. He knows their married names and even the places they had lived, but he never reveals them to me. I am sure I know why.

After I return to Australia I realise it was probably not a good idea to look for my father. It is obvious he has aged into a far worse version of the man my mother has described. I find myself shuddering all over again at the thought of his blood running in my veins. One day it occurs to me that perhaps Laurens van der Post might be my father, not Tony. I invent a scenario in which my mother meets Laurens, she becomes pregnant and when he disappears she quickly marries Tony to get herself out of a sticky situation. For a few days I dream about having this famous writer for a father. I even venture the possibility my ambition to be a writer is inherited. Eventually I do some research and to my disappointment I discover that at the time of my conception Laurens van der Post was on Special Mission 43 deep in the Javanese jungle. A few weeks later he was captured by the Japanese and remained in a prisoner-of-war camp for the rest of the war.

Shortly after returning from England, I visit my parents in their new home at Yerrinbool in the Southern Highlands. Ursula is full of amusement when I tell her I think Tony is still carrying a torch for her. I go for a walk with Nigel. He has to walk every day now because he is recovering from a mild heart attack and recently had an operation to remove blockages in the arteries in his legs. The path takes us through the bushland that surrounds the Baha'i school. The rain is falling as soft mist. We chat about my trip and about Tony.

'So what did you think of him?'

His question surprises me. I want to tease him by asking him 'compared with you?'

I don't give him a direct answer. Instead I say, 'I am so glad you brought me up as your daughter.'

I sense he is blushing but I have looked away, to save him the embarrassment of knowing I am observing him being prideful.

I will see Tony once more before he dies in 1995. On my second visit in 1989 I take Naomi with me. This time he walks around the village introducing both of us as his daughters. Naomi thinks this is very funny, but it makes me angry. Not only is it an absurd assertion but I am furious at the idea of him claiming Nigel's daughter as his own. In the pub he starts to tell us an obviously dirty joke.

'That's enough,' I say, pointing my head in Naomi's direction.

'Oh dear,' he says. 'Getting out of line, am I? Wouldn't be so straight-laced if I had brought you up.'

'Well, then, I'm pleased you didn't,' I snap back.

Over the next few years we correspond and talk on the telephone intermittently. I visit Britain from time to time but without telling him. I decide I can't cut him out of my life completely since I am the one who opened Pandora's box. I speak to him in hospital the day before he dies. I imagine he never guesses just how much I dislike him.

A year later, on another visit to England, I track down and meet both my half-sisters. It takes time to convince them I really am their sister as Tony had never breathed a word to either of them about my existence. In fact, he had never told them he had been married to anyone before their mother. When I told them, each separately, that he had died, they both said the same thing—that they were pleased to be finally rid of him. Later they confirmed he had beaten them and their mother viciously on many occasions. They also confirmed what I had thought about their brother Michael. He had killed himself. All Michael had ever wanted to be was an artist and, when Tony refused to let him go to art school 'because only poofters go to places like that', he shot himself.

I realised then I had never understood just what a gift I had been given when Nigel took my mother away from Tony and I became part of the life they made together.

Ingrid and Tony Piercy

Diana and Eileen, Oxford, 1996

The legacy of a life of love: Ursula and Nigel's descendants, 2003

I LOVE YOU PAST INFINITY

Chapter Fifteen

Nigel, Naomi, Ursula and Eileen, 1988

Thou art my light and my light shall never be extinguished.

—Baha'u'llah

Yerrinbool, 1992

HE IS SPRIGHTLY, still upright, with few apparent signs of ageing except for the deepening pink around his eyelids and a slight clouding of his irises. Each day he gets up early while she is still sleeping. Makes himself the same breakfast as the day before, eggs and toast, and says one of his obligatory prayers. If he's left in peace for long enough he says the long one. As soon as she calls out to him he brings her toast and coffee in bed. He sits on the edge of the bed and asks how she is feeling. He goes for his daily walk, except on her bad days, does the shopping, cooks the meals, mows the lawn occasionally, and even does the washing. In the cooler weather he frequently digs the garden, which never seems to benefit much. He makes beds and plants seedlings, sometimes carrots and sometimes strawberries. Usually his crops fail because he doesn't tend them regularly. He fetches things for her, her books, her knitting and her newspapers. All the while they talk of what their life has become, their Baha'i activities, the books they read, the friends who visit often, the children and grandchildren, seventeen in all now.

Since they arrived here, just after he retired twelve years ago, and not long after Cila died, their work for the faith has never ceased. They came to this little Southern Highlands village as co-caretakers of the Baha'i Yerrinbool School and Convention Centre. When they could no longer manage those duties because of Ursula's failing health, they built a little house across the road from the school. Their home is constantly filled with people, not only with family and friends but with Baha'i visitors from all over the world. He still writes letters. They hold fireside meetings and attend functions at the centre. It goes on like this year in, year out, until the height of summer in his seventy-eighth year. Under the burbling rhythm of their lives a dark force has been gathering. One morning he brings breakfast to her in bed and the next he is in hospital with a severe heart attack.

Whenever I go to visit my parents I can't wait for the moment when I first catch sight of his face. Age has only made him more handsome, more benign, with that crooked nose and carefully shaped English gentleman's moustache and the gentle blueness of his eyes. Driving down today to see him in Bowral Hospital I am terrified this image may have changed, but there he is, propped up on his pillows in pyjamas that match the colour of his eyes, dispensing gentle wit and largesse to all around him. He looks healthy enough, I see with some relief. I realise now I can hardly ever remember seeing suffering in his face. Perhaps when a child was in danger, like when two-year-old Stephen nearly choked on a grape, or when he had to put Whisky down. I never saw the pain he must have felt leaving his ageing parents, knowing he would probably never see them again. I rarely saw him flinching at my mother's tirades, never heard him complain to any of us. He hid it all. It was his duty not to foist his suffering on to others. What we know now is that, although he looks healthy enough, his heart is no longer capable of keeping him alive without help. In order to survive he has to undergo an urgent heart bypass, which takes several days to organise.

On 14 February Michael comes down to the Royal Prince Alfred Hospital in Sydney where Nigel has been taken by ambulance to await his operation. He gets Michael to go and forage for a piece of paper and a pencil. While they chat about the cricket results, Nigel sits quietly drawing, then folds the paper into quarters. Just as he is finished Ursula arrives. Nigel gives her his handiwork. It is a Valentine's Day card. My mother's eyes are full of tears. She looks at Michael. 'Never once since we met has he ever forgotten—not even this of all times.'

On the front of the card Nigel had drawn a heart with an arrow. Inside were the same words he had written for twenty-five years: 'I love you past infinity.'

The night before the operation we all visit him—Charmian, Naomi, Michael, Diana and Robert, David and I. Stephen is now the headmaster of a primary school in northern New South Wales and hasn't been able to come down in time. We tell Nigel we love him. He is bright and cheery, making silly little puns to wipe the anxiety from our faces. He tells Charmian he is worried about what will happen to

Ursula if he doesn't survive the operation. He says it would be hard for whoever she might want to go and live with. He takes Charmian's hand. 'I know she can be difficult, but I am still very much in love with her,' he says. 'I have never stopped loving her, never for one minute.' David is the last to visit and as he turns round to wave goodbye, Nigel gives him a thumbs-up signal.

He is still giving us this gift of love, so our mood is positive although slightly concerned. But his worn-out heart doesn't have the strength to get going again.

The next day most of the family gather in Naomi's little flat in Neutral Bay. At ten past eleven the telephone rings. It is the surgeon wanting to speak to Ursula. She listens intently and speaks only once, to thank him for calling. After she hangs up she relays what he had told her. Nigel has not been taken off the bypass machine yet because they are having some difficulties re-starting his heart. They are going to attempt a few more things and he will call back within half an hour. He rings back fifteen minutes later. She listens intently for a few moments and then she asks, her voice clear and strong, 'Are you telling me I have just lost my husband?'

She hands the phone to Diana so the surgeon can repeat what he has just said. Charmian gets my mother a glass of water. We would be able to hear the hum of the traffic from Military Road except for the drumming that fills our ears. Even with the blinds drawn to keep out the morning glare, the thick heat in the room makes it hard to breathe.

My mother sits still on the chair looking hard at the telephone, which is now back in its cradle. We wait for her to be the first to say something, for our own lips are suddenly sealed by the unspeakable. We brace ourselves. She will certainly start to wail soon. It is what we all expect. We know because her loss is certainly greater than ours. She will shake and weep, and scream she cannot live without him. Which one of us will have the strength to help her deal with her agony?

Time ticks in slow motion. Naomi's old fridge clicks and whirrs.

'Could you pass me my handbag?' she says at last.

She reaches into her bag and takes out not her cigarettes but her Baha'i prayer book. Michael switches on the reading lamp beside her chair. Her hands are steady as she opens the book and flicks through to the page she is looking for. She holds the book up to the light and reads as if a cloud of serenity has engulfed her being. Her voice is powerful, unquavering.

'Glory be to Thee, o Lord my God! Abase not him whom Thou hast exalted through the power of Thine everlasting sovereignty, and remove not far from Thee him whom Thou hast caused to enter the tabernacle of Thine eternity.'

Ursula and Nigel

Our faces are wet but our reaction is almost noiseless. She closes the book and puts it down on her lap. She looks around the room at each of us in turn.

'I am going to pray every night to God until he lets me join him,' she says smiling. We smile back our understanding.

The room goes dark and the fridge is chopped into silence. There has been a power failure.

'I knew he would come round to say goodbye,' she laughs. And suddenly everybody laughs, and then the silly stories about him come tumbling out. We stretch out our arms to each other all over the room and cry. Except for me. For some reason I cannot cry.

***

DAVID DOESN'T WANT me to see him. Maybe I am too caved in to have the strength to argue, but I am sure it is really because I need to keep hold of that last pyjamaed image, his face beaming with love out of the whiteness of the ward.

We have gone to pick up his personal belongings and a family member is needed to identify him, which David, generous as always, spares me. We wait in a special room with another couple. They do not look at us or we at them. This moment is much too weighty to engage with strangers, even with those who are experiencing the same emotions. Someone takes the other couple away and then a nurse comes in and tells us how sorry she is. Nigel made such an impact on the nursing staff in the short time he was there, and several of the nurses cried when they heard of his death. When she tells us that, after his unsuccessful attempts to revive Nigel, the surgeon had said, 'What a pity, he was a nice old boy,' I feel as if I am going to cry, but it doesn't happen. Even as Michael and I make the funeral arrangements; even on the day in Mona Vale Cemetery with the rain driving in from the Pacific, which several Baha'is say is auspicious; even when his old friend Geoff Rodwell reads the eulogy; even when I see my tall Toby with his arm around his little cousin Natalie and tears pouring down their faces; even when so many people come up after the service to say how much they loved him, even when I go home that night, I cannot cry.

Then weeks later I dream about him in some trivial domestic situation when I was still a child. I have not expected to see him again, and here he is in my dream, large as life and me not realising he is dead. He stays with me all day until evening, when I go into the garden and let myself give way to my grief.

***

THEY BRING MY mother to Raymond Terrace near Newcastle, to the neat rented townhouse with enough space to be able to wander from room to room if she wants, except she can't be bothered. Instead she sits in her old deep chair with the wooden arms and reads or does the crossword. Most of the time, though, she spends looking out of the window and smoking, so there is always a scattering of ash on the carpet around the little coffee table.

Someone has put her pictures up on the walls, and unpacked her photographs, the little knick-knacks, the brass bell, the silver cups her grandfather had engraved, Mama's turquoise menorah, the picture of Abdul Baha. None of it looks right, she thinks. It's like a film set, a place that's made to look like home, but if you were to walk behind the walls there'd be an empty space where the memories are supposed to be.

She knows they mean well. She should have been firmer, should have refused. At first she supposed they were right. How could she look after herself now he has gone? She has no way to get about to do her shopping or visit the doctor. She tries to tell them she would manage at Yerrinbool with the help of the new caretakers—they wouldn't have minded running errands for her or taking her into Bowral.

'You'll be better off with your family looking after you,' Diana and Michael say. 'And you won't be so lonely.'

Someone does come round most days, Jenny or Michael, who live five minutes away, and Diana and her girls. They bring her cooked meals and chatter away. Even when she knows they're coming, often she doesn't bother to comb her hair or put on lipstick. What if they do see that her cardigan is unevenly buttoned and her trousers smudged with ash? She will not be jollied, no matter how important it is to them. And now we are all becoming impatient.

'I wish you wouldn't talk about suicide to my girls. They love you and it really upsets them,' Diana complains on one occasion.

She knows they are all discussing how they are going to solve her problem—no, not her problem, the problem of her. Did they expect it was going to be easy, that they could wave some practical magic wand, come round with a couple of books and a casserole, suggest she start writing her memoirs, knit herself a cardigan, paint a picture? Next thing they'll want her to go on the aged-care bus to bingo. The heavy weight that lies inside her won't be moved by a few well-meaning platitudes. No, she thinks, not even a block and tackle of words will do it this time.

What they don't realise is she has nothing to recover for now. They don't say anything about her loss. Rarely even speak his name. She is thankful for this at least, for she could never give a name to her grief. She wouldn't have expected this, she who could articulate in fine detail all the conditions that had ever assailed her. What was it Diana's Robert used to say to her? 'G'day, Urs. How are you? What's it today? Is it your legs, your back, your head?'

Could they possibly understand how it would only demean her grief to have to put it into words? How even her thoughts are emptied of his presence and this feeling must continue to remain undescribed except for the prayer she says over and over: Come and take me so I can be with him.

Hers is a spiritless body. It lies like a heavy pancake on the surface of the bedcovers ignoring the pillow mounds. Her cheek is flattened into the blanket. At night she crawls under the eiderdown and presses the edges around the contours of her body so the duck feathers encase her. There is no space as heavy as the hole made by grief. There are no subtle colour ranges, no pretty shades to ease you into black. The feeling she could describe to them is the one of being robbed. He hadn't told her how ill he was until it was too late. If he had undergone the operation when the doctors told him to he would have survived. He would still be alive. But he had procrastinated because he worried about not being able to look after her.

It is this that keeps my anger with her on the boil. She should have understood. He is no longer here and it is all her fault.

Still, she and I don't argue anymore. At family gatherings we stand aside from each other with cool politeness. Her self-indulgence and attention-seeking give me a pleasurable anger, a sense of righteousness. I am saying to myself, see, I was right, it was you all along. You drove the rift between us. Your self-centredness is the reason you find it hard to love me, not the fact I am unlovable.

Eventually she moves back to Yerrinbool. We usually visit her in pairs for courage. Naomi and I often go together. Naomi has returned with her little girl from Britain after her marriage failed. She and I work together in a stock-footage film business I set up in 1986. Naomi spends weekends cooking and freezing gourmet meals to take down to Ursula.

I go on my own only once. They are having a community memorial service for Nigel in the hall at the Baha'i school. She hardly speaks to me except to ask me to find some tablets for her. In my mother's bathroom cupboard there are many bottles. I find the one marked Valium. I tell her they are too old, more than twelve months.

Her head shakes tightly. 'Don't tell me what to do. Don't come down here once in a blue moon and try to take over.'

I fetch her some water and she doesn't thank me. She slurps it greedily and then turns her face away. It is as if I don't exist. I go to the window and open the curtain slightly so I don't have to look at her. A willy-wagtail amuses itself by bouncing through Nigel's unkempt strawberry patch. She whines for my sister to telephone. It is because I cannot or will not comfort her. She tells me that last time Naomi came she cleaned the whole house and that Stephen's children have beautiful manners. But when we walk across to the school she becomes her animated outgoing self, receiving the mourners' solicitations with grace and dignity.

***

YOU HAVE SAID this all your life: 'I feel as if I'm going to die.' It lost its punch a long time ago and no doubt you have guessed as much by this time. The last time we speak to each other was when you ring me at work six days before your seventieth birthday. You want to make sure I understand the seriousness of what you are saying. 'The ambulance is here, Eileen. I think I'm having a heart attack. Will you tell the others?'

I wonder whether I managed to hide the weariness in my voice. I hope I sounded as though I didn't think you were faking it. I did as you asked.

I call the family and a sort of communal sighing goes on down the telephone lines. You want one or some of us beside you all the time.

'Why don't you come and live down here?' you once asked Diana after you had moved back to Yerrinbool from Raymond Terrace. You posed the question as if the task of Diana and Robert selling their house and moving with four children to this quiet backwater with practically no employment opportunities was something they could do easily, and for no more reason than giving you some company. You made a weak attempt to make it sound as though you really thought it would be to their advantage. When Diana laughed out loud at your suggestion, even you chuckled at your own absurdity. Besides, Diana had made it quite clear you understood perfectly well the ramifications before you moved so far away from everybody.

When you ring you actually ask for Naomi, but she is out and you have to make do with me. I remember your tone quite distinctly. You are trying to sound casual but there is a tremor in your voice which I mistake for theatrics. Perhaps what I really hear is a little bit of triumph. Anyway, they discharge you from hospital the next day, which supports the consensus you aren't ill, just lonely.

Michael rings Naomi the next Monday just after we have started work. It is a beautiful late spring morning and I have just made myself a cup of tea when Naomi comes into my office. She repeats what Michael has said to her.

'Mummy's dead.'

Her eyes are wide as though she is drowning. Her head is high and drawn back, and as she spins the words across my desk, they echo up into the fluorescent tubes. 'Mummy's dead.' I am thinking this can't be possible because in the past whenever you told us you were going to die you never did. By doing this you have become immortal. So this has to be another one of your tricks. Your little ploy last week hasn't worked, so now you have resorted to a new twist, one that we can't possibly ignore.

Naomi is saying something to me, her face slightly contorted.

'Did you hear me?'

I nod. 'What happened?'

The community nurse had arrived on her regular visit to find you lying in your bed, a book in one hand and your reading glasses in the other. All I could think is, it is an amazingly peaceful way for such a traumatic life to end. I remember wondering why I don't feel like crying. It took two weeks after Nigel died for me to cry but I had felt it building up inside me, refusing to come out. Now I seem to be feeling nothing except a vague sense that something has fallen away. Perhaps it is a recognition of motherlessness, or maybe it's relief your suffering is finally over, or even that our battles can be done with at last. The only thing I can define is guilt because your dying is not causing me the same suffering as his death. Perhaps this is my ultimate test, the one in which my love for you is measured and once again found wanting. Could it be that it was never there for either of us and all my criticisms of you for not being able to show me love were sheer hypocrisy in the face of my own lack of love for you?

David and Naomi and I drive down to Yerrinbool, but of course they have already taken you away. The three of us sit in the living room wondering what to do next. It will be hours before someone else arrives. We go peering around the rooms of the house, picking things up here and there. It feels as if we are still children, expecting you and Nigel to come home any moment and catch us poking about through your things.

Naomi picks up your handbag. I remember thinking she has always been much braver than I—less compliant, more vocal—more loved by you. She opens your purse and shows us its contents. I take a sharp breath. There are several hundred-dollar notes.

'We could go to lunch at the White Horse Inn in Berrima,' she says. 'It's where Diana and I took her the last time we were down. Only this time she can pay.'

'Do you realise what day it is?' Naomi asks as we are waiting for our order to arrive.

'Oh, my god,' I say. 'It's her birthday. She would have been seventy.'

We look at each other and think about you. It is a lovely lunch and we thank you for it. You are all we can talk about and then we go back to your empty house with the table by the window covered in an array of dried-up plants in plastic pots, yesterday's Sydney Morning Herald on your footstool folded to the crossword, your last cigarette butts in the ashtray. Your dishes from your last meal sit neatly in the washing-up rack. I find myself wondering what was the last thing you watched on television.

Michael arrives just after we return from Berrima. On the Saturday morning before you died he and Jenny had driven down with their girls Rebecca and Alice for the weekend to make sure you were ok after the fright you had earlier in the week. You sent him into Bowral with a shopping list. He questioned why you were asking for two family-sized bars of chocolate when you had once told him the doctors said chocolate was bad for your heart.

'I always ration it out,' you argued with him. 'I only have a couple of pieces a night.'

Michael says you were in high spirits as they left on Sunday afternoon. You said you were looking forward to reading the new book Diana had sent you for your birthday. You stood on the porch and waved goodbye to them. The last people to see you alive.

Michael goes into the kitchen and comes back after a few minutes. His face is half smiling, half bewildered. He is shaking his head.

'She ate it all.'

'What?' we ask.

'The chocolate. She promised she wouldn't but she ate it all, not one but two whole bars. No wonder she had a heart attack.'

Your funeral is a sunny celebration at the Bowral Cemetery with the buggies on the golf course next door squeaking all the way through the service. Naomi's three-year-old daughter Jess relieves her boredom by throwing little lumps of clay at your coffin. I am sure you would find this as funny as we do. A Baha'i friend reads the eulogy, which turns out to be mostly about how you were lucky to have been married to someone as wonderful as Nigel. I guess you would have agreed with him, but you would probably have been quite miffed as well. It is supposed to be your life we are celebrating. I am sure you would understand why we all have to avoid making eye contact as he lists the attributes Nigel brought to your relationship. The afternoon is filled with a lightness and a sense of rejoicing that you and he are no longer separated.

Afterwards we go back to the house. Your will leaves your estate equally divided among the six of us and we have to sort out who is going to have what. Our family is very dispersed and so we need to take advantage of the rare opportunity of being all together. If anything represents a tribute to the values you and Nigel have instilled in us, it is the spirit of generosity and love towards each other that fills your little house that afternoon. The distribution of your modest belongings is a gift-giving occasion when little items are offered up to the individual who would be most appreciative of that particular treasure.

I have to confess I refuse anything of yours that is offered to me. If it had once belonged to Mama or Granny Hall or Nigel I accept it, but I am still too angry with you to want to own anything that belonged only to you. The strength of my anger under the circumstances surprises even me.

Michael goes into Mittagong to get some Chinese take-aways for us all. Towards the end of the meal we have a discussion about an appropriate inscription for your tombstone.

As we are trying to come to a decision Dicey, Stephen's Baha'i wife, says, 'I can think of something, but it's naughty.'

'Go on, tell us,' we egg her on.

'How about "I Told You I Was Sick"?' she giggles.

This leads Michael to suggest 'Death by Chocolate'. I am sure if you were present you would have joined in the laughter. Maybe you are.

The words that we finally choose for you are 'Abide then in thy love for Me, that thou mayest find Me in the realm of glory'.

Nigel's grave: clockwise from front, Naomi, Diana, Michael, Eileen, Stephen and Charmian

Ursula with Eileen and Diana, Hyde Park, London, 1947

Chapter Sixteen

THE EYE OF THE LENS

The meaning
of our existence
is not invented
by ourselves, but
rather detected.

—Viktor Frankl, *Man's Search for Meaning*

QUITE A FEW of the important revelations in my life have happened while I was doing the ironing. I was probably twelve the first time I cleared my mother's ironing basket as a bribe to get her into a good mood. Then, as now, I relieved the monotony by listening to the radio as I worked. As I look back on my life I am amazed by the number of times I have heard something really significant while I am doing this chore which I hate with a passion, particularly because it's not something I do very often. One day a few years after my mother's death, as I was dealing with a mountain of creased clothes, I heard an interview with a woman who had struggled with and conquered addiction. She revealed how one of her hardest issues had been coming to terms with the fact that her parents found it almost impossible to show their children any love. The woman told the interviewer, 'Do you know, I cannot remember a single instance of my mother holding me.'

Without warning I began to sob. I was crying so much I couldn't see what I was doing and I had to put down the iron. Although I had never thought about this before, I realised that I too had no memory of my mother holding me. The closest Ursula and I ever got to affection was a perfunctory kiss on the cheek whenever we met. I tried to imagine the difference it would have made if just once she had put her arms around me, or even told me she loved me. Now I understand why I love hugging and cuddling so much. But I had to wait until I was an adult before I knew what it was like to be embraced by someone.

Towards the end of 2001, again while I was ironing, I heard another radio interview that revealed something about Ursula's past none of us, not even my mother, had known. The interviewee was J.D.F. Jones, whose biography of Laurens van der Post had just been published. Of course I was interested in this because Laurens had been engaged to Ursula, who had often described to us how fate had intervened to end their relationship. She told us she had met him in Jerusalem when she was only sixteen and he had asked her to marry him, but shortly after his proposal he had disappeared. Ursula heard he had been killed. She had no way of knowing the British army had sent him out to fight the Japanese in Java. Later, when she was living in London with Nigel, she was told that after the war Laurens had come back to Jerusalem to find her.

I was intrigued by the idea of finding out more about this famous man who had once loved my mother enough to ask her to marry him. Laurens's family had authorised J.D.F. Jones to write the biography but, as he delved into the man's life, the story he unravelled was very different from the one the world had come to know. The public image was of a man who 'had won renown in an outstanding range of roles: as a war hero, writer, explorer, mystic, environmentalist, Jungian, behind-the-scenes diplomat, and friend and confidant of the great—famously including both Mrs Thatcher and Prince Charles.' What his biographer found was that many of the most remarkable aspects of Laurens's life were not as he had given the world to understand. The biography 'looked behind the façade that Sir Laurens so skilfully created and suggested he became a prisoner of his own creation.'

But what really made me sit up and pay attention was the biographer's revelation that Laurens had a penchant for proposing to very young women as a means of seducing them. It was even rumoured several illegitimate children had been born as a result of these various liaisons. In one confirmed instance in 1952, the parents of South African friends had asked Laurens to chaperone their youngest daughter Bonny on a voyage to London where she was to study ballet. Laurens had seduced the fourteen-year-old on the ship and then set her up in a bedsitter in London close to where he lived with his mistress Ingaret. 'This is not Sex, this is Romance,' he said and Bonny believed him, as Ursula had done ten years earlier. He eventually married Ingaret after he divorced his first wife, who lived in South Africa with his two children. In 1954 Bonny returned to South Africa to give birth to Laurens's daughter. Her parents forced him into making a large financial settlement on Bonny and her child by threatening to have him charged with statutory rape if he refused.

It had never occurred to me to doubt Ursula's version of the circumstances of their accidental separation. She believed that Laurens had been sent away on a secret mission and had not been allowed to contact her before he left. As the details of Laurens's philandering were revealed, I realised his proposal to my mother was probably just a ploy to seduce her. I am sure Ursula did not guess Laurens never had any intention of marrying her or that his severing of contact may have been deliberate.

I thought J.D.F. Jones might be interested to hear about Ursula's 'engagement' to Laurens so I contacted him through his publisher. He replied saying that I was probably right in thinking my mother was just one of his many young conquests.

In one of his letters to me he wrote, 'bear in mind that I have got to know Laurens very well over the past four years. He was, in an old-fashioned phrase, a cad. And I have plenty of evidence, from several continents, of him siring a child and then vanishing hot foot. (I have today spoken with a London lady who knew Sybil—the Java secretary in 1946–47. He promised to marry Sybil, then decamped.)'

J.D.F. had recently heard from a sixty-year-old man in South Africa, who was also convinced Laurens was his father, and he suggested I too might be another in the growing line of Laurens's illegitimate children.

'Not so,' I wrote back. I had already established that, according to the date on my birth certificate, Laurens must have been in Java at the time of my conception. In response J.D.F. pointed out it was quite common practice at the time to have the date on a birth certificate changed in order to 'legitimise' the birth. It was just a matter of paying the official concerned a small bribe. It had been discovered that the details on the birth certificate of the South African man were incorrect.

Of course I had never considered that my date of birth might be false. J.D.F.'s suggestion threw me into a spin. The more research I did the more confused I became. I assembled all my documents and photographs, my birth certificate, my mother's autograph book, letters from Tony and Ingrid, Tony and Ursula's marriage certificate, the photograph of Tony and me taken for the *Congleton Guardian*, other photographs of Tony's daughters, and an image of Laurens downloaded off the internet. I spent hours, days even, looking for clues, but I found nothing that would conclusively confirm which man was my father and if, in fact, my birth certificate details are false.

The certificate states what it always has—that I was born at the Haifa Government Hospital on 4 January 1943—it is dated 15 January 1943 and the official's signature is illegible. Both my parents' nationalities are shown as British. I assumed by this that my mother's marriage to Tony had given her automatic British citizenship. My religion is listed as Christian ('C. of E.'). Another notation on the certificate indicates a ration card was issued to me on 25 February and another that I was baptised by Angus Nicholson on 14 April. So there is nothing odd about the certificate or the chronology to show that anything was out of order. However, there is nothing to disprove the theory that the date of my birth may have been changed. And when I looked at my parents' marriage certificate I did notice something interesting. They were married on 4 March 1942. If J.D.F.'s conjecture were correct, then the date they had chosen to be my birthday was exactly nine months to the day after they were married. Was this significant or was it mere coincidence?

It appears Laurens left Jerusalem early in 1942 because he wrote to Ingaret on 12 January saying he was 'going farther away. I can't even give you an address.' In what must have been the shortest of whirlwind courtships, only seven weeks later my mother married Tony. Why such haste? Surely she was still grieving for the lost Laurens? I can hardly imagine, even with Tony at his most charming, that he would have been able to supplant Laurens so quickly in her affections. Her own explanation was that she married him to get away from her mother. Of course Tony was debonair, supposedly well-off and, when the war was over, would take her away from Palestine and Cila. On the other hand, if she were pregnant with me, which she was hardly likely to reveal to us, then the running-away-from-home story could be a perfect way of covering up the truth.

On the surface Tony accepted me as his own daughter. I was even named after his mother. But Tony, like Laurens, was a fantasist and liar. Forty years later he was still so besotted with Ursula that she was the only one he was interested in—not me, not his grandsons. He may have named me after his mother just to prove to Ursula he had accepted me as his own child. Then, when I turned up on his doorstep four decades later, he may have decided not to let the truth get in the way of a good story, especially when he could get it in the local paper and be the centre of the town's attention for twenty-four hours.

I was also shocked to discover Tony had never mentioned my existence to my half-sisters Pamela and Diana. In fact, Pamela thought my first telephone call to her was some sort of scam. Two other things point to my not being Tony's daughter. When he came to visit our little family in London in 1947, he made no attempt to engage with me, his four-year-old daughter. He even wiped down his trousers where I had touched him. Neither did Tony show any interest in his grandsons. In all the correspondence and telephone calls we had in the years up to his death, he never once asked me how they were or what they were doing. The simple explanation could have been that he was so interested in himself even his grandchildren were of no importance. But maybe his pretended acceptance of me as his daughter didn't extend to my children. The other issue that aroused my suspicions was his quite overt display of sexual interest in me, his supposed daughter. Now this may have been the sick predilection of a lecherous drunkard or it may have been because I was not actually his daughter.

Do I look like Tony? Yes. But Laurens, Tony and Nigel were all strikingly similar in appearance—fair, tall and slim. People say Pamela and I are alike, but J.D.F. Jones thinks I am like Lucia, Laurens's legitimate daughter. Both my sons are tall and Toby has red hair like Tony. However, there is also red hair on my husband's side of the family. None of this, of course, proves anything and, short of having a DNA test, I'm never going to know the truth. What would it mean anyway, when neither of my potential paternal contenders have very much going for them as human beings? Bonny wrote Laurens more than fifty letters and he did not reply to one.

And in my heart I know that proving it conclusively would never give me the one thing I have always longed for, irrational and childish as it still is—that Nigel Charles Hall could be my father, and I could have inherited some of his goodness and integrity instead of having to work so hard to measure up to the standards he set.

***

I HAVE BEEN struggling with a piece of writing all afternoon. When I finish I am worn out but exhilarated. The piece is concerned with identity and when I read back what I have written I realise it has come from a part of me I have trouble understanding. I pick up one of my favourite books, *Man's Search for Meaning* by Viktor Frankl. Frankl was one of the twentieth century's leading psychotherapists. At the core of his theory was the hypothesis 'that man's main concern is not to gain pleasure or avoid pain, but rather to see a meaning in life.'

I read again the story of a patient who had come to Frankl suffering from deep depression as a result of being widowed some years earlier. The patient's life no longer had meaning since he lost his life's partner. Frankl asked his patient what his wife might have felt if he had died before her. His patient responded, 'Oh, for her this would have been terrible; how she would have suffered.' Frankl then suggested that by being the survivor, his patient had been able to spare his wife from the pain he himself was now experiencing. The patient said nothing but got up and shook the psychotherapist's hand and left the office. Frankl wrote of this example, 'suffering ceases to be suffering at the moment it finds a meaning, such as the meaning of sacrifice.'

For some reason this makes me think about my childhood, and suddenly I realise that the power in the piece I had just written came from my painful relationship with my mother. Rightly or wrongly, very early on these difficulties had formed the person I have now become. Until this point I had always been ready to ascribe to my childhood my faults and weaknesses—but never my strengths. Unlike my mother, who had been cosseted and protected, first by my grandmother and then by Nigel, I had been forced to strike out on my own, which had given me a foolhardy sort of courage. Dealing with my mother's temperament had made me resilient and taught me how to recognise and respond to emotional danger signals. From a very young age I had learnt the art of compromise and the rewards of demonstrating affection. Because of this I can freely lavish my friends and family with love. I can touch them, kiss them and hug them. I can tell them I care about them. All the things my mother found almost impossible to do. It came like a lightning bolt that, unwittingly, she had given me a wonderful gift, the ability to show love, which is something she had never really been able to do to anyone except Nigel. The fear that prevented her from opening herself up to her children and the affection she might have received in return meant she had denied herself one of life's greatest treasures. Her loss was, in a strange sort of way, a sacrifice she had made for us. Without it, I might have been less careful and more constrained in my own relationships.

I think of her as a very young woman unable to even put her arms around her own children. I begin to cry. The very thing she had lost she had ended up giving to me.

'Poor little thing,' I cry. 'Poor lonely little thing.'

And at that moment the anger I had felt towards her for most of my fifty odd years leaves and never returns. Even later, when I try to test myself by dredging up the most painful of my conflicts with my mother, I feel nothing but sadness for the life of hers that might have been.

***

THERE IS THIS photograph on my dressing table. I found it only recently. It's of my mother and Nigel taken in 1992 in the kitchen of the house in Yerrinbool, the little village in the Southern Highlands where they retired. Somebody snapped the pair of them while they were doing the washing up together. It was taken not long before Nigel died. He's the one at the sink and my mother is standing beside him. He's looking at her, smiling at her. His look is full of love. She's staring at the camera, probably held by one of my sisters. She's smiling, basking in the eye of the lens, basking in his love. Age has played havoc with her beauty. Her hair has lost its wondrous lustre. It's unkempt as if she didn't care any more about how she looked. Except that I know she did. The little gap between her front teeth is more defined now, and you can tell she's been a heavy smoker all her life. Her luscious lips have thinned, but she is smiling with a joy I found surprising when I came across the photograph. Sometimes now I run the tip of my finger down her cheek. There's a part of me that has begun to miss her. This is the biggest surprise of all.

When two hearts strive to beat
with one accord,
And pass through agony of
uncertainty and fear,
Sometimes together and
sometimes far apart;
And when two hearts, though
oftimes disappointed,
Survive, cemented with one
object and one desire,
To partner each in creating
life and goodness too,
Those two hearts have learnt
to beat with one accord.

Nigel's thoughts.

Acknowledgements

This book could not have been written without the support and encouragement of some very special people.

My thanks go to David Mead and Tony Mason for their input into the Hall family history, Olek Minc for his advice on the first two chapters, Viva Rodwell for her recollections of the early Baha'i period in Brisbane, my stepmother Ingrid Piercy for filling in my father's life story, Shayna Stewart for providing much peace to write in her haven by the sea, and J.D.F. Jones for his generosity and permission to draw on his biography of Laurens van der Post.

My brothers and sisters, Diana Threlfo, Charmian Powell, Stephen, Naomi and Michael Hall, have given me not only their love and constant input but also their blessing to write our mother's story in my own way. Special thanks to Diana whose contribution was her prodigious memory and unflagging patience.

I would like to thank Dr Andrew Spillane, Dr Fran Boyle and the staff of the McCrone Ward at the Mater Hospital, who made it possible for me to complete this book under difficult circumstances.

I am specially blessed by the support of my writing friends Charlotte Wood, Lucinda Holdforth, Rebecca Hazel and Vicki Hastrich, whose wit, intelligence and love are a never-ending source of inspiration.

Special thanks also to Fran Moore for smoothing the path, Sarah Odgers for her fabulous design and Mary Trewby whose superb editing skills gave the manuscript a special shine.

Hazel Flynn recognised the story in my mother's life and has been there for me through all my trials and tribulations. I could never have written this book without her constant encouragement and brilliant perception.

David, Suzanne, Peter, Nigel and Toby—thanks for all your patience, love and support.

Further Reading

Viktor Frankl, *Man's Search for Meaning*, Washington Square Press, New York, 1978.

Edward Horne, *A Job Well Done: A History of the Palestine Police Force 1920–1948*, The Book Guild, London, 2003.

J.D.F. Jones, *Storyteller: The Many Lives of Laurens van der Post*, John Murray, London, 2001.

Marion A. Kaplan, *Between Dignity and Despair: Jewish Life in Nazi Germany*, Oxford University Press, Oxford, 1998.

C.J. Lambert, *Sweet Waters: A Chilean Farm*, Chatto & Windus, London, 1952.

First published in 2006 by Pier 9, an imprint of Murdoch Books Pty Limited
www.murdochbooks.com.au

Murdoch Books Australia
Pier 8/9, 23 Hickson Road, Millers Point NSW 2000
Phone: +61 (0) 2 8220 2000 Fax: +61 (0) 2 8220 2558

Murdoch Books UK Limited
Erico House, 6th Floor North, 93/99 Upper Richmond Road
Putney, London SW15 2TG
Phone: +44 (0) 20 8785 5995 Fax: + 44 (0) 20 8785 5985

Chief Executive: Juliet Rogers
Publishing Director: Kay Scarlett

Commissioning Editor: Hazel Flynn
Concept and design: Sarah Odgers
Cover design: Toyoko Sugiwaka
Project Manager: Paul McNally
Editor: Mary Trewby
Production: Maiya Levitch

National Library of Australia Cataloguing-in-Publication Data:
Naseby, Eileen. Ursula : a voyage of love and drama
1. Hall, Ursula, 1924- . 2. Bahais - Australia - Biography. 3. Mothers and daughters -
Biography. 4. Women immigrants - Australia - Biography. I. Title. 297.93092

ISBN: 978 17404 5751 4
ISBN: 1 74045 751 X

Printed by 1010 Printing International Limited in 2006. Printed in China. Reprinted 2007.

All images courtesy of Eileen Naseby, except illustration on page 68, which is courtesy
of David Naseby